Larger Than Life

STAR
★★★★★★★★★★ AMERICAN CULTURE / AMERICAN CINEMA
DECADES

Each volume in the series Star Decades: American Culture/American Cinema presents original essays analyzing the movie star against the background of contemporary American cultural history. As icon, as mediated personality, and as object of audience fascination and desire, the Hollywood star remains the model for celebrity in modern culture and represents a paradoxical combination of achievement, talent, ability, luck, authenticity, superficiality, and ordinariness. In all of the volumes, stardom is studied as an effect of, and influence on, the particular historical and industrial contexts that enabled a star to be "discovered," to be featured in films, to be promoted and publicized, and ultimately to become a recognizable and admired— even sometimes notorious—feature of the cultural landscape. Understanding when, how, and why a star "makes it," dazzling for a brief moment or enduring across decades, is especially relevant given the ongoing importance of mediated celebrity in an increasingly visualized world. We hope that our approach produces at least some of the surprises and delight for our readers that stars themselves do.

ADRIENNE L. McLEAN AND MURRAY POMERANCE
SERIES EDITORS

Jennifer Bean, editor, *Flickers of Desire: Movie Stars of the 1910s*

Patrice Petro, editor, *Idols of Modernity: Movie Stars of the 1920s*

Adrienne L. McLean, editor, *Glamour in a Golden Age: Movie Stars of the 1930s*

Sean Griffin, editor, *What Dreams Were Made Of: Movie Stars of the 1940s*

R. Barton Palmer, editor, *Larger Than Life: Movie Stars of the 1950s*

Pamela R. Wojcik, editor, *New Constellations: Movie Stars of the 1960s*

James Morrison, editor, *Hollywood Reborn: Movie Stars of the 1970s*

Robert Eberwein, editor, *Acting for America: Movie Stars of the 1980s*

Anna Everett, editor, *Pretty People: Movie Stars of the 1990s*

Murray Pomerance, ed., *Shining in Shadows: Movie Stars of the 2000s*

Larger Than Life

Movie Stars of the

1950s
★★★★★★★★★★★★★

EDITED BY

R. BARTON PALMER

RUTGERS UNIVERSITY PRESS

NEW BRUNSWICK, NEW JERSEY, AND LONDON

LIBRARY OF CONGRESS CATALOGING-IN-PUBLICATION DATA

Larger than life : film stars of the 1950s / edited by R. Barton Palmer.
    p.   cm. — (Star decades : American culture / American cinema)
    Includes bibliographical references and index.
    ISBN   978–0–8135–4766–4   (hardcover : alk. paper)
    ISBN   978–0–8135–4767–1   (pbk. : alk. paper)
    1. Motion picture actors and actresses—United States—Biography.   I. Palmer,
R. Barton, 1946–
    PN1998.2.L37   2010
    791.4302'80922—dc22
    [B]   2009043156

A British Cataloging-in-Publication record for this book is available from the British
Library.

Visit our Web site: http://rutgerspress.rutgers.edu

Manufactured in the United States of America

For Grace O'Keefe Berry,
who may be a star herself one day

CONTENTS

☆☆☆☆☆☆☆☆☆☆☆

ACKNOWLEDGMENTS
★★★★★★★★★★★

The research for this volume would have been impossible without the released time provided by the English Department and the College of Architecture, Arts, and Humanities at Clemson University. A huge debt of gratitude is owed to Dr. Lee Morrissey, departmental chair, and Professor E. Clifton Egan, dean. Funding for travel, books, and other media was provided by the Calhoun Lemon family. As always, I am much appreciative of their continuing support for my professional activities, which, especially in the current economic climate, would be otherwise very difficult to sustain. Murray Pomerance and Adrienne McLean, the editors of the Star Decades series of which this present volume constitutes an entry, have provided excellent advice and guidance. Their judicious and thorough copyediting has prevented many an error and infelicity. Leslie Mitchner of Rutgers University Press and her staff have, as usual, been a joy to work with through the various stages of planning and production. The not inconsiderable work of putting together the various parts of this book was eased considerably by the patience and understanding of Carla and Camden Palmer, who have tolerated the editor's not always pleasant preoccupation with a variety of time-consuming tasks. And I would be remiss if I failed to mention that it has been a joy to revisit as a scholar the films that, as a youngster growing up in the 1950s, I remember from a seemingly innumerable number of Saturday nights spent at the now mostly vanished theaters of Stamford, Connecticut (the Avon, the Plaza, the Palace, and, preeminent for its fascinating Art Deco interior, the Ridgeway). My aunt and uncle, Pauline G. and Gilbert A. Barton, generously shared with their nephew their weekly date with Hollywood's offerings, giving rise to memories that are among the most magical and inextinguishable of my childhood.

Larger Than Life

INTRODUCTION
★★★★★★★★★★★
Stardom in the 1950s

R. BARTON PALMER

By the end of the 1940s, the Hollywood film industry had established itself as an integral part of American popular culture through the production, distribution, and exhibition of celluloid entertainment for general national (and international) audiences. Because the value of such releases depended, for obvious reasons, on filmgoers seeing films as unique or innovative, marketing campaigns often emphasized the supposedly pleasurable differences that each "coming attraction" somehow embodied. But Hollywood's business model also depended heavily on sameness and predictability, qualities as necessary for producers (who needed to be sensitive to economies of scale) as they were for exhibitors (who required a constantly changing supply of films of consistently high quality). Crucial to the satisfactory maintenance of a dialectical balance between the absolutely new and the tried and true were a stable system of diverse genres and the contracted availability of established star performers. Hollywood's balance between sameness and difference finds a microcosmic reflex in what critic Richard Maltby calls the "two bodies" of the star: the perdurable (if existentially varying over time) form of the performer consumed and enjoyed across a series of productions, as well as the transitory incarnation of that same self as a character customarily limited to a single film (380–84).

Stars, of course, were not all that the industry had to offer the paying public. Over almost three decades, the studio system had developed a flexible approach to providing every film with a variety of attractions: compelling narrative; appealing spectacle; and provocative but ultimately conservative themes. The onscreen (and, complexly, also the offscreen) presence of those charismatic, culturally evocative personas called stars had long been crucial to the industry's continuing profitability. Stars, in fact, were absolutely essential to the very notion of Hollywood. Hollywood produced films, but, just as important, also produced itself as a fantasy, extending the glitz, glamour, and charisma it put on the screen to "real life." The Los Angeles suburb was both a thriving business center and an idealized world of the imagination, a "tinseltown" inhabited by endlessly captivating celebrities whose "private lives" were carefully surveilled and shaped by studio publicity machines. And so, in addition to performing onscreen, stars played themselves, constituting the indispensable population of a world continually produced as pleasurable fantasy. It had been so since the 1920s.

Much else, however, had changed in America by the beginning of the 1950s. It is true that escapist entertainment of the glamorous Hollywood variety remained popular, especially in the performance-oriented genre of the musical. As this volume establishes, the musical held onto much of its audience through most of the decade (which was also, arguably, the great age of the Broadway musical), but a steep decline had already begun that would accelerate in the 1960s. Escapism, of course, was also available for those who wished it across the spectrum of other postwar Hollywood genres, including westerns (which often retreated into an idealized national past), melodramas (in which life's vexing personal problems found satisfying solutions), comedies (whose entertainment value often flowed from a riotous anti-realism), and war films (which sanitized, anatomized, and celebrated the global victory so recently attained). All the stars discussed in this volume consistently, if not exclusively, worked on projects conceived as what studio heads considered solid entertainment of these kinds.

★★★★★ Lighter and Darker Strains

But popular taste at the time came also to include a desire for a deeper, more serious, and confrontational engagement with life's troubles. The wholesale conversion to a wartime economy had posed a serious challenge to traditional social values (and especially gender roles), altering the understanding many had of society and their places in it. The reversion to peacetime occupations for men and women was accompanied by a reassertion of the importance of the traditional family, particularly for the middle class. Among other postwar adjustments, both social and economic, however, this conservative retreat soon uncovered deep dissatisfactions. The retrospective stereotype of the American 1950s is that it was a placid decade marked by untroubled acceptance of collectivism in both economic and personal life, an age of conformity to social norms and lasting loyalty to organizations. But the 1950s were also vexed by public issues that simmered often just beneath an only apparent surface calm, held in check for the most part by a consensus desire for their repression. As demonstrated throughout this volume, sometimes these tensions received eloquent expression in the films of the era, an aspect of Hollywood's cultural importance that was crucially dependent on the richly signifying images of the industry's stars.

What was new in the postwar period was that there were strident demands at the time, especially from young filmmakers like Elia Kazan and Stanley Kramer, for a cinema that would be more authentically engaged with what viewers might understand as "real life." The industry, however, refused for the most part to deal openly and directly with the troubling questions of the day (especially segregation and McCarthyism), though Hollywood did produce a limited number of usually low-budget films (only some featuring valuable stars) that dealt with Cold War politics and racial matters. Hollywood's experience with "A" production social-problem films in the late 1940s, including Kazan's *Gentleman's Agreement* (1947) and *Pinky* (1949), was somewhat disappointing. These critically acclaimed productions were often quite popular (*Gentleman's Agreement* was Fox's highest grossing picture in 1947), but, often wracked by controversy, Hollywood in the 1950s had enough political troubles of its own without looking for many more.

For example, at the very beginning of the decade, Joseph L. Mankiewicz's *No Way Out* (1950) offered an unforgettable confrontation between a rabid racist (Richard Widmark) and a young black doctor trying to establish himself in a northern urban hospital (Sidney Poitier). The film features a disturbingly violent race riot that recalls a similar outbreak of white hostility toward blacks in 1943 Detroit. Poitier went on to build a substantial career during the following two decades, becoming one of Hollywood's most acclaimed and bankable actors. But there would be no more roles in which he would play a black family man threatened in his home by a pathologically prejudiced white man. Instead, Poitier would be mostly limited to projects that weakly endorsed conventional liberal pieties or only superficially explored racial stereotypes (*Go, Man, Go* [1954] and *Band of Angels* [1957] are useful examples). Hollywood simply could not conceive of many profitable ways to utilize him or the few other African Americans who attained something like star status (Harry Belafonte, Dorothy Dandridge, Ossie Davis, Ruby Dee, Eartha Kitt, and Ethel Waters chief among them). In fact, catering to a mostly white clientele to whom "Negroes" were, in Ralph Ellison's telling formulation, "invisible," 1950s Hollywood offered few opportunities of any kind for actors of color, beyond their participation in the occasional all-black musical production (*Carmen Jones* [1954], *St. Louis Blues* [1958]) or, often playing a servant of some kind, as a supporting dramatic player (for example, the memorable appearance of Waters in such roles in *The Member of the Wedding* [1952] and *The Sound and the Fury* [1959]).

If the movies of the1950s mostly shied away from the more controversial areas of national and international politics, some of the era's most notable releases at least launched the celluloid examination of psychological "truth," with more searching dramatizations of the inner life than had previously been brought to the screen. Issues of happiness and identity were treated within the flourishing genre of the family melodrama, in which the discontents of the most personal of relationships found telling, if usually rather traditional, dramatization (*Magnificent Obsession* [1954], *All That Heaven Allows* [1955], *The Man in the Gray Flannel Suit* [1956], and many others). But this character-centered view of human experience found its most culturally significant expression not in a single genre, but in the innovative, ultra-naturalistic style of acting known as the Method that, after developing in the New York theater, exerted a considerable influence on performance (and even the concept of performance itself) in Hollywood during the 1950s. A new generation of Method-trained actors—most notably Dana Andrews, Carroll Baker, Martin Balsam, Marlon Brando, Montgomery Clift, Lee J. Cobb, James Dean, Mildred Dunnock, John Garfield, Julie Harris, Kim Hunter, Karl Malden, E. G. Marshall, Kevin McCarthy, Paul Newman, Gregory Peck, Eva Marie Saint, Rod Steiger, Maureen Stapleton, Jo Van Fleet, Eli Wallach, and David Wayne—rose to prominence and "sought out roles that led to suffering, both emotional and physical," challenging conventional notions of what constituted entertainment (McCann 6). As several chapters in this volume illustrate, the Method complicated the relationship between the actor's two bodies by identifying "the actor's own personality not merely as a model for the creation of character, but as the mine from which all psychological truth must be dug" (Vineberg 6). The Method, to put it somewhat crudely, aimed at transforming performance into "being," and so the more astute practitioners of this style—Brando, Clift, Dean—often delivered performances that threatened to collapse the distinction between star and character, even as they emphasized an affecting presentation of bitter, sometimes neurotic inwardness that suited the industry's profitable investment in family melodrama.

However, many—perhaps most—Hollywood films of the decade did not indulge in such powerful, disturbing anatomies of the self. As Murray Pomerance has pointed out, the big box-office successes of the decade were solid entertainment of the kind the studios had been purveying for decades rather than provocative art. Not one of the decade's biggest earners represents "the work of filmmakers most critics and scholars now most frequently placed at the pinnacle of filmmaking at the same time" (5). As America began to enjoy the first stages of an unprecedented peacetime prosperity, the studios took care not to offend the more traditionally minded among their audience, continuing to fund and support an industry-created office, the Production Code Administration, which had been founded

In *Fear Strikes Out* (Robert Mulligan, Paramount, 1957), Anthony Perkins gave an affecting performance as a major league ballplayer driven to mental illness by the relentless perfectionism of his father (Karl Malden). Courtesy of the Academy of Motion Picture Arts and Sciences.

in 1934. It was the task of the PCA to vet and shape projects at various stages in their development and production in order to forestall, insofar as possible, legal restrictions (including banning) at municipal and state levels and to satisfy special interest groups, most notably the lay Catholic organization the Legion of Decency (founded in 1933 and arguably enjoying its most vigorous and powerful decade in the 1950s). The legion demanded what one of its most concerned and articulate members, journalist Martin Quigley, termed "decency in motion pictures," threatening condemnation and boycotting of, and even protests against, releases that its raters regarded as dangerously immoral, perhaps even an "occasion of sin." American society began to move unexpectedly to the left on cultural issues during the 1950s, and the film industry would in 1968 abandon the Code and institute the current ratings system. In part, this change was provoked by Code-defying directors in the 1950s like Otto Preminger (whose *The Moon Is Blue* [1953], in which the word "virgin" was uttered for the first time in a Hollywood film in relation to sexual inexperience, was released without a Code seal and to large box office returns, and whose *Man with a Golden Arm* [1955], even more successful, ignored the Code prohibition against representing drug addiction, providing singer-turned-leading-dramatic-man Frank Sinatra one of his most powerful roles as a junkie attempting to kick the habit).

For the most part, however, and despite some stylistic and formal influence of European movements such as Italian neorealism (especially shooting on location), commercial films eagerly promoted an idealized and conservative vision of American society, a collective, representational ideal in which the industry's gallery of named, recognizable performers played indispensable roles. What made stars the most popular and acclaimed of these recognizable performers is that on one level they customarily (but not always) represented important and appealing or intriguing social types. As the essays collected here show, however, stars, in the words of Richard Dyer, are "always more complex and specific than types," which, as it were, only constitute "the ground on which a particular star's image is constructed" (*Stars* 68). Stars represent more than an attractive gallery of ideal and idealized versions of figures familiar from everyday life. In fact, their images are just as often linked to the signification of potent contradictions as they are to the incarnation of broadly accepted ideals of looks, manner, and social values.

★★★★★ A Hollywood Low and the Postwar American High

In 1946, Hollywood rode a cresting wave in ticket sales, and its many stars never enjoyed greater popularity worldwide. Box office receipts hit an all-time high ($325 million) as returning servicemen fueled a dating boom, and consumer goods, which might have competed for the money in very full wage packets, were not yet available in sufficient quantity (see Schatz 353–94 for complete earnings figures; the financial account of Hollywood offered here reflects his analysis). Weekly attendance at film theaters, in fact, almost equaled the nation's population, at the time close to 140 million. This staggering figure indicates how important moviegoing had become for the many who must have attended religiously many times a week. Studio profits ran close to $120 million, nearly doubling the record figure of $60 million set just one year earlier. Gross revenues were an astounding $1.45 billion (also a record), and this success was largely fueled by a string of five films that each earned more than $5 million in domestic rentals, far exceeding even the most optimistic industry expectations.

Each of the films was in some sense both a genre exercise and star-driven: *The Bells of St. Mary's* (1945), a religious melodrama featuring two of the decade's most popular performers, Bing Crosby and Ingrid Bergman; *Road to Utopia* (1945), a musical and the latest in an ongoing franchise of similar "road" movies, starring (again) Crosby, as well as Bob Hope and Dorothy Lamour (a trio that by 1945 had become a kind of composite star); *The Jolson Story* (1946), a musical biopic starring Larry Parks and Evelyn Keyes, two of the most recognizable performers, minor league stars, if you will, from one of the so-called "Little Three" studios, Columbia Pictures; *Duel in the Sun*, a western starring, among a cast of name performers (Joseph Cotten, Lionel Barrymore, Lillian Gish, and Walter Huston), Gregory Peck and Jennifer Jones, two of the decade's most acclaimed and popular stars; and *The Best Years of Our Lives*, a postwar melodrama with three featured stars, Fredric March, Myrna Loy, and Dana Andrews, and a strong supporting cast of experienced name performers (Virginia Mayo, Steve Cochran, Ray Collins, and Hoagy Carmichael).

These last two films did hint at new directions for the industry, perhaps because they were each projects overseen by one of the era's most aggressive and successful independent producers. Made by an established industry master, William Wyler, *The Best Years of Our Lives* seems a precursor of the more serious kind of fare urged on the industry by the likes of Kazan, Kramer, and Nicholas Ray. Dana Andrews's performance as an ex-flier who experiences great difficulty in readjusting to civilian life features a moving "interior" sequence in which the demons that haunt the disillusioned former navigator are exorcised, requiring the small-scale, dialogue-free facial acting in which Method-trained actors specialized. This intense moment of self-discovery, triggered by the outpouring of repressed memories, anticipates similar scenes in a number of famed 1950s productions: James Dean in *Rebel without a Cause* (1955) and *East of Eden* (1955); Paul Newman in *Somebody Up There Likes Me* (1954) and *The Left-Handed Gun* (1957); Montgomery Clift in *A Place in the Sun* (1951) and *I Confess* (1953) as well as *Suddenly, Last Summer* (1959); Marlon Brando in *The Men* (1950), *A Streetcar*

Named Desire (1951), and *On the Waterfront* (1955); Anthony Perkins in *Fear Strikes Out* and *The Tin Star* (both 1957), among a number of others.

The sensational success enjoyed by *Duel in the Sun* certainly predicts the shift in audience tastes toward the less Victorian treatment of the sexual life that becomes such a prominent element of 1950s cinema (a trend that would be exploited by a number of stars: especially Elizabeth Taylor in *Cat on a Hot Tin Roof* [1958] and *Suddenly, Last Summer* [1959]; and Paul Newman, also in *Cat*, and in both *The Long, Hot Summer* [1958] and *The Young Philadelphians* [1959]). Similarly, *Duel* arguably breaks new ground in building its narrative around a distinctly antiheroic (if also attractive and somewhat sympathetic) protagonist, a strategy that would soon underlie the profitable notoriety of Marlon Brando's Stanley Kowalski in *Streetcar Named Desire*. As a result of *Streetcar*'s critical and box office success, as well as the respect accorded Brando by those in the business, the antiheroic protagonist would become one of the most characteristic figures of 1950s cinema.

The national economy in the early postwar era managed to maintain momentum as wartime production was shifted to satisfying (after creating) consumer demand, inaugurating a decade and a half of unprecedented growth that expanded the middle class and provided most Americans with a lifestyle that was comfortable and even rich beyond the wildest dreams of their parents. As a result, the 1950s were, in the estimation of a prominent historian, William O'Neill, an "American High," but not, as it turns out, for the film industry. The most noteworthy crisis was political: the continuing investigation of purported communist influence in the industry by the House Un-American Activities Committee in the early years of the decade, which led not only to a bitter, divisive confrontation between right- and left-wing members of the filmmaking community, but also to the jailing of ten "unfriendly" witnesses and a blacklist that lasted for years, ruining many careers (including that of Larry Parks, the star of *The Jolson Story*) and polarizing the film community, with notable stars lining up on the right (John Wayne, Dick Powell, and James Stewart, for example) and on the left (Humphrey Bogart, Gene Kelly, and Lauren Bacall, among others). More destructive in the long run, however, was the fact that production costs, fueled by rising wages in a time of inflation, rose steadily in the postwar era, while earnings fell substantially. By 1950, studio profits were down to about $31 million, only about 25 percent of what they had been in 1946, while, perhaps even more disastrously, the profits of exhibitors had declined about 60 percent, forcing the closing of many theaters.

The decline in the film business had multiple causes that created something like an economic perfect storm. Income from foreign markets did not meet expectations (in some countries, like the United Kingdom, Hollywood profits were frozen and could not be exported to the United States, as the British film business experienced similar hard times of its own). Because it was an economic as well as a political barrier, the falling of the Iron Curtain (a process completed by 1949) deprived Hollywood of its customary and profitable markets in Eastern Europe. And there was a destructive competition in Los Angeles itself between two rival labor unions. With the eventual victory of the International Alliance of Theatrical and Stage Employees (IATSE), some workers received fatter paychecks, but this proved to be no general boon as union employment in the industry fell precipitously because the growing financial crisis forced Hollywood to cut production and eliminate the jobs of many contract workers.

Such developments by themselves would have posed a serious enough threat to the industry. Even more disastrous, however, was the fact that Hollywood, through large-scale social changes it could not have anticipated and could hardly adjust to quickly, began to lose much of its traditional main market: middle-class urbanites who lived within walking (or public transportation) distance of downtown theaters and were not averse to paying the higher admission prices at these first-run venues (which, owned and operated directly by the major five studios, for two decades had generated a very high proportion of the gross earnings of "A" production releases). A severe inner-city housing shortage hit the country in the immediate postwar years, and the unexpected solution to this problem was quickly found in relatively cheap suburban developments. The building boom beyond city limits was largely fueled by the government loan programs mandated in the G.I. Bill.

This profound social change may have been a terrific boon to the nation's millions of veterans and to the housing industry, but it spelled disaster for Hollywood. Suburban areas were usually far from movie theaters and frequently off public transportation routes, making a trip back into town to see a picture often inconvenient and expensive. Furthermore, the public had become acclimated to "going to the movies," that is, dropping in at theaters whenever convenient and without regard for feature showtimes. Driving in from the suburbs made this kind of filmgoing impractical for most. Movie attendance, as a result, became more of an event than a casual activity, requiring greater planning and effort. These trends did not favor the industry during the 1950s, but exhibitors would manage a turnaround of sorts in the 1960s as more theaters became established in the suburbs.

To make matters worse, one of the most significant developments of the early postwar years was the appearance of a home-centered and (at least apparently) free substitute for moviegoing. The broadcast services provided by television, and the popularity of the new medium, expanded rapidly. By the end of the 1950s, most families in the country owned a set which they turned on for a gradually increasing number of hours every week. Furthermore, with the establishment of a consumer economy devoted to the production of "durables" and the emergence of entertainment alternatives from boating to bowling, Hollywood's traditional customers began to spend more of their discretionary income on washing machines, vacation travel, and do-it-yourself projects than on going to the movies. Deserted by their patrons, thousands of theaters around the country closed their doors forever. Some observers thought that America had finally wearied of the motion picture.

For Hollywood's stars, however, the appearance of television proved more a blessing than a curse. With its emphasis on both live drama (produced in and broadcast from New York) and filmed series (which were often transplanted from radio), television created an immense demand for trained actors, especially those of proven appeal. Television offered great opportunities for work, even if the pay did not approach what name actors and stars could make in Hollywood. Important stars from the 1940s (Loretta Young ["The Loretta Young Show" (1953)], Dick Powell, David Niven, Ida Lupino, and Charles Boyer ["Four Star Playhouse" (1952)], Jack Benny ["The Jack Benny Program" (1950)], Groucho Marx ["You Bet Your Life" (1950)], Abbott and Costello ["The Abbott and Costello Show" (1952)], Robert Cummings ["The Bob Cummings Show" (1955)], and Robert Young ["Father Knows Best" (1954)], among many others) found renewed career life on the small screen as they sought out additional sources of income, grew too old for leading parts, or otherwise slipped from fashion.

Conversely, a number of actors who had found little success in Hollywood discovered in television the path to a stardom that had otherwise eluded them. One of film noir's most effective bit players, Jack Webb, turned producer and transformed one of the Hollywood productions in which he appeared (*He Walks by Night* [1947]) into a showcase for his acting talents. "Dragnet" became one of 1950s television's most successful and influential crime drama series, even enabling Webb to return to feature filmmaking as star and producer (*Pete Kelly's Blues* [1955]). Similarly, Lucille Ball, a comedienne whose talents for slapstick and zany comedy had been wasted during her years as an RKO contract player, developed a television series with her husband, musician and part-time Hollywood actor Desi Arnaz. "I Love Lucy" (1951) enjoyed phenomenal success in its initial run and subsequent, seemingly endless syndication well into the next decade and beyond. Like Webb, Ball also took her newly fashioned persona back to the big screen (*The Long, Long Trailer* [1953]). Fifties' Hollywood bit players Lee Marvin, Clint Eastwood, and Steve McQueen would all go on to achieve movie stardom (and more in the case of Eastwood) as a result of their work in anthology television drama and then, taking on starring roles, in popular television series during the 1950s.

★★★★★ The Move to the Package-Unit System

There was a further, though less surprising, blow that the five major studios (Paramount, Warner Bros., RKO, MGM, and Twentieth Century–Fox) had to endure. For three decades an essential element of the majors' success had hinged on the vertical integration of their business model, in which production, distribution, and first-run theatrical exhibition were organized under one corporate umbrella. After decades of legal wrangling, the U.S. Supreme Court ruled in 1947, in what came to be labeled the "Paramount Decree," that vertical integration was in restraint of trade and therefore illegal.

As a result, the major studios during the next few years were all forced to sign consent decrees that led to their divestiture of theatrical holdings. Without a secure market for their product, the studios could no longer function as "factories" turning out hundreds of films annually by methods that were similar to (if always different in important respects from) the industrial assembly line. A gradual shift was made to one-off production (the so-called package-unit system), "a short-term film-by-film arrangement," in the words of Janet Staiger, designed to service a market no longer controlled by group rentals. As she relates, producers now were more required to "differentiate the product on the basis of its innovations, its story, stars, and its director" (Staiger 330, 332). One of the results for the industry was that the contract system for those working both above the line (creative personnel) and below (technicians) gradually disappeared. Once again, such a radical change in the approach to production planning, though it posed difficulties for the industry, actually strengthened the position of many of Hollywood's stars, as they became in general even more important than in decades past to the promotion of each film's unique, special appeal. It is no accident that some industry regulars like John Wayne, Cary Grant, Kirk Douglas, and James Stewart took advantage of this freedom from exclusive studio contracts to explore new approaches to their image and screen roles, coming to enjoy either a renewed or a strengthened popularity.

One of the most notable "small films" of the decade was 1955's "best picture," *Marty* (Delbert Mann, United Artists). In the title role, Ernest Borgnine was outstanding as a love-starved New York butcher. Courtesy of the Academy of Motion Picture Arts and Sciences.

If Hollywood's stars welcomed the advent of television, the film industry was encouraged to differentiate its product in order to gain a competitive edge. On the one hand, Hollywood could outclass the fuzzy black-and-white images and tinny audio then available on the tube. On the other, insofar as public taste and the PCA would allow, the studios could emphasize serious, gritty drama that, while increasingly an important presence on the Broadway stage of the era, could not in many cases be featured into productions for the small screen. Unlike the broadcast networks, Hollywood was not answerable to either program sponsors or Federal Communications Commission (FCC) protocols.

The pressing need for product differentiation led filmmakers to innovate with two dissimilar kinds of films during the 1950s, while never breaking decisively from the "general entertainment" model that had sustained the industry since the 1920s and even earlier. More traditional, even retrograde, in both story and their dependence on glamorous, extravagant spectacle, were the blockbuster Technicolor films shot in one of the era's several innovative widescreen formats. Often remakes of, or closely similar to, the epic spectaculars of late 1920s cinema, these films were filled with stars (often appearing in cameo or restricted roles) and featured elaborate, expensive production values (especially the proverbial "cast of thousands"), and they did not neglect the big-screen appeal of the scantily clad human body, a representational strategy "covered" as it were by the fact that the stories they told were period pieces. The decade's run of biblical and historical epics, including *Quo Vadis* (1951), *Demetrius and the Gladiators* (1954), and *The Ten Commandments* (1956), treated religious subjects and fully exploited the titillating possibilities of ancient dress (or, at least, Hollywood's idea of it). Such films needed impressive human figures more than actors and offered opportunities for performers with obvious physical gifts: Yul Brynner, Joan Collins, Victor Mature, Robert Taylor, and preeminently Charlton Heston. The big-budget Technicolor musical also continued as a staple, starring both familiar faces and bodies from earlier decades—Fred Astaire, Cyd Charisse, Bing Crosby, Doris Day, Judy Garland, Gene Kelly, Frank Sinatra, for example—as well as introducing new stars as disparate as opera tenor Mario Lanza and rock 'n' roll sensation Elvis Presley.

The blockbuster's "other" was the small-budget black-and-white film, whose appeal was hardly what is now termed "eye candy," but rather an affecting, dramatic, stylistic engagement with arty, politically engaged, or perhaps even adult themes. An amazing trend-setting success in the immediate postwar era, as already mentioned, was achieved with the film noir and the social problem drama, two closely connected and sometimes indistinguishable genres that featured not only the thematization of discontents with American society but also the complex intersection of opposed stylistic regimes: expressionism and documentary realism, a mixture found in the Broadway theater of the period as well (and, in film, influenced by the rise of the "art house" cinema, especially European modes such as neorealism and, by the end of the decade, the French New Wave). Such films usually required actors who were tough, urban types, good-bad guys with sophistication and pep. To some degree, the industry's need in this area was filled by actors who had made a reputation for such portrayals in the 1930s and 1940s, among them Humphrey Bogart, James Cagney, Henry Fonda, Glenn Ford, John Garfield, Sterling Hayden, Van Heflin, Arthur Kennedy, Alan Ladd, Fred McMurray, Robert Montgomery, Edmond O'Brien, Vincent Price, Edward G. Robinson, Barry Sullivan, and Richard Widmark. But an emerging generation also found opportunity here: Ernest Borgnine, Marlon Brando, Raymond Burr, Broderick Crawford, Kirk Douglas, Dan Duryea, Farley Granger, William Holden, Burt Lancaster, Robert Mitchum, Jack Palance, Robert Ryan, Rod Steiger, and Eli Wallach, among others. Such productions required actresses of a complementary type to incarnate scheming femmes fatales or hard-bitten women with more than a little experience. Memorable performances of this type during the 1950s were delivered by an interesting mixture of established, even older performers (such as Joan Bennett, Rita Hayworth, Ida Lupino, Barbara Stanwyck, and Claire Trevor) and a younger generation of talented actresses, including Lauren Bacall, Anne Bancroft, Yvonne DeCarlo, Rhonda Fleming, Ava Gardner, Gloria Grahame, Jane Greer, Susan Hayward, Janet Leigh, Marilyn Monroe, Kim Novak, Lizabeth Scott, Jan Sterling, Gene Tierney, Shelley Winters, and Joanne Woodward.

The flourishing of film noir and the social-problem film through the 1950s was certainly unexpected. This production trend was blamed by some for the industry's continuing precipitous drop in gross earnings. Critic Manny Farber, for example, complained that Hollywood had moved away from the "old flowing naturalistic film to embrace 'mannerist works' that betrayed the accepted function of the corner theater (an institution itself fast disappearing), that 'simple mansion of leisure-time art'" (in Sklar 89). In any case, the small films of the 1950s, including some striking noir productions (Orson Welles's *Touch of Evil* [1958]) and deglamorized, gritty dramas like *Death of a Salesman* (1951), *Come Back, Little Sheba* (1952), *The Rose Tattoo* (1955), *Patterns* (1955), *Marty* (1955's Oscar winner for Best Picture), *The Rainmaker* (1956), *A Hatful of Rain* (1957), *The Three Faces of Eve* (1957), *12 Angry Men* (1957), *The Bachelor Party* (1957), *The Diary of Anne Frank* (1959), and *Middle of the Night* (1959), were showcases for ostentatiously excellent acting especially, but not exclusively, of the Method type. With the larger sphere of Hollywood production, small films constituted collectively something that could arguably be called a "cinema of performance" that decisively affected the conception of screen acting, accelerating a turn toward increased naturalism. Method acting is alive and well in American

In *Sunset Blvd.* (Billy Wilder, Paramount, 1950), Hollywood took a look at its own history, especially its reliance on star performers. Gloria Swanson memorably incarnated a star of the silent era whose career was cut short by the transition to sound pictures at the end of the 1920s. Courtesy of the Academy of Motion Picture Arts and Sciences.

filmmaking of the twenty-first century, a testimony to the lasting influence of this aspect of 1950s performance on later generations.

But in terms of acting culture more broadly considered, the 1950s in Hollywood were much more than a decade that witnessed the first real flourishing of a style that would have such lasting influence. As the essays in this volume illustrate, the period was also characterized by what we might call industrial trends, including the continuation of the traditional concept of the leading man (the handsome, charming, affable actor with a resonant voice who looked better in evening clothes than with his shirt off and who could be readily slotted into different action, dramatic, and comedy roles). Tony Curtis, Rock Hudson, Jack Lemmon, James Mason, Ray Milland, Gregory Peck, Spencer Tracy, and many others who enjoyed starring roles during the era belong to this general type, which is capable, of course, of considerable variation; the notable "pretty boys" of the era— Robert Wagner, Troy Donahue, Hudson, Tab Hunter, and Guy Madison— constitute an interesting and important subgrouping, one that was crucial in engaging adolescent and young adult filmgoers. The postwar era's rougher version of the leading man, like Kirk Douglas, Charlton Heston, Burt Lancaster, and Robert Mitchum, also were often flexible enough to play in a variety of genres. All the actors on this list appeared in westerns, romances, and comedies. In terms of actresses, the 1950s saw a number of interesting developments. There was the advent of a group of blonde "bombshells" of outsize physical proportions (the female equivalents of John Wayne, Charlton Heston, and Rock Hudson to some degree). These so-called "mammarians" included Jayne Mansfield, Marilyn Monroe, Jane Russell, and, in some sense, Judy Holliday and Kim Novak. Traditional leading-lady types, however, also found work and success, often continuing careers begun in the 1940s: Joan Bennett, Joan Crawford, Bette Davis, Olivia de Havilland, and Barbara Stanwyck chief among them. Some, notably Susan Hayward, made an impact on 1950s cinema through searing dramatic (rather than strictly romantic or comic) performances. Three of the decade's most unusual films (*With a Song in My Heart* [1952], *I'll Cry Tomorrow* [1955], and *I Want to Live!* [1958]) featured Hayward as either a performer or a criminal who finds herself unable to fulfill the dream of domestic happiness that 1950s culture suggested women pursue.

Other notable stars of the era were *sui generis*, from Jerry Lewis—partnered for most of the decade with Dean Martin, and whose zaniness was exceptional (though with roots in the work of other film comedians like Chaplin, Laurel and Hardy, and The Three Stooges)—to Audrey Hepburn's stylish sophistication. Her popularity testifies, as this volume suggests, to the growing interest during the 1950s in both Europeanness more generally (witness a number of "travelogue" productions staged in Europe such as *Roman Holiday* [1953], with Hepburn, and *To Catch a Thief* [1955]) and French fashions in particular (for which Hepburn became a kind of onscreen model). She is one of a number of exotic, sexy European actors and actresses to capture the interest of American filmgoers in the 1950s, as the successful work in Hollywood of Rossano Brazzi, Gina Lollobrigida, Sophia Loren, Anna Magnani, and Yves Montand demonstrates.

Of course, the reading of such images, as Hepburn's case usefully exemplifies, is far from simple. The stars themselves always exceeded the general type to which they in some sense customarily connected. And so their significance for Hollywood history can only be explored through in-depth case histories. Star personas, moreover, take shape across a career that molds and shapes—sometimes radically altering—the meaning of their presence, a meaning that is also constructed extratextually (through interviews, fan magazine articles, celebrity experiences, entertainment "news").

With in-depth discussions of Fred Astaire, Marlon Brando, Montgomery Clift, Bing Crosby, Doris Day, James Dean, Audrey Hepburn, Charlton Heston, Judy Holliday, Rock Hudson, Gene Kelly, Jerry Lewis and Dean Martin, Jayne Mansfield, James Mason, Marilyn Monroe, Kim Novak, Gregory Peck, Frank Sinatra, and James Stewart, *Larger than Life: Film Stars of the 1950s* focuses on the most notable stars of the decade, offering a varied and useful survey of acting styles, performance histories, and the construction of star images in what was beyond a doubt one of the richest periods of classical Hollywood filmmaking. The fifties was a time of change for actors, most notably, perhaps, as the practice of long-term exclusive contracting came to an end, making them increasingly independent. But it was also a time of stability, as box office results demonstrated the continuing importance of stars to the filmgoing public. Careers were lengthened for those who had joined the industry in earlier decades. And new careers continued to be launched. It is clear that the stars of 1950s Hollywood helped ensure that the industry itself, then radically reorganizing its business model in the face of a disastrous downturn and widespread social change, would retain its prominence in American culture. As the 1950s opened, the studio system might have found itself in devastating crisis, but its stars, enjoying an outsized popularity that suited the decade's growing fascination with widened screens filled with spectacular images, were still profitably "larger than life."

Montgomery Clift
Hollywood Pseudohomosexual

TISON PUGH AND BARRY SANDLER

One of the silver screen's foremost leading men in the 1950s, Montgomery Clift inspired devotion from his female fans, the vast majority of whom little suspected his homosexuality. Surprisingly, during an era that seemed to exult in conformity and repression, he made little effort to conceal it within the intimate confines of the Hollywood community. Clift's close friends and family knew of his queer sexuality, though some were quick to modify it. In an interview with biographer Patricia Bosworth, Clift's brother Brooks describes his brother's sexuality: "Monty was a bisexual . . . I met two girls he got pregnant. He was never exclusively one thing or the other; he swung back and forth. Because we'd been raised in

Courtesy of the Academy of Motion Picture Arts and Sciences.

Europe where homosexuality was more or less accepted, he never felt ashamed—until much later when he grew up" (Bosworth 67). Director Herb Machiz ascribes the anguish of Clift's personal life to his sexuality: "The real tragedy in most homosexual lives and for a person as sensitive as Monty was having to accept the tremendous disappointment of never finding a mate worthy of him" (Bosworth 254). In the closeted world of 1950s Hollywood, however, as well as the outside world, Clift's sexuality could not be openly addressed, despite his abstention from marriage.

At the same time, between homosexuality and heterosexuality are various shades of gray, and Clift's characters in his film oeuvre—strong yet sensitive, with a saturnine sensuality simmering just beneath the surface— frequently exhibit a type of masculine sexuality that one might call *pseudohomosexuality*. This term suggests the ways in which some men fail to convincingly embody normative sexuality and display characteristics that cast them with gendered suspicion. Barbara Ehrenreich outlines the ways in which marriage defined a man's sexual normativity in the 1950s:

> The average age of marriage for men in the late fifties was twenty-three, and according to popular wisdom, if a men held out much longer, say even to twenty-seven, "you had to wonder." . . . By the 1950s and '60s psychiatry had developed a massive weight of theory establishing that marriage—and, within that, the breadwinner role—was the only normal state for the adult male. Outside lay only a range of diagnoses, all unflattering.
>
> (Ehrenreich 14–15; see also 16–28)[1]

Falling somewhere between the poles of heterosexuality and homosexuality, such pseudohomosexual men as bachelors, priests, wimps, and, of course, closeted homosexuals could become marked with queerness despite their attempted performances of normative sexuality.

Queer male stars such as Anthony Perkins, Rock Hudson, Farley Granger, and Montgomery Clift frequently exhibit pseudohomosexual masculinities as part of their star personas. Whether in Perkins's murderous maternal obsession in *Psycho* (1960), in Granger's homoerotic relationship with his fellow killer in *Rope* (1948), or in Hudson's tongue-in-cheek romp as a straight man playing gay to win Doris Day's affections in *Pillow Talk* (1959), pseudohomosexual screen personas often obliquely reflect the sexuality of the actor playing the role. For Clift, pseudohomosexuality explains much of his enigmatic appeal as a leading man, in that his dazzling good looks and magnetism drew audiences in, yet his fans rarely saw him in the role of a successful heterosexual romantic lead, and in the few cases they did, he invariably met a tragic or unfulfilled end. Whether arbitrary or by design, Clift's roles conveyed the image of men self-contained and unobtainable.

Within the restrictive cultural context of 1950s cinema, such roles in traditionally feminine and masculine film genres (from melodramas to westerns
and war movies) deploy the enigmatic coding of the pseudohomosexual to
create a man of mystery for audience consumption.

☆☆☆☆★ Hollywood, Homosexuality, and the 1950s

A culture with a significant homosexual population, Hollywood in the 1940s and 1950s faced the paradox of relying on queer talent
to make films that could not openly depict homosexuality. As a result,
queerness was often coded into films, simply through the subjective sensibility of the filmmakers, with those creative forces cloaking its actual content (see Russo). For example, Farley Granger describes how the sexuality
of the lead characters in *Rope* was treated as an open secret: "We knew that
they were gay, yeah sure. I mean, nobody said anything about it. This was
1947—let's not forget that. [The homosexuality of the characters] was one
of the points of the film, in a way." Arthur Laurents, the film's gay screenwriter, comments further on its queer themes: "I don't think the censors at
that time realized that [*Rope*] was about gay people. They didn't have a clue
what was and what wasn't. That's how it got by" (*Celluloid Closet* DVD).
Although much of Hollywood blinded itself to homosexuality, queer
themes nonetheless appear with relative frequency in films of the 1940s
and 1950s, and in terms of casting, queer actors like Granger were often
picked to play pseudohomosexual roles.

Public attitudes about homosexuality in the 1950s wavered between
confusion and intolerance, although some notable medical iconoclasts
attempted to enlighten and encourage acceptance. Alfred Kinsey's publications, including *Sexual Behavior in the Human Male* (1948) and *Sexual Behavior in the Human Female* (1953), revolutionized social views of sexuality,
especially in regard to his theories of a continuum of human sexuality, with
heterosexuality and homosexuality as opposite ends of a spectrum. Kinsey's
research underscored a potential for latent bisexuality in just about everyone. Sigmund Freud, whom Clift portrayed in John Huston's wan 1962 film
biography, died in 1939, but his influence on debates regarding sexuality
continued in the decades after his death, especially with the 1951 American publication of his 1935 letter to a distraught mother in which he wrote,
"Homosexuality is assuredly no advantage, but it is nothing to be ashamed
of, no vice, no degradation, it cannot be classified as an illness" (Freud 786).
In terms of social change, many queer GIs returning from World War II
relocated to large cities and formed gay communities and organizations. In

the early 1950s, the gay rights group known as the Mattachine Society was founded. These fledgling steps for queer emancipation were accompanied by increased paranoia and suspicion about homosexuals, notably in the House Un-American Activities Committee and Joseph McCarthy's witchhunting Permanent Senate Subcommittee on Investigations (see Rizzo).

With homosexuality gaining wider exposure but with acceptance still long delayed, surrounding social tensions often focused on whether a given man was or was not homosexual, and thus the effects of pseudohomosexuality might threaten the identity of even the straightest of men. For example, Norman Mailer, writing in the 1950s for the gay magazine *One*, confronts the fear of his own latent homosexuality: "There is probably no sensitive heterosexual alive who is not preoccupied at one time or another with his latent homosexuality, and while I had no conscious homosexual desires, I had wondered more than once if really there were not something suspicious in my intense dislike of homosexuals" (qtd. in Ehrenreich 129). In 1950s America, where conformity was a seal of social acceptance, the Red Scare was at its height, McCarthyism and political witch hunts destroyed lives, and films such as *Invasion of the Body Snatchers* (1956) exploited dread of the enemy within, pseudohomosexuality played on the persistent fear of an internal invasion by the Other.

In regard to Clift, the popular press continually addressed the questionable nature of his sexuality in articles about him, pondering his life as a bachelor, his potential girlfriends, and his famed reticence about discussing his personal life. The titles of many of these articles—including *Photoplay*'s "What's It's Like to Date Monty Clift?" (Tricia Hurst, July 1949), "Tall, Dark, and Different" (Elsa Maxwell, September 1949), "Montgomery Clift's Tragic Love" (Jane Corwin, May 1954), "Forget the Mystery, Meet the Man—Monty Clift" (George Kingsley, December 1954), and "Hollywood's Most Shocking Rumor" (Cameron Shipp, August 1958)—play upon the public's fascination with Clift's romantic life, as well as the possibility of his secrets. In an article in the *Saturday Evening Post* entitled "Hollywood's New Dreamboat," Stanley Frank pokes fun at Clift's masculinity, calling him a "marshmallow delight" and observing that the actor "does not generate sparks of broad-shouldered virility from a torso pegged to a twenty-nine-inch waist." Frank also describes how Hollywood press agents created a story about Clift as a world-class skier, ostensibly to project a persona of athletic masculinity: "The attempt to build him up into an outdoorsy he-man drew a loud snicker from Clift. 'I'm just learning to ski,' he said. 'I lower the tone of every hill I go on'" (27 August 1949, 109). This account, possibly apocryphal, nonetheless hints at studio concern regarding

Clift's masculinity and the actor's self-deprecating response to such fabricated machismo.

Key phrases and terms that obliquely connote queerness frequently appear in these articles. In a story in *McCall's* called "Montgomery Clift . . . Strange Young Man" (January 1957), Eleanor Harris quotes one of Clift's friends, who says that the actor "suffers from a Narcissus complex" (32), and his twin sister recalls that he was "very sensitive even as a child" (70). These descriptions of narcissism and "sensitivity" tacitly adumbrate homosexuality, in that such terms have long been stereotypically applied to gay men. Indeed, in Barbara Long's obituary in *Vogue* magazine ("The Winner Who Lost: Montgomery Clift," 15 November 1966, 70–74, 86), Clift's sexuality is anatomized by an anonymous friend:

> He attracted masochists, and he himself was a sado-masochist. . . . Actually he was almost pre-sexual, and his sex fantasies were so completely psyched out we wouldn't have seen the sex in them. I always thought whenever he embraced a friend, male or female, that he was really reaching out for that oceanic thing that newborn babies have with their mothers. Whatever his problem, whatever the root of it was, we'll never know, but he never got past infantilism.   (74)

This pop-psychology analysis proposes numerous diagnoses of Clift's sexuality, uniting in a vision of him as an infantile bisexual yet somehow asexual sado-masochist. As a whole, this exegesis dances around the truth of Clift's sexuality, yet never quite touches it. Furthermore, that this friend is anonymous suggests at least the possibility that the speaker was homosexual, and possibly one of Clift's lovers. Long does not describe her source in any detail, but she later mentions that two of the guests at Clift's funeral were from Cherry Grove on Fire Island, a town known as a gay mecca (see Newton).

Clift was famously reticent about discussing his love life, which subsequently fanned the flames of gossip around him. For example, Jane Corwin notes in "Montgomery Clift's Tragic Love" that "on the subject of girls, Monty remained skittish with interviewers" and then resignedly comments: "Customarily, however, Monty diverted questions about rumored romances by speaking, instead, of his work." Elsa Maxwell's "Tall, Dark, and Different" opens with this teaser hinting at Clift's pseudohomosexuality in his wily escapes from a hypothetical female: "She served him coffee—he disappeared into the kitchen! She mentioned movies—he plunged into politics! She said goodbye—he left in the service elevator! Which isn't surprising—she was entertaining Clift!" (38). This miniature melodrama illustrates the difficulty for women in nabbing a pseudohomosexual boyfriend. Maxwell also rationalizes Clift's lackluster love life: "I did not, although it shames me as a reporter, ask him about his girlfriends. He does not take kindly to personal, prying questions. . . . Where Monty is concerned, though, I can think of no girl who would understand his personality or his philosophy" (86). For the popular press of the 1950s, Clift was both sexual due to his incredibly good looks yet asexual in that he refused to divulge amatory fodder for interviewers. George Kingsley offers this homogenizing, if somewhat infantilizing, interpretation of the star's sexual appeal in "Forget the Mystery, Meet the Man—Monty Clift": "[his] sadness is one of the qualities that makes him so enormously attractive to female moviegoers. It seems to arouse their maternal instincts" (92). Clift is seen as the perfect child, and one of the defining features of children is their culturally presumed asexuality.

In terms of his personal life, Clift obviously struggled with the need to cloak his homosexuality within the more accepted cultural coding of pseudohomosexuality. For her biography of Clift, Patricia Bosworth interviewed one of Clift's former girlfriends, Phyllis Thaxter, who describes the asexual innocence of their relationship: "Monty and I loved each other very much, but it was a romantic kind of love—I never went to bed with him. . . . But we finally thought—well, maybe we *should* marry. It seemed like a good idea." Bosworth then recounts the scene of their breakup: "Then one afternoon while she was still living at the Clifts, Monty sat [Thaxter] down and said, 'I've been thinking about it, darling, and I can't get married. It just wouldn't be right.'" Thaxter then continues: "He seemed so serious and a little sad, as if he knew something I didn't. I didn't ask questions; I just said all right and we never mentioned marriage after that" (73). It is not difficult to read the queer subtext of this scene, as it tells the familiar story of a gay man and a straight woman, in which the man's secret desires subvert any hope of marital fulfillment. In the closeted world of the 1950s, society demanded that homosexuals perform pseudohomosexuality, yet at times these performances could only go so far. Pseudohomosexuality protects yet constrains, and these tensions are similarly evident in Clift's films.

★★★★★ Montgomery Clift's Pseudohomosexual Melodramas

Much of Clift's appeal as an actor stems from his beauty; as Richard Dyer remarks, echoing a sentiment shared by many of his fans, "When I see Montgomery Clift I sigh over how beautiful he is" (*Stars* 162). Largely due to his good looks, Clift makes an ideal lead for films intended for a female audience. Primarily known as "tearjerkers" and "women's

movies," melodramas typically focus on feminine perspectives and heightened emotionalism. Robert Lang argues that the melodrama is foremost "a
drama of identity" that addresses the protagonist's autonomy:

> A woman (or a woman's point of view) often dominates the narrative of the
> family melodrama because individual identity within the patriarchal con-
> text—always defined by a masculine standard—is problematic for women.
> The dominant ideology asserts that, whether or not a woman is at the cen-
> ter of the narrative, what is at stake in the melodrama will be a question of
> identity—of a failure to be masculine, or a failure to accept the repressive,
> subjectivity-denying terms of patriarchal femininity.   (Lang 8)

Many of Clift's melodramas, including *A Place in the Sun* (1951), *I Confess*
(1953), *Indiscretion of an American Wife/Stazione Termini* (1954), *Raintree County*
(1957), and *Suddenly, Last Summer* (1959), focus on (or at least include) this
issue of female identity formation. Notably, Clift's characters in *Indiscretion
of an American Wife* and *Suddenly, Last Summer* play secondary roles to the
female characters in distress—respectively, Jennifer Jones's Mary Forbes
and Elizabeth Taylor's Catherine Holly. Clift undeniably plays the lead in *A
Place in the Sun*, *I Confess*, and *Raintree County*, but his characters in these
films are highly emasculated from patriarchal authority and take on a feminized cast. Each of these melodramas, whether with Clift in the lead or secondary to a female lead, features him as somehow incarnating a form of
pseudohomosexuality.

In *A Place in the Sun*, Clift's pseudohomosexual persona coincides with
the film's focus both on the role of the outsider trying to fit into a social
order he does not belong in and on the ideological constraints placed on
working-class sexuality. When George Eastman (Clift) joins the manufacturing firm of his wealthy uncle, his cousin Earl (Keefe Brasselle) warns
him, "There's a company rule against any of us mixing socially with the
girls who work here. My father asked me to particularly call this to your
attention. That is a must." Despite the fact that the firm manufactures
women's swimsuits—in effect, manufacturing heterosexual desire for
women—George is trapped in a "look but don't touch" world. Sexual desire
is monitored throughout the film: the police send George and his girlfriend
Alice Tripp (Shelley Winters) home when they are caught necking in a car,
and Alice worries that her neighbors will learn of their affair. "Mrs. Roberts
is right next door," she whimpers before melting in George's arms. Despite
the carnal nature of his relationship with Alice, George's sexual development appears arrested in other scenes. During a phone conversation with
his mother, she admonishes him to behave: "I know you'll be a good son."
The seductive Angela Vickers (Elizabeth Taylor) then teases him for his

emasculation: "Did you promise to be a good boy—not to waste your time on girls?" When George and Angela's love finally ignites, it seems real and alive, the most natural of Clift's screen romances. This is due less to his gift as an actor to manufacture it than to his lifelong platonic friendship off-screen with Elizabeth Taylor, with whom he shared honesty and affection, feeling no pressure to perform. This comfort with Taylor sustained and vitalized Clift as her romantic co-star in two additional films, *Raintree County* and *Suddenly, Last Summer*, and brought a depth and credibility to their onscreen relationships that fortified his allure and allowed him to perpetuate the pseudohomosexual persona in a viable context.

A Place in the Sun tells the story of a socially marginalized man attempting to assert his position in industry and concomitantly to establish his masculinity, but it is apparent from early in the film that Clift's Eastman is the feminized object rather than the masculine agent. Laura Mulvey's famous assessment of the gendered dynamics of gazing—"Pleasure in looking has been split between active/male and passive/female" (Mulvey, "Visual Pleasure" 162)—is overturned in this melodrama, with Clift serving as the feminized object of the gaze. When he first walks into the swimsuit factory, he is greeted by a wolf whistle; when Angela meets him while he enjoys a solitary game of pool, he offers to let her play, but she purrs demurely back, "Oh no, I'll just watch you." Gazing at him from behind, she then queries, "Do I make you nervous?" George replies succinctly, "Yes." Angela is quite literally in the driver's seat of their relationship, picking him up and chauffeuring him in her car, and George readily complies. Such images of weakness are fixed on him throughout the film, as his sense of reason is continually subverted by his physical urges and visions of grandeur. The tragic irony for George, replicating, albeit in class rather than sexual terms the irony for Clift in reality, is that the ideal life with the perfect woman is, alas, unobtainable, and this awareness lends sadness and depth to both the character and performance. At film's end, George's desperate attempts to establish himself as a man culminate in his being convicted and executed for Alice's accidental death, and Clift's pseudohomosexuality merges with the character's inability to rise from working-class to upper-class man. Both economically and sexually, George is doomed to disappointment and then death.

Alfred Hitchcock's *I Confess* merges murder with melodrama, but with the identity of the murderer known from the film's beginning, its melodramatic core takes prominence. The heart of the film is encapsulated in a question voiced by potential cuckold Pierre Grandfort (Roger Dann): "What does one do when one's wife is in love with a priest?" Pierre's wife Ruth

(Anne Baxter) still loves Father Michael Logan (Clift), despite his vow of celibacy. In an emotionally charged confrontation, she tries to win him back:

> *Ruth*: Are you afraid of me? Why? Why? You're in love with me. You've always been in love with me. You haven't changed.
>
> *Logan*: Ruth, I've changed. You've changed, too.
>
> *Ruth*: You want me to pretend.
>
> *Logan*: No, I don't want you to pretend. Ruth, do you understand, I chose to be what I am. I believe in what I am. I want you to see things as they are, not go on hurting yourself.

The queer potential in this scene arises in Logan's preference for non-procreative celibacy over heterosexual passion, his refusal to pretend, and his declaration of self-acceptance. He could have easily spoken the same dialogue in a scene admitting his homosexuality to her, and the conviction with which Logan speaks it may well have been heightened by Clift's awareness of this, giving the scene a deeper layer of honesty. Logan's devotion to God must trump his love for Ruth, but again we see Clift's onscreen persona melding well with a character whose sexuality is somehow suspect. Ruth blames the war for Logan's metamorphosis from boyfriend to priest—"I didn't want to hear about the war, but the war had changed him." On the surface, her words suggest that Logan found God amid the horrors of war, but they also capture the disorienting effects of World War II on human sexuality, in which many gay men moved to metropolises after their military service ended to free themselves of the strictures of small-town life. Rather than suggesting a facile subtext of a priest hiding his true identity behind a clerical collar to avoid sexual engagement, social interaction, and self-confrontation, the transition from lover to priest depicted in *I Confess* parallels that postwar transition out of the closet for many queer soldiers who left behind baffled girlfriends when they moved to urban areas and staked out queer identities and communities (see also Pomerance, *Eye* 170–213).

Clift's charisma and looks made him an ideal romantic lead, yet his character in *Indiscretion of an American Wife*, Giovanni Doria, incarnates a suspect and brutish masculinity that is ultimately rendered ridiculous because he cannot compete sexually with a child. Despite being lured by the chance to work with legendary Italian director Vittorio De Sica, Clift clearly was miscast in the part and knew it—his discomfort seems obvious throughout. This somewhat wooden performance stands in stark contrast to his work with Elizabeth Taylor, who provided a comfort zone, and it is most evident in his scenes with Jennifer Jones, with whom he shares little onscreen chemistry. Doria jokingly assumes a masculinity rife with machismo in a conversation with his lover, Jones's Mary Forbes, telling her that he would beat her: "I'm an Italian, too. If you didn't behave yourself, I'd beat you." Mary laughs in response, but then wonders if his words are true: "You wouldn't. Would you?" When Doria subsequently hits her, Mary's nephew Paul (Dick [Richard] Beymer) is disgusted with him for striking his beloved aunt and utters with contempt, "Hitting a woman . . . I'd show him." This film reconfigures the classic erotic triangle, in which two men pursue and compete for the love of one woman, but in this instance the struggle is enacted by a man and an adolescent boy. (Given that Truman Capote wrote the dialogue for *Indiscretion of an American Wife*, this theme is perhaps not surprising, since pre-adolescent sexuality is a recurring theme in his oeuvre, including his novels [*Other Voices, Other Rooms*, for example] and screenplays [*The Innocents* (1961)]). The sexual undertones between Mary and Paul are magnified when he kisses her for promising that he can visit her in America: with a bitten apple in his hand— the classic symbol of sexual knowledge dating back to Adam and Eve—Paul is perhaps an ineffective suitor for Mary, yet his presence highlights Doria's own unsuitability for the position. Clift is only marginally taller than Beymer, and thus his physical presence does not overwhelm his competitor, despite his advantage in years. In the end, Mary chooses to return to her children—her daughter and her husband, whom she describes as a child—and Giovanni loses her as she escapes the unappealing violence apparently inherent in adult sexuality.

Suddenly, Last Summer, with a screenplay by gay writers Gore Vidal and Tennessee Williams, is in many ways the queerest entry in Clift's oeuvre. In this Southern-gothic melodrama, Clift plays Dr. Cukrowicz, a lobotomist who must determine whether to operate on patient Catherine Holly (Elizabeth Taylor) at the instigation of her wealthy aunt, Violet Venable (Katharine Hepburn). Holly was traumatized after she witnessed her homosexual cousin Sebastian being devoured alive by cannibals, and his mother, Violet, is determined to preserve Holly's idealized memory of him by erasing her recollection of the sordid events. Violet will pay any price to accomplish this, even if it means lobotomizing her niece, an offer Cukrowicz's supervisors at their financially strapped hospital find hard to turn down. Once again, Clift's pseudohomosexual qualities make him appropriate for his role, as Cukrowicz in many ways serves as Sebastian's surrogate in the film. Upon meeting Cukrowicz, Venable effeminizes the handsome doctor, calling him "Dr. Sugar," and she recognizes his similarity to Sebastian: "Such extraordinary eyes—so like him." Venable continues to notice likenesses between the two men:

Venable: You're very like him, Doctor.

Cukrowicz: In what way?

Venable: Because you, a doctor, a surgeon, are dedicated to your art.

The two men are ostensibly linked through their artistic professions, since Sebastian was a poet who lived his life as a work of art. Holly later reveals that Sebastian used his mother and her to find men for him ("We procured for him . . . We both made contacts for him!"), and in this earlier scene between Cukrowicz and Venable, the viewer sees that the mother still seeks new conquests for her son, despite his death: "You would have liked Sebastian, and he would have been charmed by you." *Suddenly, Last Summer* examines both the moral dilemma faced by Cukrowicz in deciding Holly's fate and the struggle for his soul between the desperate, mercenary Venable and the wounded, vulnerable Holly. With Cukrowicz caught in the middle, he at times seems reduced to a cowering pawn in this battle of two fiercely dynamic women (and actresses). The central male figure here is subjugated to a conflicted position inherent in the material itself but underscored by Clift's onscreen passivity, which seems more pronounced than usual. That sense of weakness owing to a self-conscious awareness of disguised sexuality was here compounded by the actor's own insecurity in appearing onscreen as a romantic lead with two legendary beauties, while still bearing the disfiguring, confidence-shattering scars from a serious automobile accident two years earlier.

Despite the homosexual subtext at its core, *Suddenly, Last Summer* is ostensibly a heterosexual melodramatic romance between Cukrowicz and Holly. Paired with Taylor once again, Clift could rely on the affection and comfort in their offscreen friendship to help him offset anxiety in the role and make Cukrowicz's feelings for Holly seem genuine, if perhaps more empathetic than passionate. Further counterbalancing the actor's seeming quiescence and buttressing the believability of the Cukrowicz-Holly relationship and Holly's attraction to him is the fact that Clift played an establishment symbol of achievement and stability. These qualities in the character intrigue Holly, who lacks and craves both; at the same time they obfuscate the actor's insecurity. Holly kisses Cukrowicz upon meeting him, and he calls this a "friendly kiss." Despite the strictures of their doctor/patient relationship, romance blossoms, and before Holly's climactic breakthrough, in which she is cured of her illness by remembering—and thus being able to come to terms with—the details of Sebastian's gruesome murder, she begs Cukrowicz, "Hold me—I've been so lonely," and they passionately embrace. Indeed, the final shots of the movie depict the two lovers walking off together. This hetero-

Pictured here in the Tennessee Williams gothic melodrama *Suddenly, Last Summer* (Joseph L. Mankiewicz, Columbia, 1959), Montgomery Clift did his best screen work as a romantic lead when paired with his close friend Elizabeth Taylor. Courtesy of MovieStarNews.

sexual romance, however, is complicated by Cukrowicz's assumption of the position of Violet Venable's new "Sebastian." As much as the final shots establish the romantic pairing of Holly and Cukrowicz, the penultimate sequence highlights that Violet, taking onto herself the madness of which Holly has been cured, delusionally mistakes Cukrowicz for Sebastian: "Oh, Sebastian. What a lovely summer it's been. Just the two of us. Sebastian and

Violet. ~~Violet and Sebastian. That's the way it's always going to be."~~ As she ascends to her room in her rococo elevator, she continues, "Oh, we are lucky, my darling. To have one another and need no one else ever." The vision of Cukrowicz replacing Sebastian and serving as the mollycoddled yet arrogant son of the venerable southern matriarch relies on Clift's pseudohomosexual attributes, particularly those eyes that Violet believes link him to Sebastian and that Holly found so seductively blue.

By foregrounding female desire and the quest for identity beyond the constraints of patriarchal society, melodramas question social constructions of gender. Clift's pseudohomosexual characters contribute to the gendered politics of these films, creating a space to question prevailing standards of masculine identity. Even in Clift's melodramas that do not particularly play on his pseudohomosexuality, he is still cast as the outsider to the typical value system of society. In the Civil War epic *Raintree County* (1957), he plays an artistic and intelligent man, Yankee abolitionist John Wickliff Shawnessy, who sets himself apart from his community through his scholarly and creative traits. He is torn between two women—his saintly blonde, down-to-earth childhood sweetheart Nell Gaither (Eva Marie Saint) and the dark, dazzling, demented southern belle Susanna Drake (Elizabeth Taylor). Shawnessy wins the hands of both women but is mesmerized by the mysterious aura surrounding Susanna and resolves to discover her secrets—with tragic results. Clift's offscreen friendship and chemistry with Taylor again prevails, giving dimension and credibility to their onscreen pairing to sustain his status as a romantic lead. However, a case can be made here for a pseudohomosexual subtext inherent in the character's intrigue with dangerous, forbidden love. Shawnessy's willingness to be lured away from the bland, unsatisfying normalcy of a stable, conventional relationship with Nell and into the exciting, perilous, erotically charged instability of life with Susanna to fulfill his passion, whatever the risk, reflects a similar conflict and desire in homosexual men. In the end, similar conflicts in Shawnessy's physical desire and his pull to the dark side nearly ruin him; Susanna's world proves untenable and following her inevitable demise he returns to the safe, wholesome security of Nell—a victory for convention and a paean to 1950s America.

★★★★★ Montgomery Clift's Pseudohomosexuality in Masculine Genres

Clift's roles in melodramas evince a masculinity mirroring his own that is often tentative and conflicted, and in many of his other roles, pseudohomosexual edges similarly color the contours of predominantly heterosexual characters. He appeared in numerous westerns and war movies, genres that typically feature hypermasculine heroes, yet in such films as *From Here to Eternity* (1953), *The Young Lions* (1958), and *Judgment at Nuremberg* (1961), his characters display a preference for homosocial companionship, an inability to win the women they love, or some other pseudohomosexual tendency to forgo heterosexual attachment. In one such example, his widely acclaimed performance in *Judgment at Nuremberg*, a Holocaust drama of searing impact, Clift plays Rudolph Petersen, a witness for the prosecution testifying about his sterilization at the hands of the Nazis, who deemed him intellectually limited. Clift's own sense of isolation and social disengagement, his fear of being marginalized and persecuted for his sexuality, clearly connected him to the character of a lonely, devastated Jew victimized by the Nazis. It helped him understand the character in much the same way it did his tormented romantic leads in melodramas, giving weight and realism to his performance. In this film, Clift creates an image of profound anguish, and while his time onscreen is brief, it is memorable.

Clift's melodramas frequently depict him as feminized, vulnerable, and/or emasculated, and it might appear that war movies would offer him the opportunity to play more classically masculine roles. But in *From Here to Eternity*, men are more committed to the homosocial environment of the army than to their respective heterosexual liaisons. Private Prewitt (Clift) and Sergeant Warden (Burt Lancaster) both sacrifice the women in their lives—Alma Burke (Donna Reed) and Karen Holmes (Deborah Kerr)—to honor their commitments to their fellow enlisted men. In Karen Holmes's parting words to Warden, she realizes that he is "already married . . . to the army," and the homosocial foundations of the army are equated to the marital bonds between husband and wife. Indeed, except for the iconic romantic scene between Lancaster and Kerr depicting their liaison on the beach, the most touching moment of intimacy in the film occurs between Warden and Prewitt, when they drunkenly discuss their problems in love while Warden gently strokes Prewitt's hair.

Clift's own role in life as an outsider helped define and enrich the Prewitt character. Prewitt is ostensibly an individualist, one who refuses to march in lockstep with the other men, and this refusal is depicted quite literally when he must be trained to march in time with the others. Captain Dana Holmes (Philip Ober) observes that Prewitt has a "reputation as a lone wolf" and that such an ethos will not be supported in his current environment: "In the army, it's not the individual that counts." Prewitt embraces his individualism, justifying his refusal to join the regiment's boxing corps by declaring that "a man don't go his own way is nothing." Adhering to his

Clift played a soldier with a strong sense of personal honor in Fred Zinnemann's *From Here to Eternity* (Columbia, 1953). Courtesy of MovieStarNews.

credo entails his refusal to fight, but he tells Alma that he will fight for her, ostensibly privileging heterosexual passion over a solipsistic sense of ethics. Surprisingly, then, Prewitt does not fight to advance his relationship with Alma, proving his devotion to her in a public display of machismo; instead, he engages in a knife-fight with "Fatso" Judson (Ernest Borgnine) to avenge his brutal treatment of Private Maggio (Frank Sinatra). The fight itself is quite phallic, with Prewitt taunting Fatso that he will attack him with his own weapon: "See this knife? It's the one you pulled on Maggio." When Prewitt later dies, Warden eulogizes over his body, declaring, "He loved the army more than any soldier I ever knew," and this individualist who bucked the system throughout the movie is thus revealed to be the man truest to the values that the system itself ignored. The queerness of homosociality in *From Here to Eternity* is of a different valence than the queerness of Clift's melodramas, yet even in this war film his onscreen persona does not fully mesh with heteronormative masculinity.

In *The Young Lions*, Clift plays the role of Noah Ackerman, a Jew in the U.S. Army at the start of World War II, and hence a constant target of persecution and ridicule. Clift could relate to Ackerman based on his own history as a homosexual and outsider and channel his own pain, confusion, and fear into the character, bringing to the role even greater humanity and truth. This worked particularly well in conveying an awkward, self-conscious anxiety in his romantic involvement with Hope Plowman (Hope Lange), a gentile woman whose world is initially foreign to him. Clift's own unease with women as a homosexual informs Ackerman's unease with this woman from a separate socioreligious background. In some ways, Ackerman resembles Prewitt of *From Here to Eternity* in that both men find themselves at odds with the dominant ethos of the military. For instance, Ackerman's fellow soldiers deride his masculinity: "Here comes momma's helper." Ackerman determines to prove his manhood by fighting the four men who stole twenty dollars from him, only to suffer a series of bloody beatings. Before entering the army, Ackerman's masculinity is somewhat suspect because he is sexually naïve. He encounters Michael Whiteacre (Dean Martin) at the draft board and the two men become friends; when they leave the building, Whiteacre notices two young women appraising them. He sees their interest as proof of his sexual virility: "Sometimes I think I give off a scent or something—you know, arouses the female." When Ackerman responds confusedly, Whiteacre impugns his masculinity, declaring, "Your antenna's turned off" and taunting, "You're sick." He bluntly asks: "You ever had a girl?" The ensuing dialogue reinforces the view of Ackerman as sexually innocent in contrast to Whiteacre's experience with the opposite sex:

Ackerman: Have I ever had a girl?

Whiteacre (dismissively): That's what I thought.

Ackerman soon begins courting Hope Plowman, and his innocence almost cripples their romance. Ironically, he assumes a somewhat more macho persona and tries to steal a kiss, to which she angrily responds:

Hope: I suppose you think that you're such an attractive young man that any girl would just fall all over herself to let you kiss her . . .

Ackerman (moans sotto voce): Oh, God . . .

Hope: Never in all my days have I met such an opinionated, self-centered young man. Good night, Mr. Ackerman.

Ackerman then confesses to Plowman that his masculine derring-do was merely a façade: "I was afraid that if I was myself you wouldn't look at me twice." Plowman finds Ackerman's muted masculinity one of his most appealing features, stating to her father: "He's gentle, and he's clever. He's not just a man, he's a boy." Plowman's words tie in with Kingsley's assessment of Clift's appeal as an actor in arousing maternal instincts in his female audience, and the cinematic and popular-press constructions of Clift's pseudohomosexuality here dovetail.

Ackerman and Plowman become engaged, win the approval of Plowman's father, and marry. Despite the character's initial innocence, Ackerman in *The Young Lions* is one of Clift's more heterosexually successful roles. Indeed, he is compared to Whiteacre several times in the movie, and he is generally understood to be the braver and, hence, better man. Whiteacre's girlfriend, Margaret Freemantle (Barbara Rush), is disappointed in her suitor's cowardice: "I want you to act like a man. I want to be proud of you—the way Hope is proud of Noah." Whiteacre admits his cowardice openly; he freely admits his hesitation to join a war for the purpose of being shot at. In the end, the two men spur each other to masculine accomplishment, in that Whiteacre overcomes his cowardice and Ackerman returns to his family. This conclusion gives Clift the chance to play a rare role in his oeuvre: a father.

By the end of the 1950s, Montgomery Clift's now scarred good looks were fading, his internal conflicts and subsequent indulgences in alcohol and drugs were taking their toll on him both physically and mentally, and several films in which he had recently starred (*Lonelyhearts* [1958], *Wild River* [1960]) were commercial failures, thus relegating him to supporting roles. This blow to his stature and confidence was undoubtedly painful, but that pain permeated and shaped his onscreen persona and weathered appearance, giving these supporting characters enormous vulnerability and complexity. In addition, it fueled Clift's onscreen chemistry and made it electric. In *The Misfits* (1961), he and Marilyn Monroe were kindred spirits in that they were wounded, lost, and insecure; they were celebrated and ridiculed, adored and scorned, and ultimately dehumanized by years of objectification and role playing while searching for some stability, some

In *The Big Lift*, Clift (here pictured with co-star Paul Douglas) played an American airman aiding in the struggle against the Russian blockade of West Berlin (George Seaton, Twentieth Century–Fox, 1950). Courtesy of Twentieth Century–Fox.

sense of self. They clearly saw that in each other, and the connection was undeniable, turning their onscreen characters practically into extensions of themselves and giving their scenes together an honesty and raw power that make them at once both heartbreaking and transcendent.

Had Clift not succumbed to his drug habit and died in 1966 from occlusive coronary artery disease (Bosworth 370), his next picture was to have been *Reflections in a Golden Eye* (1967), the film adaptation of Carson McCullers's 1941 psychosexual novel. Clift was to play Major Weldon Penderton (the role taken over by Marlon Brando), opposite Elizabeth Taylor as his flamboyant, oversexed wife. This part would have given Clift the opportunity to play a homosexual, albeit a closeted member of the army, in a film that thematically endorses homosexuality by condemning uniformity. As Penderton, he would have defended those who resist social norms: "It's morally honorable for the square peg to keep scraping in a round hole rather than to discover and to use the unorthodox one that would fit it." The blatant symbolism of these lines—in which the traditional "square peg in a round hole" cliché becomes replete with sexual and sodomitical meanings—argues forcefully for appreciating sexual diversity. Penderton's words also celebrate the homosocial community of the army: "There's much to be said about the life of men among men." The possibility that Clift would have played Penderton points to the ways in which his onscreen pseudo-homosexual persona, after years of channeling his own internal conflict and sexual confusion into his fictional characters, was merging with his real-life identity as a gay man.

An actor's onscreen persona is merely an illusion, yet it is an illusion that nonetheless can speak important truths. The delicate alchemy of casting the right actor in the right part cannot be distilled into a science, but the real-life conflicts of an actor that are human and recognizable can indeed be harnessed and imbued in the character being played, even when camouflaged, to make that character more honest and credible, as is clearly evident in Clift's work. The pseudohomosexuality of the 1950s informs and reflects the fluid gendered dynamics of so many of Clift's roles, and, in so doing, defines his enduring place in film history.

NOTES

1. Ehrenreich credits psychiatrist Lionel Ovesey with coining the term "pseudohomo-sexuality" (24–25). For more analysis of men, masculinity, and pseudohomosexuality, see her "Breadwinners and Losers: Sanctions against Male Deviance," in *The Hearts of Men*, 14–28.

2 ☆☆☆☆☆☆☆☆☆☆☆

Charlton Heston and Gregory Peck
Organization Men

R. BARTON PALMER

Consider the following two stories about film acting that involve two of 1950s Hollywood's most popular male stars: Charlton Heston and Gregory Peck. Working with veteran director George Marshall on one of his first westerns, *The Savage* (1952), Heston was uncertain about how to play a short scene. According to the script, he was to ride his horse close to the camera, dismount, and utter a single, and apparently simple, line of dialogue. The young actor, so Heston reported years later, worried that the line did not suit his character, and he proposed a substantial revision.

Marshall listened with apparent understanding and sympathy to what turned out to be a lengthy and complex pleading, then turned to the earnest neophyte and said: "Look, kid, in this business, the most important thing is not whether you act, but can you ride a horse to your mark."

Marshall interpreted, correctly it seems, Heston's concern with character and interiority as signs of an enthusiasm for the so-called Method, an acting style then a common preoccupation of aspiring actors, especially those who, like Heston, had done their apprentice work on Broadway and in live television. The director closed their discussion with this sardonic comment: "In this shot, that's your motivation; just hit the damn mark. Ok?" Writing his autobiography, Heston saw this exchange as a defining career moment. "I got the message," he writes, "I hit the mark. Acting is partly a question of focus" (Heston, *Arena* 119). He had learned that screen acting was (at least in the first place) not feeling, but action, that is, doing what he was told with enough precision that the camera could capture the image the director desired. He had also absorbed the lesson that a successful career in Hollywood might depend on taking orders—and no pointless back talk or discussion. After his brief and unproductive "creative" dispute with Marshall, Heston would become a loyal organization man during his entire Hollywood career.

It turns out that Gregory Peck had a similar encounter a few years earlier with a veteran director that he also remembered long afterward, if a bit less fondly. Like Heston, Peck had moved to screen work from the stage. And for years after becoming a substantial star, in fact, he continued to think of himself as a serious (that is, stage) actor, working when his film schedule permitted with the La Jolla Playhouse in his hometown near San Diego, which he had founded with fellow actors Mel Ferrer and Dorothy McGuire in 1947. Intent on honing his skills in classical repertory and current productions, he too had become attracted to the Method, undertaking training with one of its less orthodox but very popular masters, Sanford Meisner. Heston never studied with Meisner and in his autobiography never speaks about training or workshopping with any of the Method's famous gurus. Yet, so pervasive was the influence of this brand of naturalistic acting that, while filming *The Savage*, he had adopted the form of preparation that is perhaps most characteristic of Meisner's approach. The famous teacher believed that actors should build a performance by discovering the inner truth of their character, which they could then project, rather than by consciously designing movements and inflections. Dialogue should reflect that inner truth; if it did not, then it should be altered in order to achieve a greater sense of truthfulness. In this theory of preparation, identifying the motivation (object, intent, desire, etc.) of the character at different moments in the narrative was crucial. It was this process that Marshall had rejected so decisively when directing Heston, who was apparently unsure of both his character's motivation and the dialogue that should reflect it. Peck approached his performance as the amnesiac and possible murderer Dr. Anthony Edwardes for Alfred Hitchcock's *Spellbound* (1946) with the same preparation technique in mind.

The famed British director showed as little patience for this approach as Marshall did a few years later. Hitchcock seems to have regarded the Method as both trendy (in the worst sense) and also useless for screen work because resources other than the actor's voice and body were available to create character. Confident during the shooting of *Spellbound* (1946) that his carefully designed editing pattern, along with music, would lend the required meaning to the actor's celluloid presence, Hitchcock asked Peck in one close-up simply to void his face of all expression. Try as he might, the actor found he could not comply. As Peck's biographer Gary Fishgall comments, "That told him nothing about what to feel; only how to look. It was too technical for him" (Fishgall, *Peck* 97). This was a mark he could not hit. Much like Marshall, Hitchcock cared most about the actor's looks, especially insofar as they marked him as belonging to a type that filmgoers would find sympathetic. Even more important, perhaps, he was concerned about the actions and movements he had designed at the storyboard stage; the requested "blank look" apparently fell into this category. This formal structure, it seems, was often simple. Hitchcock once confessed: "My kind of picture is made up entirely of looks and reactions," certainly an oversimplification of the kind the director was accustomed to utter for dramatic effect, but true enough in its own way (Gottlieb 173).

Peck, in contrast, had trained himself to imagine the interior feelings that allowed these movements to be produced. To achieve such authenticity, the actor had to experience (by a process of sympathetic imagination) a state of mind that would make his character's lines and action ring true. To Hitchcock, that process was a matter of profound indifference. His only concern was that his actors should simply do as they were instructed; and, as noted, he determined what that instruction would be long before the cameras began to roll. To Peck, however, screen acting was much more than hitting his mark, and he could never be satisfied with just this "focus," as Heston calls it.

★★★★★ Looking for That Inner Truth

Interestingly, Peck in retrospect felt somewhat uneasy about the inadequacy of his performance for Hitchcock in *Spellbound:* "You do it

his way. I don't think I was at my most effective with him—not because I
didn't like him as a director, but because I was not quite flexible enough . . .
to do everything he wanted and at the same time provide my own inner
truth. Because it's quite possible to act the other way about, from the externals *in*. Many, many great actors do this" (qtd. in Haney 120). After further
experience in the art of screen performance, the actor was able to recognize
clearly the different interests of performer (who needed his "inner truth")
and director (who only needed to be given "everything he wanted").

Peck could now see that thinking about appearance, demeanor, gestures, movement, vocal inflection, and so on might constitute a useful
beginning. For him, however, the process of preparation still had to arrive
eventually at a plausibly fabulized interior self (or at least moment of consciousness) so that the requisite externals might be authenticated. Otherwise, acting would be only a superficial impersonation, lacking the force of
truth that some form of "being," however shallow, limited, and confected,
might lend it. He would, in short, give directors what they wanted, at least
to the best of his ability, but he remained determined to provide his characters with an inner being that made them his own. He would not be happy
with just hitting the mark, however important, as he acknowledged, that
might be. Peck would conform only as much as he found necessary to work
successfully.

Let's be clear. This was not at all the lesson Heston had taken away from
his brief clinic on screen acting with George Marshall. As he tells the story,
after making *The Savage*, hitting the mark in the most literal sense was all
that mattered to him. Carefully controlled action, as Heston admits, was
only part of acting, but apparently for him it was the most important part.
He never discusses any other form of preparation, even in his acting "diary,"
nor did he afterward show any interest in either of the two principal vari-
eties of the Method (see Heston, *Diaries*). For example, in his autobiography
he has much to say about his work on *The Ten Commandments* (1956), which
was a particularly challenging location shoot. Playing arguably the most
enigmatic character of the Old Testament (and a central figure in three
world religions) could be understood as offering considerable difficulties,
and so his "personal preproduction was extensive."

How, then, did Heston approach playing Moses? His preproduction was
in part something he vaguely refers to as "research," which perhaps
included some attempt to understand and get inside his character. Did he
read the book of Exodus or study the approach taken by Theodore Roberts
in the 1923 version? He never says. In fact, the only details Heston does
recall (or at least think worthy of mention) concern the "fifteen or twenty

costumes" he had to be fitted for, as well as the "nine distinct makeups" that had to be "designed, redesigned, and finally tested," with no little contribution from him (*In the Arena* 128). Similarly, in speaking about his work on *The President's Lady* (1953), where he played Andrew Jackson, the actor recalls that "as we developed several make-ups, I began to feel more and more comfortable underneath them" (124). He admits to making a serious mistake in what was to be his second portrayal of Jackson, as the forty-six-year-old American general defending New Orleans against the British in *The Buccaneer* (1958). Consulting with Wally Westmore, Heston advised the makeup director to give the general, as he admits, "a shock of white hair and latex wrinkles suggesting a Jackson of at least sixty" (*In the Arena* 178), making this central figure from American history substantially older than he had been at the time. It is an interesting confession, suggesting as it does both the casualness of his approach to the part (not being certain how old the general was at the time seems an extraordinary lapse) and also his seemingly exclusive commitment to externals. For surely playing a sixty-year-old man would require a very different physical approach (even in terms of gross externals that Heston was good at providing, such as posture and walk). Were such aspects of performance truly of less importance than latex wrinkles?

In any event, Heston's memoirs suggest that he conceived acting as hitting the mark in two related senses. First, acting involves actions, especially those that required practice, skill, athleticism, and courage to perform. His account of the various difficulties faced and overcome in both the staging and photographing of the chariot race sequence in *Ben-Hur* (1959), arguably the most effective and complex action sequence ever staged in any film, overflows with an enthusiasm that is never evident in his accounts of the other, less physically demanding productions in which he was involved. The enduringly amazing celluloid result speaks not only to the technical brilliance of Wyler and the crew (especially famed stuntman Yakima Canutt), but also to Heston's strength, coordination, and steely nerves. Second, portrayal of character for Heston was as a kind of inspired impersonation, a process, dependent on issues of physical appearance like costuming and makeup, whose end result was an internal feeling of comfort rather than a projected sense of authenticity that might register more or less unconsciously in the small movements of his face and his vocal inflection.

Such hard-to-define marks of being, such flickers of intense emotion, could be recorded in a close-up, but would be irrelevant to stage acting because they would be invisible to most in the audience. If the one-shots in *Ben-Hur*'s chariot race capture facial expressions that ring true, this is likely

No other Hollywood actor of the period but Charlton Heston possessed the strength and athleticism to manage a four-horse chariot, the essential element of the spectacularly successful *Ben-Hur* (William Wyler, MGM, 1959). Courtesy of the Academy of Motion Picture Arts and Sciences.

because, actually performing this stunt, Heston was able to project a deep sense of authenticity without even trying; no search for sympathetic understanding was necessary. The dramatic scenes in this film, however, are another matter entirely, and it is quite evident that the canny veteran director William Wyler did his best to cover for the young man's quite limited ability to portray even intense and rather uncomplicated emotion. The chariot sequence is framed by two scenes that bear this out and are quite striking in their own way. Having maneuvered his erstwhile friend but now bitter enemy, the Roman Messala (Stephen Boyd), into the chariot competition, Wyler stages what Method performers call a "private moment" before the race begins. Alone and unobserved, Heston as Ben-Hur is framed in the entrance to the amphitheater, to all appearances enjoying the prospect of confronting his enemy but anticipating the hardships and dangers of the struggle to come. To express what the narrative suggests is the character's overloaded emotional state, however, Wyler simply has Heston, whose back is to the camera, cover his face with his robe and bow his head. The camera never shows his face, and hence any chance for beginning the film's set-piece action with an affecting and character-revealing close-up is discarded.

Why was the scene handled in a way so uncharacteristic of Hollywood practice in general and Wyler's filmmaking in particular? The only plausible explanation is that Heston was simply incapable of providing a facial expression that satisfactorily expressed the deep emotions his character must have been experiencing. This explanation is seemingly clinched by the sequence that follows the race, which is staged and shot in an even more extraordinary fashion. Defeated and dying from the horrible mangling he suffered during the race's exciting conclusion, Messala is laid out on a table, awaiting the amputation of both his legs. Ben-Hur arrives to witness his enemy's end and stands above and to the right of the table with others of Messala's party; the group is easily accommodated within a medium shot that would allow Ben-Hur's reactions to be recorded in the same frame with Messala's last words. The Roman has one more trick up his sleeve. Ben-Hur had thought that his mother and sister had died in prison, but Messala, eager to get in the last blow against Ben-Hur, reveals that they are still alive. Both, however, are now lepers, forced to live in poverty and despair in a wretched valley where those afflicted with the disease are sent.

Once again, the narrative, true to its origins in novelistic melodrama, presents the protagonist with a moment of sudden *éclaircissement*, eliciting powerful, primal emotions that should register on his face: joy that his family still lives, horror at the fate they have endured and are enduring, surprise at Messala's ability even with his dying words to inflict such terrible pain on him, and impotent anger at the unmerited persecution of those he holds dear perpetrated by the man who was once his most beloved boyhood friend. As Boyd, in a bravura portrayal of a man whose hatred dominates even his natural fear of death, wheezes out the fateful words from his broken body, Wyler has Heston turn his face away, in a gesture that simply expresses (inappropriately?) the young man's reluctance to face the truth. It seems clear why, throughout his career, Heston, unlike Peck, tended not to be favored with close-ups or even with scenes to play in which he was required to register emotion with more than body posture. His earliest screen projects find him playing standard melodramatic parts in which he is required to respond to a love interest (Lizabeth Scott in both *Dark City* and *Bad for Each Other* [1953], Eleanor Parker in *The Naked Jungle* [1954]). Such films required love scenes, and in this, according to the apt formulation of Michael Druxman, he "usually appears as wooden as a cigar-store Indian" (Druxman 12).

Had such dramatic roles been the only ones that the industry could have offered him, Heston would likely have had a very short career in filmmaking indeed. The fact that he became a star in the era suggests how the industry had shifted away, at least in part, from its focus on character-driven intimate

narrative in which the display of conventional forms of emotion in inter-
personal encounters was central. Heston may have proved unable to act
with his face in the manner of screen melodrama or to play romance in the
fashion customarily expected of leading men in the early postwar era, but
he was certainly skilled at portraying a larger-than-life, traditional form of
masculinity. In films whose narratives work to demonstrate the inner bank-
ruptcy of this gender style, Heston could only play an antiheroic foil, as he
does in *Ruby Gentry* (1952), a film whose focus is the barely restrained sexual passion of the female protagonist (Jennifer Jones), who is trapped by
her marriage to an ignorant clod (Karl Malden) and her desire for a handsome but shallow young man (Heston).

But few actors, if indeed any, of the era were as well equipped in terms
of looks, physique, and temperament to play sympathetically macho, even
aggressive or brutish males. An insolent lean, a broad smirk, a sardonic tone,
a confident stride, and an impression of contained physical energy commu-
nicated by his deep, resonant delivery of dialogue are his performance trade-
marks, especially in the 1950s. There is no mistaking the alpha-maleness of
his presence, and his large body (especially those very broad shoulders)
could easily fill the screen, a distinct advantage in an era enamored of the
various forms of widescreen cinema. He was at his best when his assigned
character made the most of these qualities, most notably, perhaps, in the first
part of his performance in *The Ten Commandments* as a haughty Egyptian
prince, an impersonation that nicely rhymes with Yul Brynner's arrogant,
stubborn Pharaoh in the second half of the film. Though he found himself
with few opportunities to play against this rather restricted type, Heston
proved surprisingly expert at reducing his own persona to humorous
absurdity in *The Private War of Major Benson* (1955), in which he plays a ram-
rod-stiff ex-army officer unexpectedly put in charge of a military academy.
The actor found the property so attractive, in fact, that he stretched himself
thin by fitting the shooting into idle periods of the *Commandments* production. Heston's Major Benson, however, is a one-dimensional character,
nothing much more than the amusingly exasperated butt of adolescent
pranks. Heston required no motivation to hit his mark this time. Benson was
a character that he could play with only a few choice external gestures and
some fabricated bluster, mostly "being" himself more or less.

✰✰✰✰✰ A Personality Actor with a Difference

In 1950s Hollywood, such a limitation might be more of an
advantage than a handicap. For the most part, stars of the period were "per-

sonality actors," who, as Fishgall puts it so well, invested "each role with a range of general qualities, a way of moving, speaking, looking, and behaving," thus only partly becoming the characters they played (*Peck* 147). Despite his interests in confecting a second inner self for marking the difference between his character and himself, Gregory Peck was arguably as much a personality actor as Heston. And it is also true that, as a result, he found a number of roles beyond that range in which he was clearly limited, if not as limited as Heston. For example, when he was required, for John Huston's ill-starred adaptation of Melville's *Moby Dick* (1956), to play the larger-than-life Captain Ahab, American literature's most obsessive Romantic hero, Peck found himself unable even to suggest the larger metaphysical aspects of the character. He was quite conscious of his failure either to understand or to project Ahab's mythic stature and was likely both chagrined and also flattered by what the film's screenwriter, Ray Bradbury, publicly proclaimed about his abilities: "Gregory Peck is never going to be a paranoid killer or a maniac devourer of whales" (qtd. in Fishgall, *Peck* 186). Interestingly, however, in his explanation of failure Peck did not fix on "externals": a strained "disturbed" vocal inflection for the monomaniacal character that he could never get right because his delivery was too deliberate; a makeup and costuming scheme that made him look uncannily like Abraham Lincoln; dialogue that for the most part lacked any mythic qualities (Bradbury was famed as a science fiction writer, not as a Melvillean epicist). Instead, Peck faulted his own inner resources, his unfulfilled search for sympathetic understanding: "I was unable to overcome the feeling that Ahab was an old lunatic" (qtd. in Fishgall, *Peck* 186).

As Peck's career took shape in the 1950s, his principal type emerged from the trial and error of moving from one project to another, often, because of contract obligations, with little choice as to roles. Peck made what now seems an extraordinary total of eighteen films during that decade (while Heston, it should be noted, stayed even busier, appearing in an even more remarkable twenty-two theatrical releases, mostly as the featured character and acting in thirty-four half-hour or hour-long television dramas). If Heston's specialty was action films, especially costume epics, Peck emerged as especially suited to play, in dramas of different kinds, gentlemanly, passionate, well-educated, and somewhat refined professionals, capable of passion but not overly romantic, who were eager for success and other conventional rewards of masculine accomplishment. In two principal genres of the 1950s, the westerns and war films of the small- to medium-budget variety that constituted much of his screen work during the decade, he could play a one-dimensional version of the single-minded obsessive type, sometimes good, sometimes bad: a martinet cavalry officer in *Only the Valiant* (1951) who discovers a better way to lead men; the captain of a British man-o'-war who is eager to wreak havoc on Napoleon's navy in *Captain Horatio Hornblower, R.N.* (1951) and who must disobey orders in order to accomplish his larger mission; a self-destructive, depressive pilot who learns to be more humane in *The Purple Plain* (1954); and a rancher eager to avenge the murder of his family and whose anger is eventually assuaged in *The Bravados* (1958).

Peck's screen persona was flexible and sympathetic enough to enable him to play in a variety of genres: psychological westerns like *The Gunfighter* (1950), high-minded literary adaptations like *The Snows of Kilimanjaro* (1952), light romantic comedies like *Roman Holiday* (1953), serious dramas like *The Man in the Gray Flannel Suit* (1956), and even "A" production war films like *Pork Chop Hill* (1959). Other performers—such as Dana Andrews—often turned in skilled performances in the kind of roles that Peck, in Hitchcock's *Spellbound* and *The Paradine Case* (1947), simply could not bring off with any conviction or subtlety.

Peck's interest in Method techniques differentiated him from other sympathetic, conventionally handsome leading men who had broken into pictures in the early 1940s and continued to be featured players in the late studio period. This interest aligns him more with those of the next generation, who, generally entering the business after stage experience, were even more thoroughly imbued with Method ideas, such as Marlon Brando, Montgomery Clift, Ben Gazzara, Joanne Woodward, Karl Malden, James Dean, Carroll Baker, and Paul Newman. For Peck, getting into character (when the production called for a "rounded" portrayal, not always the case for him in the 1950s) involved an often elaborate and extensive process of sympathetic understanding that proceeded from a careful reading of the script (no need for input from the director), a process of which the actor has left extensive records.

Peck's annotated shooting script for the most famous role he was to play during his career, Atticus Finch in *To Kill a Mockingbird* (1962), exemplifies the kind of deep reading and performance design that by the end of the 1950s he had become accustomed to practicing. Here is just a small sampling of his commentary:

> Atticus above little emotions . . . but capable of passion . . . imperturbable . . .
> a little bigger than most men, has conquered animal emotions . . . irritation,
> he is above it . . . no aggressiveness . . . wrath yes . . . establish the way you
> talk to the children [in the first scene with Mr. Cunningham] . . . every scene
> positive . . . never bored . . . never tired . . . not on the shelf . . . establish her

authority [Calpurnia] . . . first came warmth and humor, establish here his intelligence [in scene where Atticus learns of Tom's arrest] . . . [with line "So was I"] *Mean it!!* [underlined] It's a stinking matter . . . [in scene where Atticus talks about Scout's getting her mother's jewelry someday] tender but manly . . . [In the scene with the Judge, GP changed the line "Well, thanks for the business" to "I'll take the case. I know what we will be up against. I'll be ready."] [GP changes Judge's line "I thought I'd let you know it's your case" to "I'm thinking about appointing you to take his case," gives GP a chance to affirm his interest] . . . [GP tells himself to "visualize lynching" at the end of this scene] . . . [same scene] be alive with the problem . . . [in courtroom scene GP tells himself "that dirty S.O.B. Ewell is *in my mind* and *poor Tom*"] . . . [in scene with Ewell GP tells himself, *"Don't compromise,* show his hard side, explains Atticus's character, it will mean something"].

(in Palmer 203)

This extensive preparation served Peck well. He had to struggle with energy and unflagging purpose to impose his conception on *To Kill a Mockingbird*, not only interrogating, and accordingly modulating, his own performance in the service of authenticity, but successfully lobbying with the film's director and producer (Robert Mulligan and Alan J. Pakula), and even the studio, Universal Pictures. He barraged his fellow filmmakers with extensive comments and suggestions, first about the script and then about the film's rough cut (Palmer 192–203). He was no longer a neophyte working for a domineering Alfred Hitchcock, one of the giants of the industry, but a proven box-office attraction who had taken advantage of the accelerating shift to independent production in the industry and had moved, if only in part, to the other side of the camera.

The result speaks for itself. He won the Academy Award for Best Actor (which he was pleased and honored to accept). More important, perhaps, the American Film Institute ranks *Mockingbird* twenty-fifth on their top 100 release list, while, perhaps more interestingly, recognizing Gregory Peck's Atticus Finch as the "greatest screen hero" of all time. In *The Organization Man* (1956), William H. Whyte wrote, "If the [organization man] goes against the group, is he being courageous—or just stubborn?" Peck's going "against the group" proved not only "courageous" but, perhaps more to the point, admirably self-serving. Peck the actor and producer was intent on imposing, insofar as possible, his vision on films that would be made within (not in spite of or outside) Hollywood institutions. If he became a rebel (or, perhaps better, something of a self-righteous prima donna), his rebellion, like that of Atticus Finch, was a strictly limited crusade, an assertion of self that ended in his rooting himself even more firmly into the inner circles of Hollywood.

In contrast, Heston's focus was always on the mark set for him by the director and producer. Significantly, in an era when even older actors like Cary Grant and James Cagney explored the possibilities of either incorporating or getting more deeply involved in production, Heston remained satisfied with working for others. He never struggled before, during, or after production to impose his individuality on any film. In the words of Albert Zugsmith, the producer of *Touch of Evil* (1958), who appreciated his against-type impersonation of a Mexican detective as part of an impressive featured ensemble (including Orson Welles, Janet Leigh, and Akim Tamiroff), Heston was a "thinking actor . . . a nice man, but of greater importance a 'team player' who makes no waves during production"; his reward was constant employment and a lengthy career (qtd. in Druxman 11).

The making of *The Big Country* (1958), in which Heston played the second lead to Peck's featured character, provides an interesting contrast in their work with William Wyler, a demanding craftsman who was notoriously unreceptive to complaints or suggestions from the cast. After several takes with a close-up that (perhaps not uncharacteristically) Heston had difficulty doing, Wyler moved on to the next shot, even though the actor pleaded for another take. The director ignored Heston's pleas for guidance, simply responding: "Chuck, if I don't say anything, that means it's O.K. All right?" (Heston, *Arena* 168). Heston demurred; there was no further discussion. The result: beginning in the 1950s Heston was a featured player (if not really a star in the strictest sense) in "some of the most successful pictures to ever adorn theater screens—in fact, three of them—*The Ten Commandments* (1956), *Ben-Hur* (1959) and *Earthquake* (1974) [which ranked for a time] among the twenty all-time top-grossing pictures" (Druxman 11). And yet, as Druxman goes on to explain, Heston was "never considered by his industry to be truly viable when it comes to attracting patrons to the box office," the reflex, perhaps, of his onscreen presence appearing "stiff" and short on "warmth and vulnerability" (12). But in the role of larger-than-life heroic figures, especially in historical reconstructions, Heston in his prime had few, if any, rivals.

✮✮✮✮✮ Making (No) Waves

Peck had a much different experience with Wyler. His company had invested heavily in *The Big Country*, making him a de facto co-producer. As he was to do later during the making of *Mockingbird*, Peck tried to use this leverage in order to make sure that the film presented him in the best possible light. Reviewing the dailies at one point, he asked Wyler to do a reshoot because he was unhappy with his performance. Wyler had no patience with a request that might delay the shooting schedule, unnecessarily in his view. "I'm not going to do another retake. We don't need it," he said, and with no little impatience. An angry Peck stormed off the film's location in Stockton, California, and did not stop until arriving at his home in Los Angeles. With his co-producer and star now unavailable, Wyler determined to shoot the rest of the film at the studio. Peck at first refused to report, but then, considering how his fit of pique was hurting his reputation in the business, finally agreed, though he had to give a party for Hollywood notables after the shooting wrapped in order to show publicly he had made the peace (Haney 274–75).

In this instance, Peck shows the other side of his unyielding desire for self-promotion and self-expression (we might find it interesting that in reviewing the rushes, he did not lobby for retakes of any of the shots that did not include him). Instead, he showed a strong stubborn streak, one that might well have compromised his career had he not been persuaded by his wife to apologize indirectly. Walking off the set in the middle of a production, when every minute of on-set time costs a pretty penny, was then as now close to an unforgivable professional misstep.

Interestingly, these sharply contrasting reactions to Wyler's authoritative (arguably officious) style find their reflex in the fictional world that *The Big Country* brings to life, in which Heston appropriately plays the loyal organization man (a figure whose strength derives from faithful service to his somewhat megalomaniacal employer). In contrast, Peck is the outsider easterner who is at first willing to accept the *autres moeurs* of the barely civilized wilderness in order to marry a rich rancher's daughter, whom he met and wooed while she was resident back east. But when pressured to abandon his own code of conduct and behave instead in accordance with all the values that define the "western man," he refuses to go along, eventually ending the engagement. Heston's character, in contrast, has always embraced the regional ethos unquestioningly. Interestingly, he is a ranch foreman, eager to do the bidding of his employer, not, like Peck's easterner, an independent spirit. At a crucial point, however, Heston's character questions the wisdom of continued obedience to a notion of personal honor (and an urge for self-aggrandizement) that will surely prove mutually suicidal for all concerned. In the end, however, he does not go "against the group," while Peck's character goes his own way and succeeds in surviving, while simultaneously profiting from, the ensuing social wreckage. Peck is the nonconformist, Heston the organization man whose loyalty, maintained against his better judgment, leads him to a bitter end. And—an indication

of the film's untraditional, ungeneric engagement with social questions—
Peck's "dude" is the lead, while Heston's "cowboy" is the supporting role.

The conflict between masculine styles in the film (one, as Raymond
Williams would have it, traditional, the other "emerging") not only effectively makes use of the screen personas that the two actors had established
during the 1950s. This conflict also interestingly works over the vexed
issue of the need for, but limits to, individuality in a world where the pressure to "go along in order to get along" was thought by many professional
sociologists/observers like William H. Whyte and Robert Lindner (whose
book *Must You Conform?* was published in 1956) to be alarmingly increasing.
Considered as contending images within a single film, and as actors who
established very different screen selves during the same era, Gregory Peck
and Charlton Heston offer, in the revealing formulation of Richard Dyer,
"star images [that] function crucially in relation to contradictions within
and between ideologies, which they seek variously to 'manage' or resolve"
(38). In embodying these contrasting styles, the performances of Peck and
Heston in *The Big Country* interestingly reflect their extratextual lives as
Hollywood performers, positioning the film to be read as an intriguing allegory of Hollywood in the 1950s.

★★★★★ An Axiom of the Cinema

On an institutional level, we can understand the differences
between Peck and Heston as embodying an important aspect of the transition
from Classical Hollywood to New Hollywood, with the older version of the
actor as simply an appropriate element in the image (hitting his mark, so to
speak, as Marshall and Hitchcock might say) slowly giving way to a new version (strongly influenced by developments within the serious American theater) of the actor as a character marked by a palpable sense of authenticity.
In part, as numerous commentators on the era have remarked, the New
Hollywood that emerges in the course of the 1950s constitutes what is in
effect a cinema of performance, in which the actor as character (and the character of the actor) becomes a focus of attention (see the chapter in this volume on Marlon Brando for further discussion on this point). In this scheme,
the younger man (Heston) would be something of a throwback (it is interesting that he was so comfortable working with industry legend Cecil B.
DeMille, who was more than five decades his senior). Peck, his somewhat
older counterpart, in contrast, aligns himself with the Young Turks, "rebel"
male stars like Clift and Brando who, as Graham McCann suggests, were "in
search more of 'authenticity' than of stardom" and dramatized the rejection

of society's demand "to conform to traditional values and familiar types" (3, 6). In its own generically bound fashion, *The Big Country* stages a revolt against the climate of conformity that is as revealing of the anti-establishmentarianism simmering just beneath the surface of an ostensibly tradition-bound 1950s culture as the more famed youth films of the era such as *The Wild One* (1953) or *Rebel Without a Cause* and *East of Eden* (both 1955).

It is also tempting to cast Peck and Heston as performer versions of industry stereotypes (one in the process of losing purchase and the other emerging) that were prominent in French critical analysis of Hollywood in the period. Peck is the auteur since, as his career progressed, he became increasingly committed to his vision of whatever film he was making, including especially his own role in it, while remaining barely tolerant of authority figures who might contest that vision. Heston is the *metteur-en-scène*: an uncomplaining employee, with no vision of his own, who could be depended on to do a commendable job while making no trouble in the process. Following this line of thought, it would be easy enough to make some neo-romantic point about the unconventionality of the true artist at Heston's expense. Peck would be the rebel who, persevering, rises to the top of his profession riding the energy of his irrepressible individuality, while Heston would be cast as the "organization man," the 1950s nightmare version of what happens to male individuality in an increasingly rationalized collective. In the words of Whyte, who is certainly the most widely read Jeremiah of the period, the organization man "feels an obligation to the group" and thus goes along even though he can "sense some moral constraints on his own free will" (15). In both *Ben-Hur* and *The Ten Commandments*, Heston convincingly portrays this type, with the irresistible will (or unignorable presence) of the divine determining both action and, ultimately, also character.

We might also laud Peck's professional perfectionism (for which others, of course, might occasionally have to suffer) and look less favorably upon Heston's somewhat superficial preoccupation with the look rather than any more deeply "inner" approach to character portrayal. The critical and popular consensus is that Peck turned out to be the better actor than Heston. But this might well be a question of differing degrees of interest in and dedication to those aspects of the craft that earn awards and peer esteem. However extraordinary they are, "athletic" performances do not often receive Best Actor Academy Award nominations (Heston's for *Ben-Hur* is an interesting exception, the result in part, perhaps, of the film's sweep [eleven awards total] of the competition that year). Film theorists have paid little or no attention to what exactly are the so-called athletic aspects of action performance, but it is clear enough that this is an area of screen acting in which, however underrated and underappreciated, Heston excelled. Later in his career, Peck is simply unimaginable in parts like that of the medieval vassal Chrysagon, charged with building and holding a frontier castle against a host of enemies in *The War Lord* (1965). The embattled nobleman, mature and cynical, is memorably incarnated by a physically dynamic if aging Heston, who did many of his own stunts (he was forty-one years old during production).

The contrast in reputation between the two actors could also be understood in terms of that most interesting of neo-romantic concepts: talent. Druxman reports (without citing a specific source) that one actress who worked with Heston considered him "the world's highest paid non-actor," a judgment that may be apocryphal, but, given the critical consensus about his performances, certainly expresses something of a truth. Peck, in contrast, would be the craftsman who, making the best of an ability that was in its own way rather limited, worked tirelessly at both self-improvement and self-promotion, becoming one of postwar Hollywood's best loved performers. Heston, it is true, also improved in the course of a long career his ability to portray (rather than simply embody) character. To dismiss Heston, however, is to ignore the important, unforgettable role he played in a 1950s cinema dominated in part by large-budget historical dramas or actioners in which the technical and acting resources of the Hollywood cinema were deployed in excess in order to compete with the industry's small screen rival. With its unreliable black and white images, its tinny sound, its shoestring, even shoddy production values, its commitment more to drama and music hall entertainment than to engaging spectacle, television occupied a very different position in the era's spectrum of popular culture. Because of his featured roles as part of large, talented acting ensembles in three of the most popular and critically acclaimed epic productions of the decade (*The Greatest Show on Earth* [1952], *The Ten Commandments*, and, preeminently, *Ben-Hur*), Heston became an iconic image of the era. Those three films just mentioned are impossible to remember without him, just as the next decade's *To Kill a Mockingbird* inevitably brings to mind Peck as Atticus Finch. Heston's physical presence, impressive in part because unusual, complemented by the gracefulness of a much smaller man, evokes the somewhat retrograde production strategy of the era, its fascination with what Aristotle terms *opsis* and we now call eye candy (compare his appeal to that of silent-era screen idol Douglas Fairbanks).

Heston was an ideal type to be exploited by the directors from Hollywood's honored past (DeMille and Wyler) who were called upon, as crisis gripped the industry, to re-create the visual splendor of the early studio period, in part, of course, by remaking two of its most honored and financially successful productions. In such a cinema, Heston's obsession with externals (especially, it seems, the right makeup), while easily mocked when compared to the round character realism of a Method performance, seems not so misplaced after all. In the late silent and early sound era George Arliss and Paul Muni significantly advanced the biopic's commitment to impressive and affecting historical reconstruction, working mostly with externals, or from the outside in. Druxman is surely correct to observe that "the number of contributions Heston has made to this genre dwarfs the combined real-life portrayals of both these fine actors" (12).

In part, this may be because Heston proved able to negotiate the connection between what Richard Maltby calls the "actor's two bodies" in a way that proved particularly effective for audiences of the era. One way of looking at the process of stipulation involved in acting (the transaction according to which the audience accepts the actor's implicit presentation of himself as "another") is to identify the ways in which the actor's body, the presence of his real self, might constitute a "distraction from the fiction" (Maltby 380). Of course, this distraction is what provided the psychological and erotic fuel for the star system. Stars, that is, always appear as themselves, no matter what characters they are also ostensibly incarnating. And so this recognition of their "real selves" inevitably limits the sense in which the fiction of the narrative can be understood as fiction (rather than simply as the display of an already known, attractive persona).

But this persistence of the self in performance, so to speak, has another effect. As we have been here exploring it in its postwar naturalistic guise of the Method, acting can be understood not only as an abnegation of self (always partial and temporary) but also as the corresponding confection of a convincing alternative that we term the character. In the case of "personality actors" like Heston, the abnegation of self is always problematic, making it impossible for the actor to disappear completely into a role. For Hollywood, however, the sense in which the actor's real body always remains present and obtrusive conversely offers "the means by which viewers invest in the existence of characters as if they were real people" (Maltby 380). The paradox is that the heightened recognition of the actor's *real* body furthers the desired effect of investing the *fictional* character with reality and solidity. This is especially true when that character, drawn from history, is most easily recognizable and memorable in terms of externals and is imaged in narratives where "rounded" characters would be irrelevant at best, distracting at worst. Do we really want a Moses in *The Ten Commandments* suffering from the same moral crises, anatomized in a series of private moments, as Terry Malloy (Marlon Brando) in *On the Waterfront* (1954)?

In a cinema that profitably turned toward the spectacular gigantism of the cinematic past (DeMille had his most impressive decade of achievement since the 1920s) while embracing technological improvements designed to heighten the affect of the image (particularly widescreen processes), Heston was destined to become a central figure, incarnating something like the ancient idea of the hero (Achilles, Aeneas, Hercules). He was destined to become, in the famous formulation of French critic Michel Mourlet, "an axiom of the cinema":

> By himself alone he constitutes a tragedy, and his presence in any film whatsoever suffices to create beauty. The contained violence expressed by the sombre phosphorescence of his eyes, his eagle's profile, the haughty arch of his eyebrows, the prominent cheek-bones, the bitter and hard curve of his mouth, the fabulous power of his torso; this is what he possesses and what not even the worst director can degrade.   (qtd. in Maltby 381)

George Marshall told the young Heston that it was important for him to hit his mark. By the end of the 1950s, however, it became apparent that his presence alone could sustain larger-than-life narratives, making it unnecessary for him to do much in the way of acting.

Heston's portrayals are heroic in a more traditional sense, one that encompasses the sweep of Western culture. He could manage, without really trying, what is in some respects a more impressive feat: resuscitating a long-dead Michelangelo, bringing to real life for the first time the legendary El Cid, or providing Moses with the impressive presence that makes believable his orderly leading of the assembled tribes of Israel out of Egyptian bondage. To be sure, this is an ability (the star presence solidifying the fictional) possessed by other actors of the period. In both *Lust for Life* (1956) and *Spartacus* (1960), Kirk Douglas uses his own impressive physicality to authenticate spectacular historical recreations, even, in the former film, showing how such incarnational display can be provided with a Method-produced expressivity, as both the outsized artistic achievement and the inner psychological turmoil of Vincent Van Gogh are brought memorably to the screen. *Spartacus* even affords Douglas a number of interesting private moments. Despite his impressive talents, however, even Douglas cannot rival Heston's domination of the era's resurrection of the epic form. Heston is 1950s cinema's only true axiom. No other actor is so fundamental to, so determinative of, the basic value and appeal of the gigantism at the center of the decade's profitable resurrection of the epic form that seemed (falsely as it turned out) to have reached its zenith at the end of the silent era.

★★★★★ Must We Bend, Submit, Adjust, Fit In?

Why, we might ask, would Mourlet comment that "by himself alone [Heston] constitutes a tragedy"? Is it that an essential element of the heroic is an extraordinary capacity to suffer and somehow triumph, if alone, over that suffering? Heston's film roles often suggest that this is true. His Ben-Hur is condemned to a living death in the Roman galleys, meriting special treatment by his presence alone, as the Roman admiral Quintus Arrius (Jack Hawkins)—recognizing, like Mourlet, his extraordinary physical appearance—picks him out from among the ranks of ragged and filthy slaves as a man of special character. His Moses is informed of the truth of his birth and forced to forgo the comfortable, rewarding life of an Egyptian prince for a humble exile, years of wandering in the wilderness, and obedience to an enigmatic divinity. His circus boss in *The Greatest Show on Earth* (1952) is so dedicated to serving the circus that he has no time for a romantic or personal life. His Byronic Lt. William Clark must give up his love for Sacajawea (Donna Reed) for the good of his country in *The Far Horizons* (1958). His austere aristocrat must burn down his own lovingly constructed mansion to save himself and his household from a ravening horde of ants in *The Naked Jungle* (1954). And so on.

During the 1950s, it is only in *The Gunfighter* that Peck plays a good-bad protagonist who even comes close to tragedy. Jimmy Ringo, finally staking out a path to reconcile with his wife and reclaim his role as father to his young son (aims that are entirely consistent with his developing screen persona), is ambushed and killed by a young man eager to make a name for himself. The film's narrative, however, is more heavily freighted with melodramatic probabilities. It is only that, with a palpable poignancy rather than tragic inevitability, these are foreclosed by the character's moral dubiousness. Ringo's self-confessed past selfishness and his neglect of those who depended on him make it impossible for him to claim a second chance, despite the love he demonstrates for wife and son. This love is the powerful emotion that motors the narrative and, ironically, results in his death.

With the exception of that most obvious of career missteps, *Moby Dick*, Peck's 1950s films do not end tragically. He plays characters virtuous and ordinary enough to be assimilated easily into respectable society. Or, at least, his characters demonstrate the goodness requisite for a happy ending, should one have been possible. The enduring final images in Peck's films capture archly melodramatic moments of reconciliation, coupling, and, occasionally, a painfully triumphant sense of loss: the crusading journalist resolving the moral conflict with his fiancée in *Gentleman's Agreement*; a remorseful King David receiving the signs of God's renewed blessing in *David and Bathsheba* (1951); the submarine commander, joining with his crew and buoyed by memories of his now-dead family, embarking for a final and suicidal cruise as life itself ends all around them in *On the Beach* (1959); F. Scott Fitzgerald, doomed to die young but enjoying in his final months a bittersweet romance with the adoring Sheilah Graham in *Beloved Infidel* (1959); and, most memorably, soon after the decade was done, the lawyer Atticus Finch, his case lost and his client shot dead, but his children saved miraculously from a vengeful maniac and the family restored to the safety of their home in *To Kill a Mockingbird*.

The epic hero like Moses or Ben-Hur cannot contest the metaphysical forces under the influence of which his drama of suffering and vindication play out. Large as he is in these two roles, Heston finds himself at the mercy of (or subject to deliverance by) forces so much larger than himself that they cannot even find onscreen representation at all: the disembodied God that speaks out of the rocky mountaintop in *The Ten Commandments*, the Christ who occupies the space just outside the frame in *Ben-Hur*—presences defined by their lack of presence, even as the epic hero is limited by the untranscendent obtrusiveness of his physicality, which fills the era's widened screen. The melodramatic hero like Peck, in contrast, successfully struggles against the social forces that would constrain his individuality. He effects a reconciliation of some kind through the perseverance of his desire for success or, conversely, through his willingness to retreat from obdurateness. He does not feel the need to "submit" in order to "fit in," but he does "adjust" and "bend," to answer the question posed about conformity by Robert Lindner. Lindner is most famous in the era as the author of the sociological tract *Rebel Without a Cause* that, unforgettably fictionalized, was turned into the screenplay for one of the era's most telling dramatizations of that limited opposition to establishment values so characteristic of the era. In Whyte's view, the 1950s obsession with a nonconformity staged *within* but not *against* the organization is most interestingly embodied in Sloan Wilson's novel *The Man in the Gray Flannel Suit* (1955). For Whyte, this extremely popular novel about a rising young executive who tells his boss what he thinks but refuses to become completely devoted to serving the corporation expresses the sense in which, as a fantasy at least, many in the 1950s intended to "have it both ways" (278). Offered a demanding job that will obviously allow him to be groomed for the position of CEO one day, the novel's hero, Tom Rath, turns it down because, as Whyte puts it, "he'd have to work too hard and he wants to be with his family." A believer in the traditional American value of self-actualization, Whyte sardonically comments:

Wracked by disturbing memories of the recent past and worried about his financial future, Gregory Peck, here pictured with Gene Lockhart, played the era-defining "organization man" in *The Man in the Gray Flannel Suit* (Nunnally Johnson, Twentieth Century–Fox, 1956). Courtesy of the Academy of Motion Picture Arts and Sciences.

"Blessed are the acquiescent" (278). But, the sociologist recognizes, the younger generation in the decade was not so dismissive of Rath's desire to reconcile career and family. For them, Rath was a hero, a man who stands up to the unreasonable demand of corporate life for unquestioning dedication, whatever the personal consequences might be. And an object lesson on this score is not far to seek. The boss's family life is a shambles, as he is hated and ignored by both his ex-wife and his self-destructive daughter, who are miserable despite the affluent way of life he has provided them.

Peck was seen correctly as the only actor who could incarnate Rath in the film version (1956), arguably the most socially significant melodrama of the decade. As journalist Lloyd Schorr remarked, "Gregory Peck happens to be by nature the actor in the gray flannel suit. He's stolid, conservative, hardworking" (qtd. in Haney 259). Schorr might have added ambitious (Rath exchanges a safe job with a nonprofit for a high-pressure position with a media conglomerate) and also incapable of completely submerging his personality (it is by saying what he thinks and not adopting the opinion of those on his "team" that he impresses the boss). These were the qualities of Gregory Peck, professional actor, as well. Blessed are the acquiescent indeed, but, *pace* Whyte, blessed also are those whose acquiescence is balanced by creative defiance. And doomed are those, like Rath's boss (Fredric March), who persist in their single-minded devotion to institutions larger than themselves, even those they create. They truly constitute a tragedy in themselves alone.

The relevance of this cultural development for Hollywood can be glimpsed in an allegorizing reading of *The Big Country*, in which two of that era's biggest stars can be understood as representing institutional as well as gender styles, in the broadest sense of that term. In that film, true to his screen and professional personas, Heston's ranch foreman, Steve Leech, has adopted unquestioningly the expansionist ethos of his employer, Major Terrill (Charles Bickford). In contrast, Peck's James McKay, who like the actor himself is unwilling to surrender his individuality, shows himself willing when introduced to western customs for the first time to go along with them until he discovers Terrill's commitment to mindless violence, which is matched by that of his rancher enemy, Rufus Hannassey (Burl Ives). McKay refuses to be drawn into the conflict between outsized patriarchs, and he refuses as well to allow Leech to force him into pointless public displays of masculine bravado (riding a dangerous bronco, defending his "honor" when challenged to a fist fight, and exacting a disproportionate vengeance on the Hannasseys for a minor humiliation). The most important point, however, is that McKay's noncompliance is self-limiting. He does not demur from acquiescing to the very economic system (cattle ranching) embraced by Hannassey and Terrill, only provided that he can bend its rules to suit him. So he fights the eager Leech in private (the struggle ends in a draw) and indulges in a duel with young Buck Hannassey (Chuck Connors), but with single-shot dueling pistols, not six-guns, making the contest one of courage and coolness under pressure rather than fast-draw skill.

In that confrontation, McKay shows himself both willing to risk death and also unwilling to shoot Buck down when, terrified, the younger man fires prematurely. Leech demonstrates a different kind of moral courage. After he proves unable to prevent Terrill from riding to his death in a final, pointless confrontation with Hannassey, he acquiesces to the inevitable, riding with the man who had treated him like a son and moving, at film's end, into irrelevance. Far from rejecting western values, McKay decides to settle down in the west, but not, as originally planned, through marriage with Terrill's daughter, Patricia (Carroll Baker), who loses respect for him after his unconventional rejection of the public display of masculine values.

Charlton Heston as the traditional western hero and Gregory Peck as an easterner who adapts to western ways provided an interesting contrast of masculine styles in *The Big Country* (William Wyler, MGM, 1958). Courtesy of the Academy of Motion Picture Arts and Sciences.

Instead, McKay ends the film coupled with Julie Maragon (Jean Simmons), who, like him, has refused to become involved in the suicidal feud between the two cattle barons, but, significantly, owns the water on which further development of the area must depend. The future, it is clear, will belong to the man of semi-rebellious character, who is possessed of advantages both economic and personal. The pioneering giants of the west belong to the past (the two patriarchs lie dead at film's end). And Terrill's most obvious inheritor, Heston's Steve Leech, has outlived his relevance.

Leech knows only obedience to time-honored, traditional values, whose supersedence by an individualistic ethos, respectful of but not bound by tradition, the film dramatizes. In this character, Heston offers an impressive coda to his axiomatic, epic presence within 1950s cinema. Once again, but quite poignantly, he constitutes something like a "tragedy in himself alone." Peck's McKay, in contrast, points the way toward a different notion of the heroic. An eastern opportunist, he espouses a self-serving because moderated version of the nonconformism that the rebel males of this cinematic era customarily follow to violent or self-destructive conclusions. Peck's persona is very much of the era, whose values were so soon to alter. Antiheroic versions of the nonconformist, more alienated and self-defining than either Jim McKay or Terry Malloy ever think to be, become a dominant presence in the thoroughly masculinizing Hollywood of the 1960s, deconstructing the carefully balanced dialectic between tragic and melodramatic versions of maleness that this chapter has traced in the careers of Charlton Heston and Gregory Peck.

3 ☆☆☆☆☆☆☆☆☆☆☆

James Stewart and James Dean
The Darkness Within

MURRAY POMERANCE

By Wednesday, 4 May 1955, when at 8:30 in the morning he left home to shoot *The Man Who Knew Too Much* for Alfred Hitchcock in Marrakech, James Stewart, by his wife's account the "hardest-working actor in Hollywood" (Gloria McLean Stewart, "I'm in Love with a Wonderful Guy," *Photoplay*, February 1951, 99), was the sort of personality who merited gilded treatment from studios, associates, and colleagues, not to say fans. The Paramount car, waiting outside his home at 918 North Roxbury Drive in Beverly Hills,[1] had him at the airport in time for a 10:00 A.M. departure to Chicago,

Courtesy of the Academy of Motion Picture Arts and Sciences.

where for his three-day stay at the secluded and plush Ambassador East Hotel he would have a car constantly at his disposal. In New York, for two days afterward, the Stewarts would reside at the secluded and plush Pierre (in a suite they had occupied previously), leaving on the evening of 9 May, with a pair of berths reserved on a Pan American Stratocruiser bound for Paris (where a car would also be at his disposal). Two luxurious Parisian days would be spent at the secluded and plush Plaza Athénée, again with a car, before a departure by Air France from Orly to Casablanca on 12 May; and on Friday, 13 May, at 8:00 A.M. a car would fetch them and drive them to Marrakech, where they were booked at the secluded and plush Ménara, a "hotel for tourists of good taste," as Stewart is informed in the movie itself, though not, in fact, the one his character has chosen.

Stewart's career—under the skillful management of Lew Wasserman at MCA more or less since the end of World War II—had by the beginning of this decade come to the point where he could own part of his pictures (now, along with Wasserman and Hitchcock, forming Filwite Productions) and take a hefty slice of the profit in annually deferred payments ("spread over the life of the films" [Bruck 114]) in lieu of salary to avoid tax, making him a substantial enough screen personality to have tax problems, that is, the most substantial sort of screen personality there was. During this one decade, he made twenty-five motion pictures, including, but not discussed here, *Harvey* (1950), *The Jackpot* (1950), *No Highway in the Sky* (1951), *Carbine Williams* (1952), *The Spirit of St. Louis* (1957), *Bell, Book and Candle* (1958), and *Anatomy of a Murder* (1959). Healthy, optimistic, and energetic, he was surely in a position to do the films he most wanted to do (see Fishgall, *Pieces of Time* 211–12), and had come to the resolute conclusion that doing a lot of films was a good idea: "Any actor who stays off the screen for any length of time is digging his own grave. I want to make as many pictures as I can" (to Louella Parsons, *Los Angeles Times*, ca. 1950–51).[2]

Stewart and some others like him—Rock Hudson, Tony Curtis, Elizabeth Taylor, for example—received lavish attention of the sort I have described because they were key parts of the elaborate machinery of film production, and this at a critical time, when to visit the Hollywood studios made one feel, as one observer put it, "as though he were in the midst of an ancient empire that is falling apart" (Bosley Crowther, *New York Times Magazine*, 3 February 1957, 24). Only a month after Stewart arrived in Marrakech, Thomas Pryor reported in the *New York Times Magazine* that Hollywood was actively, even desperately, searching for avatars, "the movie business' greatest and seemingly inexhaustible asset," a necessary endeavor because "time has caught up with most of the front-line stars. Middle-age paunch, disappearing or graying hair, sagging facial tissue and general diminishing of youthful vigor have blunted the romantic appeal of too many top-rated stars" (12 June 1955, 14). Although, as Gary Cooper put it, "Each star is different from every other one," Pryor emphasized the single characteristic they all shared, "some magnetic quality which sets them apart on the screen from all other actors" (14), or what Hortense Powdermaker observed as "tangible features which can be advertised and marketed" (Powdermaker 228). What appeared to viewers as an inner or "magnetic" quality, an essence possessed by the star and offered to the studio on the basis of a contract, was certainly also a treatment and a preparation provided by others, who approached, handled, dressed, photographed, coiffed, and otherwise used certain individuals in such a way as to systematically elevate them in the public eye. Addressing the cinematography of stars in *Visions of Light*, for example, William Daniels comments on how the star was typically subjected to a few candlepowers' worth of augmented key-lighting, to make her pop onscreen.

In the case of James Stewart, who moved slowly and spoke with a patient drawl, thereby invoking the image of a populist figure in whom intensive sensations of democratic fellow-feeling could be invested by viewers, or of James Dean, who squeaked and squinted, grinned and chortled, stared and waited like a faun in the woods, stars were quietly framed and lit to occupy the center of a shot; recorded with sensitive microphones that could pick up, even amplify, their every hesitating mumble; garbed with layers of comfortable, appealing texture and color; and put to work playing characters who, by arrangement, were scripted to be forthright, stalwart, dignified, or adorable if not, as we will see, spectacularly brooding, malignant, antisocial, and depressive. While "magnetism" might have been their trump, all this meticulous studio treatment did nothing but amplify and enrich it. Stewart and Dean, as performers, as males, as citizens sensitive to the culture of their age, were as different as two men could be, the one committed, in many of his roles and in the offscreen life that publicity drew for him, to support the pillars and conventions of society; and the other a rebel at heart, a clownish alien.

In his own right James Stewart in fact mounted two contrasting—in some ways, contradictory—screen personae from 1950 onward. One of these he not only displayed to the public through his image as "'exemplary husband' and family man" (Bogdanovich, *Who the Hell's in It* 245) but had developed thoroughly in his pictures heretofore (when he was managed principally by Leland Hayward), and continued in some of his pictures at the time: that of the pure-spirited, twinkly-eyed, socially abashed but genial, sweet-tempered man of the people, the American Common Man par excellence, who liked the outdoors life, nature, and simple and unaffected human relations and valued highly a "balance between the everyday world of modern movies and the world of the sagebrush and the open spaces" (Shirley Jones, in Fishgall, *Pieces of Time* 216). In mid-decade, Rod Hume described this genteel Jimmy as a "Small-Talk Star":

> He is perhaps the idea of what an average American thinks he is like—not too handsome, a little awkward, not too romantic, modest almost to a point of shyness, and a best bet to come through a winner when there is trouble. A recent poll of motion picture audiences showed that 53 per cent considered the star the typical American. . . . This is a considerable tribute to the artful artlessness of his acting.   (*Films & Filming*, July 1956, 4)

The other screened Jimmy Stewart—known, in point of fact, as "James" Stewart and offscreen rejecting the moniker "Jimmy" for the more affectionate "Jim"—was a different type altogether, a repressed and neurotic man buried beneath an apparently tranquil façade but ready at any moment to explode with vengeful anxiety and anger, or else with deeply twisted and constrained passions that could never match up with the cheery personality of the alter ego. This dark Stewart had a purposeful, even cautious way of moving instead of a carefree, "natural" stride, and a way of twisting his mouth and averting his eyes when he confronted an object of fear or loathing. "No other male film star," wrote Peter Bogdanovich, "was ever better at showing the real pain and fear caused by violence. Or, indeed, the crushing anguish of lost love" (*Who the Hell's in It* 244). Dark Stewart is to be found, certainly, in all the 1950s collaborations with Alfred Hitchcock, ably conveying "rage and disgust" (Thomas 128), but can legitimately be said to have been born in his work with Anthony Mann, a strange friend for the genteel and educated Stewart to have made, perhaps, because he was "rather crude and tough, fond of peppering his conversation with four-letter words" yet a man who inspired in the actor a "deep rapport" (Fishgall, *Pieces of Time* 214). They began their work together—which led to eight films, all in this decade, including *Bend of the River* (1952), *The Naked Spur* (1953), *Thunder Bay* (1953), *The Glenn Miller Story* (1954), *The Far Country* (1954), *Strategic Air Command* (1956), and *The Man from Laramie* (1955)—with the "splendidly crafted" *Winchester '73* (1950) (Thomas 128).

✮✮✮✮✮ A Mann's Man

Winchester '73 is, in significant part, the story of Lin McAdam, an "edgy, chip-on-the-shoulder" cowpoke and sharpshooter (Bogdanovich,

Who the Hell's in It 247) who is chasing sneering, arrogant Dutch Henry Brown (Stephen McNally), the man who killed his father. (In Stewart's westerns with Mann, he is almost always chasing someone or something, and with a sense of real desperation and grim resolve.) Running with this hunt, sometimes in parallel, sometimes crossing it, is a second pursuit, the object of which is a gleaming rifle that Lin has won in a shooting contest but that has been stolen from him by Dutch (and passed through a sequence of owners, including a trader, an Indian tribal chief, and a cowardly easterner before coming back into the hands of Dutch again, just in time for the finale). The gun, in fact, was used by Universal as the centerpiece of a sales campaign, which positioned the film as being focused on "The Gun that won the West!" rather than on Stewart, who was mocked up in publicity as being far less competent with guns than the narrative might have implied: one comic strip has the young Jimmy receiving a family heirloom pistol but being unable to make it go off, until suddenly it does, throwing him to the ground (see *Photoplay*, July 1950, 70). While for a considerable part of the film Lin is seen in a down-to-earth and respectfully playful bond with his sidekick, High Spade (Millard Mitchell), now reminiscent, now prodding, now fraternally supportive and supported, there is a violent and bleak personality lurking underneath the chumminess, an "anger beneath the surface of even the most docile man" (Thomas 127), and one day, encountering the miscreant Waco Johnny Dean (Dan Duryea) in a bar, Lin shows his fury. "Stewart, wanting to get information, grabs Duryea's right arm, twists it behind his back and slams his head down on the counter, with Duryea begging for mercy as Stewart loses his calm manner and turns ferocious," writes Tony Thomas (128), but Stewart's biographer Gary Fishgall more accurately captures the shock of the moment when he notes the chilling "look on his face as he does so, his eyes wide, his mouth turned down in a grimace, his body shaking from the exertion" (*Pieces of Time* 214).

Winchester was the beginning of Stewart's presentation of the dark self, one might argue his liberation from the romantic stereotype that had dominated his previous work (Fishgall, *Pieces of Time* 216) (most famously in *The Philadelphia Story* [1940] and *It's a Wonderful Life* [1946]). And the film held continuing importance, as well, because it was the first occasion of an actor working for a percentage deal, this arrangement negotiated between his agent Wasserman and William Goetz of Universal; soon all stars wanted the same arrangement, so that "what was initiated as a name-actor's honest sharing of the gamble with a film's financiers deteriorated into a no-lose situation for the talent," as Bogdanovich puts it (*Who the Hell's in It* 246). At any rate, the decision brought Stewart into closer communication with the producer as regarded casting, location choice, and any other feature of the process that potentially involved expenditures against the profit he hoped to see. At some other studios, this kind of arrangement began to be seen with increasing frequency, but at MGM Nicholas Schenck raged against it. For him the actor was "nobody. We took him from nobody, we lavished him with lessons and publicity, and now he's the most desired man in the world. Who taught him how to walk? Who straightened his teeth and capped them into that smile. . . . We taught this dumb cluck how to depict great emotions. And now he wants a piece of the action? No! Never!" (qtd. in Eyman 456).

The publicity for any film operates to produce an offscreen distortion: the film itself is truncated, condensed, displaced, and in this state represented as itself, but outside of itself and in an altered state. Meditating on Robert C. Allen's notion of film reception being "performed," Mary Beth Haralovich believes that publicity, too, "performs" a film (private communication, 5 July 2007). In the case of *Winchester '73*, the James Stewart depicted in artists' renditions for advertising often bore less resemblance to Lin and more to the Stewart viewers wished to believe underpinned him, the brave stalwart acting to defend civilization. The film was sufficiently popular abroad, for example, to mobilize an entire issue of *Star-Ciné Aventures* published in French for audiences in Belgium, Canada, and Switzerland; this magazine-format publication retold the entire story of the film in pictures with bubbled dialogue, in the comic book tradition, and on the cover, in four colors, stood Stewart with rifle being raised into aim, his legs spread sturdily, his eyes staring bravely ahead. Behind him, whooping Indians on horseback engaged in a charge, with one of them, long-haired in the Apache style, raising a rifle over his head in triumph. Stewart is thus configured as an Indian fighter, even though in the film he never possesses the Winchester during his encounter with Indians or for use in any other aggressive contest, since exactly his lack of the gun constitutes a rationale for him becoming aggressive in the first place.

In *Bend of the River*, Stewart's second collaboration with Mann, it became evident that, as Tony Thomas puts it, "the actor had found another screen persona, that of the quiet man with an air of edginess, who, when leaned on too heavily, erupts in anger" (143). Stewart's Glyn McLyntock was a border raider after the Civil War but has reformed and buried his past. He is now guiding a wagon train westward toward a bucolic haven in Oregon. Partnered by another former raider, Cole Garrett (Arthur Kennedy), he fights off cupidinous businessmen and ugly mercenaries, not to say hostile Indians, and braves the physical dangers of Mount Hood as he moves his wagons and cattle across virtually impassable territory in a race to beat the oncoming winter. But Garrett's principles, rugged as the rocks around him, have not been altered by time, and he finally turns against Glyn by planning to sell a load of precious food supplies, needed by the settlers, to some itinerant miners for considerable cash. In Glyn's summative battle with Garrett, just as earlier in the film when we saw him trail and slaughter a gang of marauding Shoshones, the brutal, shapeless violence locked under a civilized coating becomes disturbingly apparent. Nor does this apparently honest and good-hearted coating unquestionably sustain an appeal for us when we realize the depths of violence that have characterized this man's hidden past. Perhaps unaccustomed as yet to the psychological transformations Stewart was working onscreen, the *New York Times* rather sidestepped the issue of Glyn's sordid past, and his systematic work to repress it, by calling his a "cryptic personality" (10 April 1952, 37). And in a four-color magazine ad (illustrated by hand), Stewart is pictured as sweet, even genteel: he tenderly removes an arrow from Julia Adams's shoulder, or stands bravely with her at his side, purposive and stalwartly holding his rifle.

Stewart was "tempted," early in 1952, to shoot *The Naked Spur* for MGM (*New York Times*, 11 January 1952, 17), perhaps not only because "players always welcome the opportunity and change of pace of a trip for a film locale" but also because "MGM and the other studios have learned to plan and execute these jaunts so expertly that they are done smoothly, comfortably and not too expensively" ("On Location with 'The Naked Spur,'" *Screenland*, March 1953, 40). If Howard Kemp, his embodiment here, was not "the darkest character of his career" (Fishgall, *Pieces of Time* 233), Stewart certainly played him as unremittingly shady, and also brooding and malevolent, all this originating in events that precede the narrative and leave him eager to exploit other people for the purpose of his own private gain even as the opening credits roll. Jacques Rivette refers to his "serious face, broken up by the most basic emotions" (Rivette, "The Naked Spur" 60). Kemp's wife has deserted him and sold off his ranch, and to get a new grubstake he intends to seize the fleeing Ben Vandergroat (Robert Ryan), dead or alive, and return him for bounty. The *New York Times* rather too eagerly labels Kemp "not bloodthirsty but merely anxious" and suggests he is a "hero whose character is not particularly shining but whose conscience is obviously bothering him" (11 January 1952, 17). Merely anxious, indeed! And that conscience, because it is dark and strong in its own right, is a source of torment, not bother. Thomas suggests Kemp is "bordering-on-

Unremittingly dark, brooding, and malevolent: James Stewart as Howard Kemp, hungry for bounty, in *The Naked Spur* (Anthony Mann, MGM, 1953). Digital frame enlargement.

hysterical" (149). Vandergroat is traveling with a young woman (Janet Leigh), to whom Kemp will be attracted by film's end. Struggling with his own greed and desire for revenge upon the past, he harangues her with his intention to bring Vandergroat's dead body in for cash, but suddenly breaks down in tears and takes her to his heart instead. The past and its horrors dissolved, the two now ride off as the film concludes. An aging prospector (Millard Mitchell) and dishonored soldier (Ralph Meeker) whom Howard meets along the way, and whose lives he grossly uses to further his quest, serve mainly to illustrate his lack of compassion and civility in the context of a magnificently challenging environment (Colorado's San Juan Mountains) that offers no haven, no comfort, no touch of civilization.

Can it be said, however, as Stewart's fan Tony Thomas claims, that Howard Kemp is a darkness with a brightness inside, that at the end of the film some sheen of evil is stripped away in the cleansing wilds of Colorado so that "his true nature" can emerge from beneath? One of the riddles of Stewart's screen persona was precisely that in the 1950s, and in exactly this way, the darker characters he played were laid upon an earlier career-long presentation as a man of inherent and thoroughgoing goodness, a "true nature" that we could hope would "emerge from beneath." In the final shot of Leigh, as with sharp eyes trained on Kemp she smiles a little, we can see that she is not necessarily innocent of his real nature, nor convinced that it is good: not necessarily blind to the possibility that he will darken again. Backstage, however, Stewart's "true nature" was only noble. Fan magazines were quick to point out not only that the new fad of location filming was generally as tough as working in the studio, and quite as serious; but also that in this case it brought out the true grit of the performers. "Jimmy Stewart is a real man and a wonderful guy," wrote Millard Mitchell of his experience working in Durango:

> He had a stand-in, but he took some chances that made the rest of us hold our breath and do a little quiet praying. . . . In the chases, Jimmy at more than one time was hanging on a precipice over a rushing stream. Had he fallen, he wouldn't have had a prayer. He jumped over gulfs where a slip would have meant sudden death. And he did it all with such intensity it is doubtful he realized how much he was flirting with death. But Jimmy is that kind of a guy. An actor of the highest merit, he puts his role ahead of self-preservation.   (*Movie Time*, June 1953, 22–25)

Mitchell concludes by asking his readers to remember when watching the film that "none of his daring is faked," thus upping the ante on the viewer's potential excitement in the theater and at the same time helping to establish for Stewart a credibility and authenticity entirely beyond the requirements of his profession. If this warning intensifies our experience of Howard Kemp as a man who is true to the bone, through and through, it also elevates the sincerity of the performer who is artfully constructing him. Stewart could have performed his own stunts, after all, without us being told explicitly that he was doing so.

Exactly as happens in these stunts, by the way, Stewart's persona in the three westerns he had made with Mann so far was aligned graphically against horses, rickety wagons, crude terrain, smashing rivers, and "miles of scenic grandeur" (Richard L. Coe, "'The Naked Spur' Cleverly Filmed," *Washington Post*, 31 January 1953, 12) in order that the persistent and tormenting struggle of his dark personality against the world might be displayed iconographically. In the fourth collaboration, *Thunder Bay* (1953), the time is the mid-1940s and the locale is a tiny Louisiana village off the Gulf Coast, whither Steve Martin (Stewart) and his sidekick Johnny Gambi (Dan Duryea) have brought themselves in order to start up a wildcat oil drilling operation offshore. They come into conflict with the town's inhabitants, both over their drilling plans and over their love affairs with the two daughters of a local fisherman. In this film, Universal's first effort with a widescreen projection format (and one that singularly failed to impress critics

[*New York Times*, 21 May 1953, 39]), Stewart's presence onscreen was literally magnified, especially in relation to Joanne Dru who spends most of the narrative recoiling from his avaricious and workaholic personality. Again, he is the dark agent of progress, not the chummy companion and affable boy next door; in one telling scene, he must defend his rig against a fisherman who has come aboard secretly to plant a load of dynamite. A hurricane-force gale is raging, the Gulf is raised into walls of water, and the wind is howling, and Stewart, soaked to the skin, his face a mask of desperation and anger, must clamber among the slick poles first in order to defuse the dynamite and then in order to try to save the attacker, who has fallen overboard. In his limp body, we finally see the full strength of a man used against the elements and against a conflicting foe, and in his now empty face, filling a screen more than forty feet wide, there is an abysm equally massive. Dru has come aboard earlier, apparently to woo him; now he confronts her with a bitterly twisted mouth, convinced she planned the attack.

If he was "properly tough, harried, begrimed and laconic" onscreen here, however (*New York Times*, 21 May 1953, 39), Universal was promoting an entirely friendlier persona for Stewart behind the scenes. The *New York Times* reported that while shooting in Louisiana, the crew made exceptional efforts to befriend the community, with some of the townspeople even "asking the actors into their own homes for home-cooked meals and perhaps a friendly game of canasta when the day's shooting is over" ("Louisiana Locale," 19 October 1952, X6). Stewart gave an interview to a local reporter, charmingly recollecting the days when a "show troupe . . . would find signs tacked up on the local boarding houses reading: 'No actors or dogs allowed'" and noting, "They began taking dogs in a few years ago— and now they're even taking the actors!" This charm was repeated, and augmented, in a television guest appearance on "The Jack Benny Program," where he demonstrated that behind his argumentative, fierce-tempered screen characters he was nothing more than "a happily married man . . . a loving father, a regular churchgoer, and a gentleman, qualities that made him something of an anomaly in Hollywood" (Fishgall, *Pieces of Time* 236). Fishgall notes with irony that before the war, when Stewart's characters onscreen had all these homey qualities, "he was considerably less straitlaced offscreen."

The amity Stewart was here described as effusing so effectively to those multitudes who had hitherto suspected film people with a vengeance, and the image of the "farm boy, who loved music and America" (Fishgall, *Pieces of Time* 237), found their way onto the screen as the substance of his personification of Glenn Miller in *The Glenn Miller Story* and then of "Dutch"

Holland in *Strategic Air Command*, two far-from-dark Anthony Mann films in which he appeared to be suspended in wedded bliss with June Allyson and which recuperated his public image as the nice guy who does good and earns the admiration and respect of everyone around. Here again was the Jimmy Stewart of *Harvey* and of *The Philadelphia Story*, that kind-hearted, sensible if bumbling, always well-meaning, and considerate "good-Joe-who-can-take-it" ("Into the Wide Blue Yonder," *New York Times*, 21 April 1955, 33), that reliable companion or neighbor loyal to a fault; it was the Stewart who could show "perseverance and devotion" ("Gentlemen First," *New York Times*, 14 February 1954, X1), who could be the "big-shot romantic husband" ("Venerable Gents," *New York Times*, 8 May 1955, X1), the "solid personality" ("Ten Best of 1954," *New York Times*, 26 December 1954, X1) perfectly reflecting his status in real life as "dedicated family man, living the quiet life" ("The Glenn Miller Story," *Look*, 26 January 1954, 84–86). Even behind the scenes of his public behind-the-scenes life, however, Stewart was captivating his co-workers with his image of the patient and self-giving performer: shooting crowded ballroom scenes for *Glenn Miller* in Denver, Fishgall reports, he took it upon himself to engage the extras in between takes, recounting yarns and telling them what the cinematographer was doing so that they would not desert the production before the needed takes were accomplished (*Pieces of Time* 239). If in Cecil B. DeMille's 1952 epic, *The Greatest Show on Earth*, he had played a doctor running from the law because he had committed a murder and was now hiding out in the guise of a circus clown, the spirit of this refreshed, reinvigorated—although aging—Stewart was what audiences hoped lay under the clown makeup: that "Buttons" had killed, if at all, only by accident, or only with the best intent, or that in truth he hadn't, and that in any case the clowning would ultimately bring him a salvation he truly deserved. But now *The Far Country* and *The Man from Laramie* took him back to the West of the nineteenth century, and drew a heavy shadow over his persona once again.

He was made over into the "flawed and often unsympathetic" (Fishgall, *Pieces of Time* 241) man, a "raw-boned westerner, driven by the need to be a self-sustainer in a hard lifestyle" (Thomas 165). In *Far Country*, leading Ruth Roman's wagon train across northern Canada to Dawson City, he stubbornly proclaims again and again that he will look after himself and nobody else, finally gunning down the evil Robert Wilke and John McIntire but obstinately refusing the enchantments of both Roman and Corinne Calvet. His loner character is so tightly integrated onscreen with deft horsemanship, territorial savvy, independence, and secretive canniness, and is associated so cleanly with the forbidding ruggedness of the mountains, that even male-male friendship seems beyond him. Yet just offscreen, in the very margins of the drama, the character is drawn in less uncivilized tones in the four-color magazine advertisements prepared for the film. "Stranger with a Gun," Stewart's Jeff Webster is called, and he is described as "driven by restless longings"; alert and concerned, he poses with his rifle, and in an insert he embraces Ruth Roman's Ronda Castle with desperate passion. In *Laramie*, if he is secretive, purposive, and now so very alone that he can be victimized and severely wounded by a local rancher's gang—"Nothing quite so severe as Stewart getting shot in the hand point blank had ever been seen in such a film" (Thomas 171)—before managing to make things right and depart without emotional bonds, he is still a pleasure to watch; indeed, as André Bazin wrote in *Cahiers du cinéma*, thanks to Mann's use of Cinema-Scope, "the cowboy is more at home on the wide screen. If he moves across the whole field of vision it gives us twice as much pleasure, since we see him for twice as long" (Bazin 167). The opening-day advertisement for the film in the *New York Times* invoked movement, distance, and darkness, graphically representing Stewart as a cowboy lurking in shadows, covering his face with his gun-bearing hand and warning that he was "a man who came a thousand miles to kill someone he'd never seen!"

In all five of his westerns for Anthony Mann, Stewart wears the same rumpled hat and rides Pie, the horse he met on *Winchester '73*. As well, in virtually all of them he appears in some scenes wearing a battered tan-colored fleece-lined canvas riding jacket, increasingly stained, increasingly characterized by his presence. This was a character audiences came to know intimately, to feel at home with, to feel they could touch. And they believed they had come to the same intimate comfort with the man who was underneath.

✩✩✩✩★ Hitchcockian

All of Alfred Hitchcock's work is more civilized, more in-volved with modernity, urbanization, and the etiquettes of class than Mann's westerns, albeit Mann has a keen eye for class relations and the threat of modernity that has not yet fully crossed the prairie. The darkness that would color Stewart's characterizations in *Rear Window* (1954), *The Man Who Knew Too Much* (1956), and *Vertigo* (1958) is therefore a more pol-ished quality, evinced through nuance more than direct expression for the most part. And yet the Hitchcock performances bear direct relation to most of those he gave for other directors in the sense that L. B. "Jeff" Jefferies, Ben McKenna, and John "Scottie" Ferguson are, like Lin McAdam, Tom

Jeffords of Delmer Daves's *Broken Arrow* (1950), "Buttons" the Clown, Glyn McLyntock, Howard Kemp, Steve Martin, Jeff Webster, Will Lockhart, and Grant McLaine in James Neilson's *Night Passage* (1957), brooding and essentially unsocial human beings with a signal disturbance in their past, a gaping psychological (if not physical) wound in their present, and an obligation now to confront matters of love and society that place them under unbearable stress.

Rear Window is the story of a crippled man's detection of a brutal murder and inability to take action. Obstructed by the full-leg cast in which he is bound, photographer "Jeff" Jefferies must persuade his nurse (Thelma Ritter), his girlfriend (Grace Kelly), and his police inspector chum (Wendell Corey) that the observations he has been surreptitiously making through his window of the domestic behavior of a certain salesman across the courtyard (Raymond Burr) lead properly to a suspicion that the man has slaughtered his wife. Jeff is confined to his wheelchair, the wheelchair confined to a relatively tiny apartment, and our point of view therefore imprisoned itself in a cramped space not wholly effectual for making possible the clearest visions of the world. At the same time, through Hitchcock's camera it is possible to discover in that world a rich fabric of secret and thrilling adventures in the lives of numerous strangers who live in neighboring apartments. And so Jeff becomes the fulcrum of an intense sensation of dread and pressure, even to the degree that his dark fascination for what is going on around him provides hints of the exotic and erotic. He is a man literally locked up, now also, it seems, burdened with a girlfriend who longs for a committed relationship in the face of the fact that her aristocratic habits don't promise to meld with his workaday commitment to rove the world in search of great photographs. Stewart's screen work never eclipses his triumph in this role. At one moment he must betray a cupidinous eagerness to spy on his neighbors. "The very attitude of unwariness on the part of the people being observed gives an air of cold calculation to this business of slyly looking on. It is morbidly entertaining," enthuses one critic (Bosley Crowther, *New York Times*, 15 August 1954, X1). And at another he must sit transfixed with terror as the girl he cannot admit he loves risks her life to gain the proof he needs of the salesman's crime. When Lisa Fremont actually runs across the way, clambers up the fire escape, and enters Lars Thorwald's apartment in his momentary absence, Jeff is white with fear for her, yet cheering her on. But then Thorwald returns, and Jeff is condemned to watch through his telescopic lens as the hulking man discovers Lisa in the apartment and begins to rough her up. An expression of nightmare anguish is etched into Stewart's face, his eyes frozen open in a rictus of fear and his mouth drawn open as though to utter a way out of a fateful trap. Once again, as in Anthony Mann's films, we have a lonely man who puts off romance, denies his past, and reveals an equivocal obsession with social relationships as he is subjected to torture both physical and emotional—we can recall, watching him watching Lisa's ordeal, Will Lockhart in *The Man from Laramie*, struggling in the grip of Dave Waggoman's henchmen, as Waggoman systematically shoots his mules. In *Rear Window*, the *New York Times* reported, Stewart did a "first-class job, playing the whole thing from a wheel chair and making points with his expressions and eyes" (5 August 1954, 18). And if Jeff Jefferies is not quite the "misanthropic citizen" of *The Far Country* (*New York Times*, 14 February 1955, 24), he is a contemporary man filled with "morbid curiosity," a hero whose inner compulsions drive him into torment.

It was as a smugly controlling, if affable, family doctor that Stewart appeared in Hitchcock's remake of *The Man Who Knew Too Much*, shackled now to a talented and perspicacious wife, Jo (Doris Day), whose forced abandonment of a career in show business strains the marriage. While the family is vacationing in Marrakech, the ten-year-old son Hank (Christopher Olsen) is kidnapped and held for ransom in a political assassination plot, which circumstance forces Ben and Jo to fly to London in pursuit of him. Throughout this film, Ben McKenna shows a controlling personality, early on when he hopes openly that the child will follow in his footsteps, then systematically as he feels himself insulted by a French tourist (Daniel Gélin), stands helplessly by as this Frenchman is knifed to death in the marketplace, diffidently refuses to cooperate with the Marrakech police, and, learning of his son's disappearance, tranquilizes his wife and takes her out of the country. In a scene in the Marrakech hotel room, in early evening, as Ben pleads with the drugged Jo to forgive him and gain the strength to go with him to London, Stewart plays some of the darkest moods in his career, visibly strung taut with anxiety and grief about the child and at the same time fully aware that his marriage and love are potentially to be sacrificed if he does not manage to save Hank. Hitchcock sets the scene in shadows, taking up extremely eccentric camera positions in order to exaggerate the gloom that has enveloped Ben. At the end of the film, the child is saved, the assassination plot foiled in a gala concert at the Albert Hall; but still another anxiety awaits Ben, since he must present his family to a group of British friends who, not suspecting that anything has gone amiss, have been waiting for hours in the McKenna hotel suite. Now social status and moral correctness tax him, and he must find a way to escape giving the (correct) impression that he has been careless enough to lose his child. If

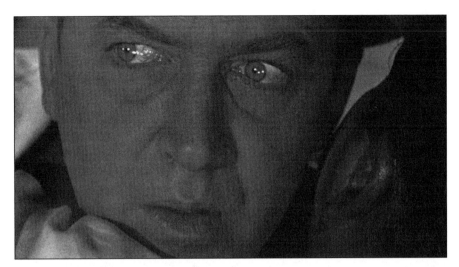

An insatiably curious American innocent abroad, receiving a dark secret. This film was shot in VistaVision, so that the screen image in some theaters would have been gigantic. James Stewart (with Daniel Gélin) in *The Man Who Knew Too Much* (Alfred Hitchcock, Paramount, 1956). Digital frame enlargement.

Ben McKenna is a tourist who deserves a comeuppance of sorts, James Stewart filming him in Marrakech was anything but: "It was as a real tourist, haunting the bazaars of then peaceful Marrakech where part of the movie was made, that Stewart gave his best performance, superbly playing himself—the insatiably curious American innocent abroad," or, for that matter, dodging the heat "in a cool café" with cigar-smoking Hitchcock, while waiting for filming to resume or being "startled" by a seamstress on her way to work, or spending an afternoon "at a small palace owned by a Romanian baron" ("The Innocent Goes Abroad: Jimmy Stewart Plays Himself on Location," *Life*, 5 September 1955, 50).

"Scottie" Ferguson haunts *Vertigo* as much as he is haunted in it. This retired detective is employed by an old friend to follow the friend's wife, Madeleine (Kim Novak), who has been taking long voyages out of town without having any memory of them and appears to be haunted by the spirit of a long-deceased ancestor. Tailing her, Scottie slowly falls in love, abandoning an old girlfriend (Barbara Bel Geddes) callously in favor of all-embracing romance with this figure of profound physical and spiritual beauty. But too soon, at an old Spanish mission, she falls to her death from a tower and, paralyzed with the acrophobia that set upon him earlier in life when he could not stop a colleague from falling to his death, Scottie can do nothing but watch in a paralyzed chill. The old friend forgives him and moves away to the east, and for months Scottie languishes in a sanitarium.

Then, moving about the streets of San Francisco, he seems to see Madeleine wherever he goes. One day a shopgirl attracts his attention and he follows her to a dingy hotel, asks her out to dinner, and slowly begins to change her so that she more and more resembles the Madeleine he loved and lost. In a stunning conclusion, he is reduced to a grief even greater than anything he has experienced before, and we are left to wonder at the gripping power of love, of obsession, of memory, of desire, and of the past as it holds us in its sway. Because of the depths of Ferguson's obsession, not to say the complications of the love story in which he finds himself and the rather casual way he carries on his detecting, he seems a man whose rational control has dissipated and who therefore struggles through life as though groping through a foggy swamp of tortured memory and awkward, hopeless feeling. This characterization, in which Stewart "manages to act awfully tense in a casual way" (*New York Times*, 29 May 1958, 24), seems at the greatest possible remove from the conventional, bourgeois family life Stewart was leading offscreen at the same time.

★★★★★ Homey

It is perhaps worth putting a little stress on one particular quality of the dark Jimmy Stewart who populates these films of Anthony Mann and Alfred Hitchcock, namely his solitary character, since the publicity apparatuses of the studios, by way of fan magazines, spent considerable effort to redress the imbalance it created. While he is charmed onscreen by women, and often by men, and while he forms intensely warm and committed bonds of friendship, he is never caught in a romantic entanglement that leads to a committed relationship that spills over the edges of the narrative. Offscreen, however, publicity worked systematically to build up and maintain his image as a domesticated man. A photo caption early in the decade gloated about his cheery domestication, noting that the "All-American boy has picked up seven pounds since his marriage to lovely socialite, Gloria McLean" (*Screen Guide*). To Hedda Hopper he explained that he didn't need to go to nightclubs because his "four children are better entertainment than Sunset Strip ever saw" ("Stewart to Reap Bounty of Family Fun This Yule," *Los Angeles Times*, December 1951). Immediately after premiering *Thunder Bay* in New York, according to one article, he "rushed back helter-skelter" with his wife Gloria, in order to celebrate the birthday of his twin daughters Kelly and Judy; a photograph by Bert Stern shows doting Jimmy and Gloria with the twins, being "shown all the flowers that 'growed' while they were away" ("A Pair Makes Two," *Photoplay*, September 1953, 68–69).

Indeed, *Parents* magazine approved the "considerable privacy" in which the cozy Stewarts were managing to live "despite their goldfish-bowl life," but noted as well that "it's still somewhat breath-taking to Jimmy Stewart to discover himself the happily married head of a family of five" (Joe Alvin, "Jimmy Stewart Tells What He Wants for His Family," *Parents' Magazine*, ca. 1952–53). Referring to Stewart's marriage, Sheila Graham's *Hollywood Family Album* celebrates him as "a guy who was searching for something real for a long time, and who couldn't be taken in by any counterfeit. . . . You get a thrill out of Jimmy Stewart's marriage. Big, lanky, lone wolf Jimmy, all settled down and father of four" ("The Domesticated Stewarts," *Hollywood Family Album*, February-April 1953, 57). Settled down, but not pinioned. *Photoplay* describes the young newlyweds as globetrotters: "Jimmy and Gloria, his bride of less than half a year, traveled some 30,000 miles in the first three months of their life together and currently eying maps and atlases and globes, they insist their travels to date were just a series of little strolls" ("Happy Hobos," *Photoplay*, March 1950, 38). And Jimmy's previous life has been packed up, so that his attentions can be focused entirely on Gloria: "His accordion is stored away in the garage; there's a 'For Sale' sign on his racing plane and he has let his amateur radio operator's license lapse" (88). Learning that his wife was pregnant with twins, he proposed to build a sleek house in Pacific Palisades but was soon persuaded to settle for "a good substantial brick affair in Beverly Hills," which had something very few Southern California houses had, a basement that Jimmy "is planning to turn . . . into a huge playroom (sound-proof) so that when Ronnie and Mike and the twins start bringing pals home, he, Jimmy, will have a place to put them. Any parent will tell you this is a swell idea" (57). As to Stewart's trademark ingenuous awkwardness or discomfort with most women and many strangers onscreen, he gave a clue to his female admirers in a *Photoplay* article, "Hold That Man," when he announced, "Men are uncomfortable when they're around an artificial type. They know the girl is acting artificially but they don't know what to do about it. So because they don't know what to do about this situation, they feel inferior" ("Hold That Man!," May 1951, 116). The bumbling boy is a role Hollywood insiders were reportedly willing to assign Stewart even years after his marriage to Gloria, and he is reported as a once "bachelor incarnate" (Fredd Dudley, "The Case of the Vanquished Bachelor," *Photoplay*, February 1955, 101) who now blissfully dotes on his children. With the newly born twins, and his two sons from McLean's earlier marriage, he and Gloria posed in June 1951 for "a traditional movie-land rite: the first family publicity stills" (*Time*). As Adrienne McLean notes of the domesticated imagery of 1950s male movie stars, so for Jimmy Stewart: "The most common 'sign' of the married male star is his children—children become visually the new props of the domestic credentials of men, especially, to interesting and ambivalent effect—and the work he does (or is supposed to do, or at least offers to do) around the house" ("Wedding Bells" 288).

It is fascinating to note that by far the bulk of publicity material produced for James Stewart during this decade was designed to work against the raw and disaffected image embodied by so many of his screen characters by emphasizing the tranquility of his marriage and home life, his homey and loving diffidence, his gentility and courtliness to all and sundry. "He is reluctant to hit anybody in a movie," drawled one paean; "his kind of person doesn't hit people" (Pete Martin, "The Shyest Guy in Hollywood," *Saturday Evening Post*, 15 September 1951, 43). He grew up a boy's boy, "member of the local Boy Scout troop," whose "small-fry dreams of greatness were concerned with mastering the mystifying tricks of such magicians as Thurston and Houdini, then taking time out from sawing women in half while he bagged grizzlies in the Rockies" (113). At home in Beverly Hills, as befits a bagger of grizzlies now thoroughly sobered, "the den is the Stewarts' favorite gathering place" ("'Slim' Pickin,'" *Photoplay*, August 1956, 57). This is a movie star without a movie star's ego: "He does not care especially for the incidental trappings of stardom," writes John Maynard in an especially "revealing" background piece for *Photoplay* ("Jimmy—on the Q.T.," October 1955, 115), and his "friends declaim as one that he is a droll fellow in a solemn, unobtrusive way" (116). If onscreen Stewart's figure is positioned and established against the craggy mountains of Alaska and Colorado, rushing rivers, vast plains, and in company with grimacing varlets and smirking criminals, what we find "backstage" is a homey and habituated man inhabiting a household that

> runs on a schedule about as exacting as that of the New York, New Haven & Hartford Rail road. Breakfast is served at a certain time, lunch at another, dinner at another. The time is always the same. . . . If the Stewarts lunch out, they do so at Romanoff's. No place else. Every Thursday evening, while in residence, they dine at Chasen's. Same table; same time. . . . Most evenings they spend either at home or at the home of one of a limited circle of close friends. The preferred diversions here are records, talk and canasta, a game for which Gloria Stewart has displayed near genius.   (116)

Nor had movies spoiled the small-town hardware merchant's son from Indiana, Pennsylvania, and although by the middle of the 1950s he had become one of the very wealthy denizens of Hollywood, in large thanks to Wasserman's skillful negotiations on his behalf—"Hollywood's new box-office champion" as of August 1956 ("'Slim' Pickin,'" 56)—still he "was never happier than when, on one birthday, he was given a fancy fitted picnic basket" (116). If he wasn't affected because of his work in movies, however, Stewart also wasn't snobbishly above the soundstage. He was a "rabid movie fan. In his converted cellar, he has a 16-mm projector, a screen and a few easy chairs, and runs whatever films he can get his hands on. Or if he hasn't got his hands on any, the Stewarts just plain go to the movies. On occasion, he runs his own pictures for the family" (116). And if committed, absorbed in his work, and devoted to home life, he is also modest in the best American bucolic tradition: even though Stewart "was extremely pleased about being named Mr. Big" at the 1956 box office, "there is no reason to believe it was ever one of his major ambitions. Perhaps it never occurred to him that an actor whose screen personality is essentially timid and reserved would pull in many more votes than the crooners, the comics, the lovers, and the cow-licked extroverts" ("'Slim' Pickin'" 59).

★★★★★ Shooting Star

James Stewart's mother, he once wrote, would see all three showings of every movie he made for three running days—nine showings: "She never missed a showing. . . . She didn't write me at once because it wasn't until the last day that she began to find out what the story was all about. Before that she just concentrated on looking at me. She felt that when she saw one of my movies we were having a visit" ("James Stewart," *Saturday Evening Post*, 11 February 1961, 76). What James Dean shared with him was an amazing capacity to warm the screen in this way, a personality that seemed to loom close to viewers as familiar, "of the family." If Dean's was not the briefest acting career in Hollywood history, it was certainly the briefest star presence, occupying onscreen but three motion pictures that opened within the slightly more than twenty-month period between 9 March 1955 and 24 November 1956. In all three performances, widely disparate though they are (Dean also had bit parts in four other films, *Fixed Bayonets* [1951], *Sailor Beware* [1951], *Has Anybody Seen My Gal?* [1952], and *Trouble Along the Way* [1953]), he embodied a masculinity utterly at odds with what James Stewart was producing at the same time: compact and muscular, not lanky and gangling; eager for physical contact, not reticent to engage; expressive, not repressed; outwardly torn, awkward, clumsy, even at times uncoordinated, and always sensitive, deeply pensive, almost feminine by standards of the day in terms of the way he exhibited an effortless physical beauty in his expressions and poses and the way he responded passively to the aggressions of other men. We can note the way Buzz Gunderson (Corey Allen) can bully him into a car race in Nicholas Ray's *Rebel Without a Cause* (1955); the way Bick Benedict (Rock Hudson) can threaten him in the kitchen of his own brand new hotel in George Stevens's *Giant* (1956); the way his afflicted father (Raymond Massey) can cow and silence him in Elia Kazan's *East of Eden* (1955).

While he lived, Dean was often a conundrum to his fellow actors, a genius to his directors, a young man living on an emotional roller coaster, who was caught up in passionate but unresolved love affairs with people of both genders. Family life was but a dream for him, and stability was anathema. Although those who knew and worked with him found Dean unrelentingly magnetic, it was only after he died on 30 September 1955 (when his Porsche Spyder crashed into a Ford Tudor on Highway 466 near Cholame, California) that his reputation began to grow and glow in Hollywood, that he became an icon, even a saint, of the screen. An English teacher from Woodstock, Vermont, for example, for whom movies were "an escape from a strenuous schedule," composed a memorial poem beginning:

> They tell me you are dead, yet I cannot
> This night believe the unbelievable;
> The restless beauty of your mind and heart
> Will not be quenched within the shallow grave.
> Your hands that moved caressing weightless things . . .
> (Evelyn Hunt, "To James Dean," *Photoplay*, January 1956, 50)

Only *East of Eden* had been released before his death.

East of Eden, a retelling of the story of Cain and Abel, has Dean as the embittered Cal Trask, convinced that his farmer father loves his brother Aron (Richard Davalos) more than him. Aron's girlfriend Abra (Julie Harris) is attracted to Cal, who knows that his long-lost mother is alive and running a whorehouse in a nearby town; she loans him money to start up a bean-growing business that will permit him to recoup money his father lost farming and thus, possibly, regain his father's love. *Rebel Without a Cause*, nothing if not one of the more influential films in Hollywood's history, recounts a period in the lives of some Los Angeles teenagers, alienated from their families, who come together to find love and trust in the face of a world where kids are reviled and displaced. Dean's Jim Stark, anguished that his parents are tearing him apart by their contradictory approaches to controlling his life, becomes attracted to his beautiful neighbor Judy (Natalie Wood) and to the soft and psychologically damaged Plato (Sal Mineo), but things turn sour when Plato gets in trouble by using a gun on a member of a youth gang, is pursued by police, and shot dead in the film's

James Dean was killed a month before the premiere of the early CinemaScope feature *Rebel Without a Cause* (Nicholas Ray, Warner Bros., 1955). Here Jim Stark is confronted by his mother (Ann Doran). Digital frame enlargement.

painful conclusion. *Giant*, the story of the fabulous Reata ranch and its scion Bick (Hudson), has Dean as a mopey and disaffected cowhand, Jett Rink, who loathes Bick but is fond of his sister Luz (Mercedes McCambridge). When Luz dies, she leaves Jett a small parcel of land, which soon begins to spout forth with oil. Jett develops the property and soon becomes a magnate, far richer than the plenipotential Bick. But wealth brings corruption and incapacity, and when the two men meet late in life Jett has abused two of Bick's children (Dennis Hopper, Carroll Baker) and has taken so thoroughly to the bottle that he cannot even stand up and fight the vengeful father. All three of these roles are written to be strong and central in their films, but Dean brings an eccentricity and charm to his performances that was absolutely unique in Hollywood of the 1950s—indeed, it remains unparalleled today. Cal Trask is inward facing, regressive, weak, and desperate, while also being innocent and beautiful as no male had ever been on the screen before. Jim Stark galvanized the consciousness of teenagers around the world, and remains *the* icon of displaced, disaffected youth; he is also tender, witty, affectionate, and accepting of the moral status of all other characters in the film, loath even to criticize his parents who are tormenting him or the boys of the gang who initially wish to exclude him as a loser. Jett Rink, for all his mumbling cynicism, seems a model of the helplessness of the poor in the face of enormous wealth and privilege, to such a degree that audiences can only cheer for him as his fortunes rise and feel saddened by his moral collapse at film's end.

Interestingly but hardly surprisingly, given the ultra-conservative temper of the times, Dean, whose performance style was flamboyant (even acrobatic), unique, and reeking with genuineness, who commanded the screen in every however momentary appearance, did not particularly find favor with the critical establishment, especially Bosley Crowther of the *New York Times*. Crowther describes his portrayal of the "confused and cranky" Cal Trask as a "mass of histrionic gingerbread":

> He scuffs his feet, he whirls, he pouts, he sputters, he leans against walls, he rolls his eyes, he swallows his words, he ambles slack-kneed—all like Marlon Brando used to do. Never have we seen a performer so clearly follow another's style. Mr. Kazan should be spanked for permitting him to do such a sophomoric thing. Whatever there might be of reasonable torment in this youngster is buried beneath the clumsy display.   (10 March 1955, 33)

No serious viewer comparing any of Dean's performances to any of Brando's will find this crude comparison apt, or agree with Crowther's later assessment of Dean as a "clumsy, uncomfortable lad" (20 March 1955, X1). Both men were free in their performance in a way that most actors hadn't been before, but Dean's sensitivity and responsiveness to the moment, at each second, is so faithful to the spirit of life that one imagines the screen itself to evaporate and the performance to leap out as a blunt reality. Michael DeAngelis discusses the theme, popular not only in contemporary opinion but lasting in critical approaches, of Brando as Dean's mentor, pointing to how even Nicholas Ray saw "the new star's behavior . . . as indicating the natural expression of the individual" by offering "a point-by-point analysis of the Brando attributes that Dean has been accused of imitating" and stipulating that "the only similarity between the two is that James also is a serious and sensitive young actor" (DeAngelis, *Gay Fandom* 85). Warner Bros., in fact, "dispensed with its roster of contract players" and undertook "a canvass of the whole country" in order to find fresh, "authentic" young actors such as Dean (*New York Times*, 4 February 1955, 17). Crowther is again disaffected by Jim Stark: "We do wish the young actors, including Mr. Dean, had not been so intent on imitating Marlon Brando in varying degrees. The tendency, possibly typical of the behavior of certain youths, may therefore be a subtle commentary but it grows monotonous" (*New York Times*, 27 October 1955, 28). This in the face of a film, and a performance, that was so tellingly poignant for conventional viewers it produced an attack from Sen. Claire Booth Luce and the Eisenhower administration, who acted to prevent its being shown to represent the United States at the Venice Film Festival. "James Dean came along at just the right time for a segment of the population whose members were still in the process of defining themselves and eager to latch on to shared symbols to distinguish themselves from their parents," writes Claudia Springer (*James Dean Transfigured* 99). But after Dean's death, Crowther managed a posthumous compliment about Jett Rink:

It is the late James Dean who makes the malignant role of the surly ranch hand who becomes an oil baron the most tangy and corrosive in the film. Mr. Dean plays this curious villain with a stylized spookiness—a sly sort of off-beat languor and slur of language—that concentrates spite. This is a haunting capstone to the brief career of Mr. Dean.

(*New York Times*, 11 October 1956, 63)

Dean won the first Audience Awards Election for his performances in *Eden* and *Rebel* (*New York Times*, 7 December 1955, 47) and was nominated for Academy Awards for both *Eden* and *Giant*, in both cases posthumously. To a reader's concern about the suitability of a posthumous nomination for *Eden*, writers to the screen editor of the *New York Times* blustered enthusiastically in March 1956 about Dean's performance being "superior," "superb," "unquestionably deserving," and evidence of "great genius and remarkable talent" (4 March 1956, X4). Warner Bros., meanwhile, was "mining cash dividends" and earning "'grosses that exceeded the receipts' the picture chalked up in its original engagement" (*New York Times*, 14 December 1955, 53).

The behind-the-scenes Jimmy developed and portrayed by publicity media was a "cat" completely focused on his acting, unaffected, chummy, serious and even philosophical, to the degree indeed that his grandmother Emma Woolen Dean's reminiscence that "in spite of all the fanfare, Jimmy only wanted to be with his family" has a certain out-of-key ring ("James Dean—the Boy I Loved," *Photoplay*, March 1956). Sidney Skolsky notes that after the flash success of *East of Eden*, Dean walked into Schwab's drugstore "in the same manner, wearing the same outfit, to the same booth" as he had six months previously when he was just an unknown "young fellow" who had the respect of his peers; "He was the same Dean. But to the customers and the waitresses he was movie star Dean" ("Demon Dean," *Photoplay*, July 1955). *Photoplay* published a reflection by Natalie Wood, barely a month after he died. "What a whale of a lot of things people don't know about James Dean. Jimmy, an oddball? Jimmy, weird? Jimmy, sullen? . . . Believe it or not, Jimmy's a sentimentalist. . . . Jimmy's proud to be an actor, don't ever doubt that. But it's not for the fame, the glamour, the money. It's the sense of achievement, the thrill of doing a good job" ("You Haven't Heard the Half About Jimmy!," *Photoplay*, November 1955).

At the same time, Dean was depicted again and again as a mystic weirdo, precisely the oddball Natalie Wood didn't meet. Looking back on his accident a year later, Rhett Rutledge waxes euphoric:

James Dean—intense believer in the occult, intense student of reincarna-tion—sped to his death last Fall on a California highway. He pursued death as if it were a beautiful woman, a Bridey Murphy who promised to reveal all the intimate secrets of the great beyond.

He did not choose the day or the hour or the means. But when the phantom he had sought beckoned in that brief instant before his sports car crashed—he took her hand.

He had been ready to go for a long time.

("James Dean: The God of a Weird and Morbid Cult,"
Exposed, September 1956, 11)

The thrill of doing a good job was not something that James Stewart doted upon when he wasn't acting, and the impression publicity gives us of him is that, indeed, acting was a job for him and not a life—a job, to be sure, that he worked at hard and in which he accomplished a stunningly rich legacy of screen performance. For James Dean, on the other hand, whose performances are so pungent and so evanescent, acting may well have been synonymous with life, and if, when he died too young, his friends and admirers tried to turn those performances into memorials they almost—and only almost—succeeded. When we see both of these men onscreen they breathe life into every scene, through timing, through reflection, through the smallest facial expressions, through tone, but now that they are gone, their delicious characters, for all the awkward wealth of feeling they inspire, leave us longing for an impossible presence. If Stewart inspired a publicity blockade that repeatedly touted his happy family life and his innocent boyhood pleasures, Dean seems to have escaped from the boundaries of the screen and the publicity handout altogether, in order to perform, most outstandingly, as a memory of a performer. Rutledge continues:

> Groups of mourning women hold spiritualistic séances in the eerie blackness, in the desperate hope of reaching Dean's departed soul, proffering their protestations of undying love and adoration. They play theme music from his films in the background to set the mood for their uncanny invocations. In cities and hamlets all over the country, high school lockers and teen-age bedrooms have been transformed into sacred altars where his photographs are surrounded by the mystic light of ever-flickering candles, symbolic of the constant worship accorded him.   (11)

"Jimmy can be paid tribute to in Hollywood or Chicago or London . . . because he LIVES in those places and will continue to do so," rhapsodized *Screen Stars* ("The Immortal Dean," November 1956, 14). Nor was conspiracy theory absent from the response to Dean's death. *Inside Story* reported early in 1957 that the 5,000 fan letters per month still being received in Dean's name, the "sock business" of his "new picture" *Giant*, and the continuing write-ups in "an endless string of fan magazines" were all orchestrated by Warner Bros., since "Jimmy's tragic death left his bosses holding a $5,000,000 bag! So they got the brightest, most macabre idea in history," that of "reincarnating" interest in the star, who would now be "'living' again only for the profits of the movie-makers" (Lisette Dufy, "The Amazing James Dean Hoax!," *Inside Story*, February 1957, 14). *Life* reported the "birth of a cult," noting that "just about anyone who ever had a nodding acquaintance with Dean is still subject to a barrage of mail, telephone calls and sometimes personal visits from his fans"; listing numerous special-issue magazines that have been "devoted entirely to Dean"; and snidely observing that Mattson's, a Hollywood clothing store where the original was purchased, "has had a run on red zippered jackets (price $22.95)" ("Delirium over Dead Star," *Life*, 24 September 1956, 80). He shared with Stewart a certain intrinsic shyness—"He was embarrassed by fame," *Life* quotes a publicist as saying; "he really wanted to be left alone." Humphrey Bogart's somewhat churlish summation: "If he had lived, he'd never have been able to live up to his publicity" (88).

NOTES

Thanks to Ron Andrus, Hope Farrugia, Lucina Fraser, and Peter Murphy.

1. The huge mock Tudor house, at the northeast corner of Roxbury Drive and Lexington Road, was razed after Stewart's death in 1997 and has been replaced by an even larger and far less characteristic domicile that hides behind a copse of olive trees.

2. Many of the popular sources cited in this article are from the Constance McCormick Collection of star scrapbooks on Stewart and Dean housed at the Cinema-Television Library, University of Southern California. Most of the material in the scrapbooks (there are seven for Stewart, two for Dean) is not documented as to source or date, unfortunately, and any textual citation with an incomplete reference is from a CMC scrapbook.

4 ★★★★★★★★★★★

James Mason
A Star Is Born Bigger Than Life

AMY LAWRENCE

The traditional reading of melodrama posits that as a genre it works on two levels—creating pathos by drawing "the audience into the character's dilemma in an act of recognition and empathy" while at the same time "distanc[ing] the audience" who, knowing more than the characters, understand the circumstances in which the characters are caught up (Gledhill 226). In melodrama, large-scale "social and economic contradictions" are "internalized as the dilemmas of . . . victims," then "externalized" (made readable for an audience) through matters of performance and style, that is, "as inarticulate gesture, overdetermined declamation, and expressionist *mise en scène*" (225). Citing the work of Peter Brooks and

---

Courtesy of MovieStarNews.

Thomas Elsaesser, Christine Gledhill reiterates that while such signs are "available to the audience," they are *not part of the characters' consciousness* (225–26).

Gledhill extends our understanding of melodrama by taking into account the figure of the star: "The star in condensing select social values becomes him or herself a theatre for the enactment of conflicting forces" (226). In doing so, the star contributes yet another layer of potential pathos while inviting "both identification and critical distance" (225). In this formulation, the audience is solely responsible for navigating the relationship between character and actor on the basis of prior knowledge (knowing more about the situation than the character does and more about the actor than is present in the text, based on previous performances, offscreen publicity, biographical information, and so on). But there is another location where the melodramatic division between emotional identification and critical distance can be made manifest.

In selected films from the 1950s, James Mason plays characters who are fully aware of the contradictions that tear them apart. Recognizing the contradictions with which they are faced and the absurdity of their desires (within the wider contexts of Hollywood and middle America) does not free them. Their pain is not alleviated by knowledge; critical distance cannot help. In his best films, Mason integrates melodramatic extremes of brutal sadism with bravura displays of suffering while his skill as a performer adds a third level of critical perspective. As his characters express an acid contempt for American institutions (Hollywood, the educational system, the family) while undergoing extravagant bouts of self-loathing and punishments mental and physical, Mason's sardonic humor serves as commentary on their (and his) position, without ever sacrificing the reality of their pain. Deconstructing one male authority figure after another (husbands, fathers, teachers), Mason also subverts the illusion of masculinity as the foundation of patriarchal dominance by exposing the agony at the heart of it. These qualities are best demonstrated in two films at the heart of the decade: *A Star Is Born* (1954) and *Bigger Than Life* (1956). *A Star Is Born* allows Mason (and Judy Garland) the chance to dissect, expose, and symbolically triumph over the studio system's exploitation and misuse of their talents. In *Bigger Than Life*, the suffocating pettiness of American suburban life produces agonizing pain, the only treatment for which is literally maddening. In both films, Mason performs the role of the "European intellectual going into a North American cultural context, carrying the capacity for critique with him" (Willemen 246).

⭐⭐⭐⭐⭐ **British Import**

At the end of the 1940s, James Mason became Hollywood's newest English leading man, following such 1930s stalwarts as Ronald Colman, David Niven, Leslie Howard, and Laurence Olivier. Although Mason was well established as the dark and brooding antihero of British costume films (*The Man in Grey* [1943], *The Wicked Lady* [1945]), Hollywood in the fifties did not know quite what to do with him. Consequently, Mason's work in this decade covers an uncommonly wide range of films with everyone from Lucille Ball to Alfred Hitchcock, Max Ophuls to Walt Disney, reflecting the transitions Hollywood was undergoing as a whole. He appeared in seventeen films in the six years between his first American film and *A Star Is Born*.

While *The Man in Grey* presented Mason "sneering like Laughton, barking like Gable, and frowning like Laurence Olivier on a dark night" (Hirschhorn 14), the two films that established the poles of his original Hollywood persona were *The Seventh Veil* (1945) and *Odd Man Out* (1947). The first provided a model for translating Mason's Byronic dash to a contemporary setting, complete with a psychoanalytic context for his character's penchant for caning women and a happy ending. The second placed Mason in a consciously "artistic" film that showcased his ability to portray a sympathetic character defined by his suffering. In a morally complicated position, Mason's thoughtful and sensitive IRA man is shot in the course of a robbery and spends the rest of the film in increasingly severe mental and physical distress.

Arriving in Hollywood in 1948, Mason quickly found himself cast as a romantic lead opposite an array of female stars. A classic Byronic figure ("mad, bad, and dangerous to know"), Mason was called upon to play lovers who were willful, driven, cold, arrogant, and disdainful. In *East Side, West Side* (1949), for example, he is Barbara Stanwyck's fortune-hunting husband. Accused of killing his mistress (Ava Gardner), he has his long-suffering wife pay for his defense. A carryover from his British films, these kinds of roles relied heavily on the actor's looks: the angular planes of his face that featured sharp cheekbones, flared nostrils, and dark eyes glowering out from under emphatic brows. Although his clipped speech (what one critic calls his "nasal contempt") gives the impression that his mouth is a thin, hard line, Mason's lips are surprisingly full and sensuous (Hirschhorn 230). As a doomed romantic brooding over a secret past in *Pandora and the Flying Dutchman* (1951) (with Gardner again), "he was almost a male Garbo," Richard Corliss writes; "his sepulchral beauty often hovered like an ancient curse over him and the women attracted to him" (32). In films like *Pandora* and *The Reckless Moment* (1949) (reviving his *Odd Man Out* Irish accent as a blackmailer-turned-chaste-lover of Joan Bennett), Mason's characters hover between good and evil. Female fans, however, were credited with knowing that "underneath the brooding exterior of the Gothic hero lies a wealth of emotions just waiting to get out" (Pearson 72). Or, as the advertising slogan for a 1953 Carol Reed film put it, Mason was "A Devil! An Angel! *The Man Between*!" Mason certainly understood this aspect of his appeal. In one of the articles he wrote for a fan magazine in the late 1940s, he described working with Robert Ryan on *Caught* (1949). "A very nice, very tall, very rugged-looking guy . . . I only met him in one scene in which we endeavored to out-glower each other." This time "he is the heavy, I the allegedly-sympathetic character," Mason notes ("So This Is Hollywood," *Motion Picture*, December 1948, 67).

Foregoing romance, the studios also cast him as a villain in a range of costume pictures. These continued a path well established by previous British imports. In *Botany Bay* (1953), Mason's sadistic sea captain (keelhauling Alan Ladd and extorting sex from convict-passenger Patricia Medina) was called both "a pale shadow of Charles Laughton" and "a fetching younger version of Captain Bligh" (Hirschhorn 122). In the remake of *The Prisoner of Zenda* (1952) Mason takes on the kind of role Basil Rathbone copyrighted in 1930s swashbucklers, conspiring to overthrow the true king and sword-fighting his way through a castle for a thrilling climax. His role in *Prince Valiant* (1954) is pretty much the same. In these films, Mason perfected a style of villainy that rested not on physical intimidation but on a quiet, mental ruthlessness. His characters in these films have much in common: they are domineering (and casually contemptuous) with women, ruthless with men, sadistic but soft-spoken, and, above all, smarter than everyone around them—and they know it.

At times the intelligence of Mason's characters marks them as leaders, admirable and sympathetic if still morally ambiguous. In Joseph Mankiewicz's *Five Fingers* (1952), Mason plays a brilliant, contemptuous spy engaged in a game of cross and double-cross only to be outsmarted in the end (he laughs at his loss). As Rommel in *The Desert Fox* (1951) and Captain Nemo in *20,000 Leagues under the Sea* (1954), Mason presents characters whose positions of command justify their imperiousness, normalizing what could otherwise be read as arrogance. As Brutus in *Julius Caesar* (1953), on the other hand, Mason revisits the passive drawn-out suffering of *Odd Man Out*, as a good man who struggles with having committed a morally questionable if politically defensible act. In either case, he is doomed.

★★★★★ **He Suffers Beautifully**

We first glimpse *A Star Is Born*'s Norman Maine (Mason) backstage in the dark. He lifts a ballerina but he cannot hold her and falls to his knees (something that happens twice in this scene). When a photographer takes a picture of Maine on the ground, Maine lunges at him, grabbing the camera. Literally reeling, Mason's movements as Maine are off-balance and off-rhythm; he sways and jerks his way from one group of people to another. He tries to mount a horse from the rear, yelling, "A horse! A horse! My kingdom for a horse!" This quotation connects him to the English theater (a tradition he will cite when he references Ellen Terry) and identifies him with Richard III, a haunted man, besieged on the field of battle and close to his finish. It is a call for help that never comes; Norman says it twice.

Maine alternates between wanting to join in with the various entertainers backstage at a benefit at the Shrine Auditorium and shaking off people who try to impede him. His drunkenness makes him unpredictable. One moment he is overly friendly and the next surprisingly vicious. When Libby, the studio's publicist (Jack Carson), intercedes, Maine throws an arm around his neck and allows the bigger man to lead him away. But when Libby puts a hand on Maine's shoulder, Maine suddenly throws a punch, staggering backward and growling, "Hands off me." Distracted by a second horse ("A horse! A horse!"), Maine is immediately smiling and laughing again, patting Libby's broad chest as he asks, "Why do you disgust me? Why do I hate you so?"

A possible answer comes when Maine proposes that Libby feed him drinks in exchange for every photo Maine agrees to pose for. Assaulted by a montage of flashbulbs, we cut to Maine happily posing in front of a series of makeup mirrors. Pressured to do more, he begins to suspect that he is being kept offstage. With both hands, he shoves Libby into a mirror, wreaking havoc. He slashes his way through curtains, knocking over one ballerina as another screams, and emerges like a man pursued by Furies with three dancers trying to hold him back. As willing to hit women as men, Norman throws the women and two stagehands out of his way, straightening his jacket as he prepares for his entrance. Finding a singing act in progress, Maine is just as willing to use physical force with Esther (Judy Garland), harshly pushing her away when she tries to lead him offstage. He only relents when she incorporates him into the song and dance. The audience for this spectacle, worried at first, ultimately misreads what we know to be emotional chaos as a delightful, lighthearted prank.

Mason, here pictured with Judy Garland, delivered a subtle and affecting performance as a star past his prime sinking into self-destructiveness in *A Star Is Born* (George Cukor, Warner Bros., 1954). Digital frame enlargement.

This opening sequence establishes Maine's volatility as his seeming open-heartedness turns to violence on a dime. He needs to be a star ("the public loves me") but despises the machinations that mediate his relationship with the audience. (He asks Libby, "How many lies have you told the public today, huh?") Throughout the opening sequence, we can also see how Mason the actor works within the circumstances of this particular production. Shooting in Technicolor and CinemaScope, director George Cukor uses complicated long takes that require a high degree of professionalism on the part of performers. This first shot with Norman and Libby lasts a minute and fifteen seconds and involves roughly ninety-three extras and two horses. Throughout the sequence, Mason weaves through crowded spaces, constructing the character of Norman Maine through posture, gesture, and the pace and rhythm of his movements as much as through dialogue. For instance, when he speaks to Libby, he rarely looks him in the eye—gazing past him (and later Esther) as if the answer to his problems, or something he has lost, is somewhere "out there."

Perhaps the scene that best exemplifies Mason's ability to emphasize different aspects of performance in order to convey the specificity of Norman's pain-filled contradictions is the scene at the Academy Awards. Roberta Pearson compares Mason's performance in this scene with Fredric March's "loud aggressive drunk" in the 1937 *A Star Is Born* (61–62). She finds March's Norman Maine forceful, cynical, sarcastic, and prepared, while Mason, Pearson argues, portrays "the character as pathetic, a confirmed drunkard and a sick man" (61–62). Although both actors were highly praised for their performances, Fredric March is a coarse instrument compared to Mason's surgical precision as he presents Norman's self-inflicted death of a thousand cuts.

In Cukor's film, twelve takes were made of Norman's speech at the Academy Awards, with six setups (Haver 150). In doing multiple takes of a scene, Cukor explained, "good (actors) will vary it every time" in order "to make it fresh" (Haver 150). Mason's changes to the speech illustrate one of the contributions an actor can make to a scene. The speech in the 1954 script begins with "My method for gaining your attention is a little unusual perhaps" and ends with the line, "I can do comedy as well" (Haver 149). In the take(s) chosen for the final film, Mason alters these lines in subtle but telling ways. Instead of Norman saying that his methods are "unusual perhaps," Mason starts to say "uncon—," interrupts himself, then continues, "unconventional"—dragging out the end of the word. By marking its beginning and end, Mason makes this one word the centerpiece of the line. The rest of the sentence—"but harsh times call for harsh measures"—arrives quietly, delivered as if to himself.

In addition to the socially inappropriate behavior of publicly intruding on his wife's acceptance speech, Norman is drunk, something indicated in subtle ways at first (his coat being unbuttoned, a stray lock falling over his forehead). But when Norman notes that it is silly to be so formal and begins to sit on the stairs, he misses the step and lands suddenly, off-balance, eliciting a gasp from the onlookers that confirms his inebriated state. In this scene, Norman is negotiating a delicate balance physically and intellectually. He astutely pinpoints the film industry's "use 'em up, throw 'em out, what have you done for us lately" ethos, shaking a finger at studio executives from his ungainly perch as he reminds them, "I made a lot of money for you—gentlemen—in my time—through the years—haven't I?" The sing-song delivery mixes childishness with rhetorical structure as Mason piles clause upon clause, adding to the script the phrases "in my time—through the years" to emphasize his years of service. When Norman arrives at the reason for his speech—"Well, I need a job now! That's it! That's the speech!"—Mason again extends and rearranges the dialogue as he rushes, stutters, and repeats the beginning and end of lines—"Yeah, that's it. That's the, that's the, that's the speech, that's uh—I need a job. That's what I wanted to say, I . . . I *need* a job!" Saying "I need a job" four times, Mason varies his reading each time, first as a declarative sentence, then as a discovery—something he has just realized the importance of, finally with exaggerated emphasis. (He underlines "need" as he turns back from his pacing by stiffening both his arms—a gesture indicating "isn't it obvious," his voice cracking as he pitches it higher for the word "job," providing an audio exclamation point.) The last time he says the line, he says it quietly, more reasonably, having regained his emotional balance. Throughout the speech,

Mason punctuates his line readings with gestures and sounds. As he leaves Esther to address the crowd, each footstep is amplified. He rises and starts pacing back and forth, looking at the ground (going nowhere, turning inward), keeping a careful rhythm. At one point, he pauses and steps warily onto a higher stair with one foot, like a child practicing balance on a curb, physically acting out the mental process of trying to figure out his problem.

Maine's understanding of how Hollywood works and his position within it does not mitigate his suffering. As Pearson notes, Norman's "intelligence and self-awareness" is coincident with the character's "greater emotional vulnerability" (72). Mason conveys this best when Norman tries, pathetically, to promote himself, acutely aware that his actual abilities have become (and perhaps always were) irrelevant. Turning away from the crowd, he both announces and muses: "My talents, I may say, are not confined to dramatic parts. I can play comedy, too."[1] Mason, of course, does both in his reading of the line, using the comically misplaced assertion to make the pathos sharper, the sardonic self-awareness to make the pain hurt more. There is no repetition or hesitation for these lines. As he says them, he reaches for the Oscar statuette Esther is holding, putting himself in direct competition with her (even claiming credit or ownership of her achievement) as a Moorish star shines behind his head. Attempting to orchestrate a finish—"Well, play something, somebody"—he accidentally slaps Esther in the face. This is a classic melodramatic moment, the emotional trapdoor where Norman's moment of victory leads instantly to emotional devastation. As an actor, Mason achieves this effect not only with his face, but his whole body. A moment of maximum physical expansion—opening his body to the camera by broadening his chest and flinging out both arms—is followed by a painfully sudden contraction when, hitting Esther, he spins away from the camera, crumpling inward (closing up his body by sinking his chest in until he is almost bowing). As he grabs his wife with both hands to make sure she is unharmed, his brash posturing to the crowd has become an anguished, wordless address to one person.

Mason's performance was immediately recognized as one of his best, but it also marks one occasion where the perception of his and his character's intelligence worked against him. Pearson, Haver, and others have criticized *A Star Is Born* on the grounds that Norman's "problem" is never explained. (The part "as written, offered no explanation for his alcoholic decline" [Haver 72].) Comparing the 1937 and 1954 versions, Pearson suggests that "both scripts fail to motivate Norman particularly well, never establishing the backstory for his alcoholism and self-destructiveness" (72). She also finds Mason's depiction of Norman's "disintegration" to be "not entirely credible" (72). Another critic, writing in 1954, argues that Mason "endows Maine with so sardonic a sense of humour and self-criticism that one cannot understand why a man of such intelligence should mind whether or not he continues to be a success in so hysterical and flimsy a place as Hollywood" (in Haver 72). Another, writing in 1979, suggests that "Maine, as James Mason has played him, seems too intelligent a character with too much humor about himself" to fall apart when met with yet another slight (Jennings 335).

But this is exactly the point: Mason plays Norman as a man who is fully aware of how petty it all is, how foolish it is to want something so corrupt and trivial, but he still wants it. What makes the aching desire all the more humiliating is knowing how paltry it is. Alcoholic self-destruction does not have to have a reason; the same intelligence, humor, and contempt attributed to Mason's Maine could be credited to John Barrymore, Cukor's model for Maine. Haver asserts that "Mason's gifts were such that he could communicate Maine's inner turmoil without an excessive amount of expository, soul-searching dialogue" (Haver 72). Screenwriter Arthur Laurents seconds this opinion when he recalls trying to account for Mason's British accent in *Caught*: "Mason didn't need justification for anything. Whatever he said, whatever he did, he was believable and riveting" (142).

Even without Norman Maine's drinking, self-loathing, or self-destructiveness, Mason would have understood the dilemmas the character faced simply by virtue of being an actor. According to Mason, he left England because he knew that actors rarely control their fate and recognized his relative unimportance in the British film hierarchy. "I knew the pecking order: Laurence Olivier, Rex Harrison [who had beaten him out for the lead in *Major Barbara* (1941)], David Niven, Michael Redgrave [star to Mason's supporting role in *Thunder Rock* (1942)])" and others (qtd. in Haver 69–70). Mason felt that in Hollywood he would "have a wider choice" of parts, although this was not to be the case, at least initially (Haver 70). Just as his last British hit, *The Seventh Veil*, had been originally conceived of and cast with another actor (Francis L. Sullivan), Mason knew that several other actors had been considered for (and were even offered) the role of Norman Maine (including Cary Grant and Humphrey Bogart). Despite the potentially humiliating circumstances, Mason looked on the bright side. "In the end it came to me and I grabbed it smartly before it slipped away" (Haver 71).

☆☆★★★ Uncooperative

Mason's career up to this point has a superficial resemblance to Norman Maine's (more flops than hits, time wasted in silly swashbucklers). But Mason was not a victim, being neither studio-bound nor studio-dependent. Compared to Maine (or Garland for that matter), Mason's relation to his career was healthy, independent, diversified. Initially prevented from working in Hollywood for two years by a contract dispute, he appeared on Broadway, guest-starred on the Fred Allen radio show, "contented himself with casual journalism," and wrote a book on cats (Morley 79–80). Even after his film career resumed, he continued to work on radio, doing several Lux Radio programs between 1949 and 1953, including condensed versions of his films *Five Fingers* and *Odd Man Out*. Making the most of his attractive voice, fashionable accent, and superb diction, Mason recorded several spoken word albums based on British literature (the poetry of Robert Browning, Dickens's *Oliver Twist*, Mary Shelley's *Frankenstein*) as well as the Book of Ecclesiastes. He also performed the dramatic narration for the ground-breaking UPA animated short of Edgar Allan Poe's *The Tell-Tale Heart* (1953). By the middle of the decade, Mason was also working regularly in television, hosting the "Lux Video Theatre" from 1954 to 1955, and starring in his own program ("The James Mason Show") in 1956.

Above all, Mason found ways to use his negotiating power to work with interesting directors and become a producer. Instead of signing with a studio, Mason "ran the gamut of Hollywood agencies" (Haver 70), trying to find the people who could construct the deals that allowed him to maintain his independence, particularly the ability to choose roles rather than have them assigned to him. Arthur Laurents maintains that it was "unfathomable why James Mason chose *Caught* as his first American picture" in 1949, but makes it clear that it was Mason who did the choosing (142). Who directed the film was also up to Mason. "[Marcel] Ophuls' acceptability to Mason was a key reason" the director was chosen for Mason's second Hollywood film, *The Reckless Moment* (Bacher 265).

Although directors loved him (Cukor called him "a complete actor . . . who has the greatest discretion," and Nicholas Ray referred to him simply as "a beautiful man, beautiful actor" [Haver 162, Ray 106]), Mason stirred up frequent controversy. The actor understood that he had made "a bad name" for himself when he was young by seeing producers as the enemy, as "men who polluted the artistic aspirations of writers, directors and actors" (Hirschhorn 15). In England, he picked fights with Gainsborough, J. Arthur Rank, and the British Film Producers Association (Hirschhorn 16–20; Morley 64–65). As soon as Mason landed in New York, he found himself in a feud with Louella Parsons, who denounced him "on her coast-to-coast radio show as 'uncooperative' and 'swollen-headed'" (Morley 78). According to one biographer (in what sounds like a description of Norman

Like many Hollywood stars of the period, James Mason found an additional (and lucrative) second professional life as a radio performer.

Maine), "James fascinated the American press with his rare mixture of belligerence, acid wit, secrecy, ill-temper and intelligence" (Morley 80).

Clive Hirschhorn, who calls Mason "incapable of effective communication with the press," describes the actor, new to Hollywood, "busy[ing] himself writing articles in magazines[,] some of which (characteristically) did not add to his popularity on the West Coast" (Hirschhorn 20, 22). (Once, after Mason and wife Pamela gave "their honest opinion of the local social scene" to a reporter, Mason had to send "telegrams of apology to almost every other actor in Beverly Hills" [Morley 98–99].) Mason's December 1948 *Motion Picture* article "So This Is Hollywood" is an example of Mason's style. The second installment in what was billed as "a startlingly frank series" begins with a statement of resistance to Hollywood's obligatory socializing, as Mason depicts himself and his wife refusing invitations "to this cocktail party and to that reception, to private showings of unreleased films that everyone is crazy about, to home movies at so-and-so's house, to television at such-and-such's" (30, 67). Facetiously addressing his shortcomings as an author, Mason apologizes, "If I had taken my duties as a correspondent more seriously, I would have made a point of bumping into a slew of film stars and asking a series of embarrassing question for the edification of the readers of *Motion Picture*. As it is, I have met six and one-half film stars" (67). He describes one of them, neighbor Glenn Ford, as "counting the days until he is free of his contract with Columbia." "Every actor who has his head screwed on the right way," Mason insists, "would rather be a free-lance than a long-term contractee." With a year and a half to go, Mason writes, Ford's studio has decided "to sweat the last ounce out of him before he is out of their clutches." In a rare example of diplomacy, Mason adds parenthetically, "The expressions 'sweat' and 'clutches' . . . are mine, not Glenn's" (67).

Mason's description of making a film at MGM shows what happens when a "characteristic" want of diplomacy is combined with cutting insight and a way with words. "The whole atmosphere of the place suggested a military junta," he wrote. "The central administration block, for example, was the colonels' headquarters—and you were never allowed to forget it. The main entrance to the studio was policed by tough-looking security men carrying revolvers" (67). At the same time that he was doing his best to stay out of studio harness, though, Mason found his independence isolating. One of the reasons he "did not particularly enjoy" his time at MGM, he wrote, was because "not being under contract to the studio, . . . I felt I was an outsider—as though I didn't belong there'" (Hirschhorn 24). This did not, however, result in an effort to dull the sharpness of his pen. Even though he thought Twentieth Century–Fox "was doing far better work" at the time than MGM, Mason referred to the former as "Penitentiary Fox," not knowing he would soon sign a two-year deal with them in order to secure the lead in *The Desert Fox* (Hirschhorn 24; Mason 67).

Mason continued to bite the hands that fed him throughout his time in Hollywood, even refusing to attend the premiere of *A Star Is Born* despite being personally importuned (and subtly threatened) by producer Jack Warner. Warner sent a telegram:

> Just learned you have not accepted invitation to be my guest. . . . There's an old adage: One must put something back if they want to continue taking something out. Assure you only good can come from your attending. . . . So why not get on the team?   (Haver 206)

Mason responded politely but did not attend (Haver 207).

Mason could be charming and immensely likable—even with the press. Despite (or because of) his feud with Parsons, he maintained a cordial correspondence with Hedda Hopper, whom he and his wife called "our first California friend" in 1948.[2] A note from 1946 also illustrates his awareness of the possible misperceptions of friendship within a celebrity culture.

> Dear Hedda, This is a hello-and-how-are-you-keeping letter. I nearly could afford to drop you now as it is quite obvious that I have retired from the film industry. So you may assume that a letter from me is motivated by the purest and most disinterested brand of love.

Hopper wrote in April 1947, "Can't wait to see you again, and whatever you do—short of murder—remember I'm on your side." Whether or not this was merely a "professional friendship"—on either side—it came to a messy end in 1953 when Hopper published reports of Pamela Mason's miscarriage and used the occasion to speculate that the couple was on the verge of divorce. Pamela Mason also found herself in legal trouble for calling Hopper "beastly" on the radio in February 1957. James Mason made his position clear, stating simply, "I couldn't agree more with my wife."

★★★★★ Domestic Crisis: *Bigger Than Life*

In the 1950s, the American nuclear family was frequently depicted as being under siege, a state that came to a head around 1955 with a cascade of films about families being held hostage in their own homes. From the big-budget, star-heavy adaptation of the Broadway hit *The Desperate Hours* (1955) to the widescreen, Technicolor *Violent Saturday* (1955) to low-budget studio flicks like *Suddenly* (1954), *The Night Holds Terror* (1955), and the bare-bones indie *Storm Fear* (1955), these films combine the domestic melodrama with elements of crime and suspense, examining small-town America and the suburban ideal through the lens of noir. The invasion of the home foregrounds the patriarchal crisis that haunts these films. Trapped in a domestic setting by his affections and responsibilities, the father must prove himself when he is at his weakest, his ability to react in a "manly" way consistently thwarted. Whether they occupy positions socially constructed as masculine (police officers, sheriffs) or confront internal cracks in their upstanding facades, these father figures fail at every turn until the last minute when climactic violence restores their standing as heads of household.

Bigger Than Life goes a step further when the family home itself is the trap and it is the father who is the greatest threat. Director Nicholas Ray had explored the consequences of paternal failure the year before in *Rebel Without a Cause* (1955), but there it is the father's "weakness" that is memorably "tearing (his son) apart." In *Bigger Than Life* the father is too strong, sees through everything, and is being ripped apart like a man on a rack. While Ray biographers credit him with being "a kind of witness to something going on in America" at this time, the insight that American domestic life was a trap was not Ray's alone (Kreidl 170). *Bigger Than Life* was just as much Mason's project (producing the film and contributing—without credit—to the script). An earlier film over which Mason exerted a degree of control, *The Reckless Moment*, explores a similar theme, this time with "the American woman" being described as "the trapped woman." One of that film's screenwriters explains that "she's not trapped by anybody, except her own responsibilities and lack of privacy. . . . That was the key: to take just ordinary life, making it impossible to handle through some terrible situation" (Bacher 272). In *Bigger Than Life*, it is the father-husband who finds himself in an impossible position: domesticity circa 1956 is killing him. Suffering increasingly acute pain, he lashes out against his life—his job, his marriage, his responsibilities as a father—questioning the ideological underpinnings of each, until his house must be literally torn apart in an effort to prevent him from destroying his family and himself.

The film is based on an account of an actual medical case about the dangers of cortisone addiction, written by Berton Roueché and published under the title "Ten Feet Tall" in the *New Yorker* (10 September 1955, 47–77). The film's "hero," distorted by the exaggerated fears of the times, becomes a metaphorical monster, comparable to other giants of the period, for example *The Amazing Colossal Man* (1957), *The Attack of the 50 Foot Woman* (1958), *Godzilla* (1954), the ants in *Them!* (1954)—and, of course, the gigantic squid in *20,000 Leagues under the Sea* (1955), Mason's most commercially successful film. Size alone, even if delusional, imperils the nuclear family (civilization as the middle class knows it) as the father threatens in raging Technicolor to break through the confines of the widest possible CinemaScope screen and crush everything before him.

When Mason was called upon to play villains, some found him subtle, others over the top. In *Prisoner of Zenda*, for instance, one writer called him "quietly effective," while another accused him of having "the sneeriest sneer in the Balkans" (Hirschhorn 104). As Gledhill points out, melodrama requires a style of acting that makes moral qualities of good and evil easily legible (something often compounded in costume pictures). For those who appreciated Mason's brand of villainy, subtlety and excess could coexist. One critic said of *Botany Bay*: "Mason gives a considerable impression of natural evil in a performance that is almost a tour de force"—a sentence that fearlessly equates the implied realism of the "natural" with the bravura display of a "tour de force" (Hirschhorn 122). But while clearly Mason can do both, I would argue that what sets his work apart is his ability to add a third dimension of critical distance.

As a character, Ed Avery presents Mason with a greater challenge than Norman Maine. Where Maine openly expresses his contempt for the superficial depths of Tinsel Town, Avery is barred by propriety and social expectations from dismissing the conventional values of middle-class America, making it impossible for him to name or acknowledge the source of his hard-to-define ailment. In *Bigger Than Life*, Mason combines intelligence and humor into what can best be described as withering disdain, the excess of which enables the audience to see the character/performance from two different perspectives. Without losing emotional contact with the pathos fundamental to melodrama, we can read "Mason" as outside the performance commenting on the character's situation. From the latter perspective, we see that Avery (like Maine) can no longer ignore the misery behind the façade of his life, but, as with Maine, all of his intelligence, wit, disdain, and contempt cannot save him from suffering.

While it was easy to imagine Mason as a movie star at sea in Hollywood, it was never easy to envision him as an ordinary person. As Pearson points out, "Mason's atypicality rendered him inappropriate for roles that required 'ordinariness'" (71). He himself thought that *Bigger Than Life* failed commercially because "the U.S. public could not accept me as [a run-of-the-mill American schoolteacher] since they knew that James Mason was an uncooperative import who should be seen only in glum foreign parts" (Hirschhorn 133). Both *A Star Is Born* and *Bigger Than Life* depict Mason's characters as outsiders—a distance increased by orders of magnitude in the suburbs of a nameless American town. As an all-American suburban dad, James Mason's Ed Avery is already a figure divided against himself.

As the film begins, Avery has been manfully hiding spasms from his students, boss, co-workers, and wife. Unable to provide sufficient material support for his family, he moonlights as a dispatcher at a cab service (the lower status underscored when Ed takes his place at a table filled with

In *Bigger Than Life* (Nicholas Ray, Twentieth Century–Fox, 1956), Mason, who plays the husband of Barbara Rush, is a father troubled by a psychotic reaction to medication.

women). Arriving home, he has already let his wife down by forgetting his contribution to the evening's party. He then fails to participate enthusiastically, and finally sums up the evening by (cheerfully) identifying the guests, his wife, and himself as dull—at which point he suffers an attack so severe it can no longer be concealed.

In classic melodramatic form, Avery's psychic pain is displaced onto his body and his house. Made up of narrow hallways, a steep staircase, and a pervasive darkness that descends from the ceilings, the shabby older residence confines its inhabitants within a series of tight frames and crowded spaces. Avery's geographically constricted life is mocked by numerous maps and bright posters advertising world travel. (The *New Yorker* story on which the film is based appeared in an issue that featured over a dozen ads promoting travel to sites as diverse as Puerto Rico, Hawaii, Mexico, France, Switzerland, and South Africa.) The house expresses Ed's pain as his wife, Lou (Barbara Rush), half-carries him to the door for his first trip to the hospital. Collapsing at the threshold, Avery clutches the door buzzer. He grimaces in pain as Lou tries desperately to pry his hand away and stop the noise. Not only concerned about alerting the neighbors—though she is that—Lou throughout the film tries to hide or deny Ed's sickness in an effort to prop him up and maintain his image as a man. As a consequence, she unwittingly contributes to his decline.

In the hospital, Avery becomes an object of study. The promise of modern medicine is conveyed through the clinical set-design with its sleek modernist décor and highly polished equipment. The doctors succeed primarily in documenting Ed's suffering. Laid out horizontally along the bottom of the CinemaScope screen, Mason-as-Ed writhes in pain as a superimposed graph translates agony into an abstract representation. Avery's condition is not really explained and not really the point. The "miracle drug" he is offered—cortisone—was specified by Roueché to be "not a cure . . . only an alleviative." It will enable him to continue his life, not alter it.

Ed begins to experience psychological side effects, characterized by a heightened sense of his own importance. An intolerable trait in a conformist era, what Roueché calls Ed's "colossal self-assurance," is the dilemma the film must resolve as it struggles to pathologize, denounce, and contain his inflated ego. Returning to school, Ed tells Lou that he feels ten feet tall but the image presents him crouched over looking through a car window. Boxed in by a frame within a frame, he is restricted by that icon of American freedom—the automobile. Seen from a low angle in the next shot, Ed rises to his full height, freed from domestic obeisance and looming over the school behind him.

Avery's egotism also distorts ideals of marital life. In an incident that Roueché refers to as "that tyrannical bath," the husband, all keyed up, decides to take a bath. Told that there is no more hot water, he suggests that his wife heat up a kettle. In the film, Lou (complaining about the old boiler downstairs in the kitchen) makes repeated trips, while Ed considers himself in the bathroom mirror. (As in most American homes, the mirror is on the door of the medicine cabinet—the place that contains the cortisone, the source of the transformation he beholds.) The person on whom Avery was based is described by Roueché as feeling at this moment "a sense of power and glory exaltation [having] become his natural state." What the film shows us is a schoolteacher who sees himself as a star.

Like *Caught* before it, *Bigger Than Life* "multiplies the indications of ordinariness" around Mason yet "only succeeds in intensifying the paradox of [his] star image" (Ellis 96–97). When Avery regards himself in the bathroom mirror, he and we recognize him as the "desperately attractive James Mason" (Ellis 96). Preening, Avery/Mason locks eyes with himself, turning his face this way and that so he can appreciate it from different angles. He holds his cigarette carefully, judging his effects. With sudden inspiration, and great satisfaction, he folds a white cloth around his neck and tucks it into his robe, transforming it into an elegant smoking jacket. Avery has become an actor, self-conscious and self-transforming. In fact, he looks like Norman Maine. At this moment, however, such elegance and self-appreciation are marked (impossibly) as impossible. The film insists that it is a sign of Avery's *sickness* that he thinks he could look/act/dress like a movie star—yet all the while we can see that he *is* a movie star. Finally fed up with being a drudge, Lou shouts that he is not in the hospital anymore (where he could be waited on hand and foot) and slams the cabinet shut, breaking the mirror and Ed's deep engagement with his exalted self/image. The assault on his image (in all senses) is shattering. Mason clutches his arms to his chest, holding his breath as Avery tries to hold himself together.

Part of the pleasure of melodrama (and the aspect that most easily crosses the line into camp) is when characters behave badly, loudly proclaiming opinions usually left unexpressed. As the cortisone swells Ed's head, it frees him to speak his mind. Look out. Annoyed by "moral midgets," at a PTA meeting Ed tells parents that children are "stupid," "lazy" "morons," the mental equivalent of "gorillas," and (in extreme low angle) espouses a quasi-fascist desire for discipline (with himself as the übermensch, no doubt). Soon he abandons his job in favor of a more exalted "career—a mission."

Unleashed on the world, Ed begins to violate social taboos. He is rude to a saleswoman at a fancy dress shop, threatening, "If we don't get a whole lot of high-class service—and in a hurry—there's likely to be a terribly embarrassing scene." While the audience may enjoy this as vicarious revenge against commercial elitism, Avery's rudeness is less enjoyable when he becomes the snob, berating the milkman for letting his bottles rattle. "You're filled with envy and malice towards me because I work with my mind," he brays, threatening to have the man fired.

Ed's most deliciously appalling behavior, of course, happens at home. Finding his friend, the school's athletic coach, Wally (Walter Matthau), talking to Lou, Ed accuses them of having an affair and refers to Wally snidely as "Mr. Muscle Beach." Deciding he has outgrown his wife ("It's a shame I couldn't have married someone who was my intellectual equal"), Ed violates the boundaries of public and private when he announces he is leaving her in front of company (Wally). Most shocking (and frowned upon) is when parents fight in front of their children. Having deprived son Richie (Christopher Olsen) of supper until he correctly answers a set of math questions, Ed discovers at dinner that Lou snuck a glass of milk to the boy while Ed was out of the room. He blows up, pounding the table and railing at her:

"Let's clear this up once and for all. I'm staying in this house solely for the boy's sake. As for you personally, I'm completely finished with you. There's nothing left. Our marriage is over. In my mind, I've divorced you." Ray uses the CinemaScope screen to turn a Norman Rockwell scene of an idyllic family dinner into a middle-class hell, with Lou on the far left, Ed on the right, and Richie caught in the middle, watching his family implode.

The climax arrives when Ed decides to unleash the wrath of God in his suburban home. When Richie steals Ed's medication and attempts to call the doctor, Ed declares the boy a thief and decides that it is his moral duty to kill him, Lou, and himself. Inspired by a sermon on the Old Testament, Ed challenges God. Lou points out that when Abraham went to sacrifice Isaac, God stopped him. Ed declaims, "God was wrong." As Ed stands above her on the stairs, holding a Bible to his chest, Lou counters with a book of her own—a photo album of Richie's baby pictures (exemplifying the assertion that "melodrama sentimentalizes ethics" [Gledhill 225]). But Ed prizes reason above sentiment (telling Lou earlier, "You just can't distinguish between the trivial and the important, can you?") and neatly shoves her into a closet. Cunningly entering the living room, he turns on the television set and waits until loud carnival music drowns out Lou's pounding and screaming as she tries to warn Richie. The front door is kicked in as Wally (having been shown this "secret" way in by Richie) rushes in and confronts Ed on the stairs. As the men struggle, they smash through the staircase banister, overturn the living room furniture, and upend the television set until Ed lies unconscious amid the wreckage and "help" can be summoned. The ending is inconclusive, any hope for the future qualified. Ed is back in the hospital and the doctors prescribe cortisone again, there being no other option. (Lou does stand up to the doctors, though, when she announces, "I am Ed Avery's wife" in much the way Esther declares herself "Mrs. Norman Maine.") Ed holds his wife and son close, but it is only an alleviative—there is no cure for what ails him.

The paradox at the heart of *Bigger Than Life* is inseparable from Mason's performance and persona. If you think you're a movie star, you're sick. If you think you're smarter than everyone else, you're insane. Being extraordinary—and recognizing it to be the case—is worse than a character flaw; it is a symptom, absurd and possibly dangerous. Anyone bigger than life must be cut down to size. At the same time, it is only when the monster within is loosed that the suburban male can flourish, finally becoming all that he can be—"James Mason," movie star: the cutting, sardonic man you love to hate, the acerbic intellectual outsider who knows just what American culture is worth—and exactly what it costs to love it.

★★★★★ *North by Northwest*

Although Mason's stardom spans several decades, with the exception of *Lolita* in 1962, his greatest leading roles can be located in the 1950s. At the end of the decade the actor condenses his patented blend of keen intelligence, critical disinterest, and unexpected emotional depth into one of his best-known performances as the villain in Hitchcock's *North by Northwest* (1959). Onscreen for less than a quarter of the film's running time, Mason justifies his star billing by anchoring the light comedy with his dark gravitational pull.

More than any of his other characters, Mason's Philip Vandamm is almost entirely defined by critical distance. He is an observer. He watches and evaluates, alternating praise ("With such expert playacting you make this very room a theater") and rebuke ("Has anyone ever told you that you overplay your various roles rather severely?"). The subject of his fascination is Cary Grant's Roger Thornhill. He can't take his eyes off him. It is the quality of this attention that gives Vandamm weight as a character. He studies Thornhill as if he were not only a mystery but a mirror. It is as if he is looking at himself.

As Thornhill and Vandamm struggle to read each other throughout the film, we are constantly invited to compare them. Both characters wear gray suits and have slicked back, gray-flecked hair; each actor has an instantly identifiable, unique British accent. On a narrative level, neither man has a home—or rather each is at home anywhere, moving from place to place as easily as they change identities. Both Vandamm and Thornhill are actors, one intentional, the other inadvertent. But while Thornhill resists when he is misidentified as George Kaplan, struggling to define and defend a single true identity, Vandamm is a master of surface. Completely at ease with the idea that all identity is fiction, he tells Thornhill when they first meet, "I know you're a man of many names but I'm perfectly willing to accept your current choice." At times, though, he seems tired of it all: one of the first things he says to Grant/Thornhill/Kaplan is "Games? Must we?" Meeting Thornhill later in South Dakota, he asks, "What little drama are we here for today?" Vandamm is right to be wary because the drama offered at the cafeteria at Mount Rushmore (the fake shooting death of Thornhill) has been staged for his benefit by one of the few people Vandamm assumes is genuine (has a single identity), the double-agent Eve (Eva Marie Saint).

The cafeteria scene hinges on the play between surface cool and emotional depth. Cary Grant provides the film's most overt displays of passion—Thornhill in the cafeteria is angry, bitter, betrayed—while Mason consistently underplays. His Vandamm never raises his voice. Tellingly, it is Vandamm's antipathy to feeling that leads to his undoing. Before he is tricked by the fake shooting, he pinpoints Thornhill/Kaplan's problem as a failure to remain superficial. "She really got under your skin, didn't she?" Thornhill gets under Vandamm's skin. Fascinated from the beginning (haunted, perhaps) by Thornhill's insistence that he is more than a series of names, a surface, a screen, Vandamm misreads Eve and Thornhill's performance of passionate hatred as genuine.

This scene is the turning point of the film. Where Grant's Madison Avenue playboy Thornhill is fighting not only for his life but for the right to be himself—something he didn't value when the film began—and in the process finds depth, genuineness, connection, Vandamm is undone by a depth of feeling he did not know he had. As a consequence, he is undermined and misled. When he is himself subjected to a fake shooting, not only is his trust in Eve shattered, but he finds that he has also lost his abilities as a critic. He forgot that passion could be an act. At this point Vandamm has his only outburst in the film (punching directly at the camera lens in the place of his ersatz attacker). The aftermath, however, is where Mason shines. Clutching his hand and staring upward, he expands Vandamm's physical pain into a broader emotional suffering which is then recast in cosmic terms.

The true MacGuffin of *North by Northwest* is not the microfilm in the statuette but Vandamm himself. Having no real motive, no verifiable identity, Vandamm occupies an existentialist no-man's-land marked by endless wandering and rootlessness. Behind a mask of wit and material comfort lies a chasm of pain. The film reaches its emotional climax at this moment of unexpected depth. As always, James Mason suffers beautifully.

NOTES

1. Mason also changed the phrase "dramatic roles" to "dramatic parts" and "comedy as well" to "comedy too." Mason's ability to play comedy is clear in these films as well as films he made in the 1960s (*Lolita, Georgy Girl,* etc.), but it was thrown into severe doubt by *Forever Darling* (1956), in which he plays an angel opposite Lucille Ball and Desi Arnaz. The angel's resemblance to James Mason is a running gag. When the wife takes him to a Mason film, what they see is a thrillingly vicious sadist in a costume drama.

2. All cited material relating to Hopper is from the Hedda Hopper file, the Margaret Herrick Library, Academy of Motion Picture Arts and Sciences, Beverly Hills.

5 ☆☆☆☆☆☆☆☆☆★★★

Reflexivity and Metaperformance

Marilyn Monroe, Jayne Mansfield, and Kim Novak

MATTHEW SOLOMON

From the author's private collection.

After several years of modeling and a few bit parts during the late 1940s, Marilyn Monroe came to the attention of moviegoers through a number of smaller dramatic and comedic parts in films like *The Asphalt Jungle* (1950), *All About Eve* (1950), *Clash by Night* (1952), and *Monkey Business* (1952). In 1952, Monroe was named "Fastest Rising Star" by *Photoplay* magazine and publicly identified as the nude model in the pinup calendar photograph "Golden Dreams." The concurrence of these two media events highlights Monroe's status as a woman who was equated with sexuality and whose name "became virtually a household word for sex" (Dyer, *Stars* 23) once she became a major movie star the following year. Monroe has been extensively—though rather unevenly (and, typically, idiosyncratically)—discussed as an icon of sex appeal, but this chapter mostly sets aside reception in order to explore the inherent reflexivity of her star image, which was constructed largely through a series of roles that foreground role-playing. As Monroe slips between performances and performances-within-performances onscreen, one is reminded of her work as an actor and her offscreen performances of the "Marilyn persona." Such roles twist Monroe's stardom in on itself like a Moebius strip that joins the seemingly facing sides of actor and character together in apparent continuity. Monroe was hardly the only star of the 1950s whose screen persona turned on reflexivity. Such reflexivity connects Monroe to the two other major stars who appeared immediately in her wake and were often compared to her: Jayne Mansfield and Kim Novak.

As Wendy Lesser points out, Monroe was almost "always assign[ed] . . . the role of actress or performer *within* the film" (205). Indeed, in every single one of her starring roles from *Gentlemen Prefer Blondes* (1953) to *Some Like It Hot* (1959), Monroe plays a professional performer. The consistency with which Monroe was (type)cast as a showgirl of one sort or another has doubtlessly contributed to the mythical status she has achieved since her untimely death from a prescription drug overdose in 1962, but consideration of Monroe as a film actor must contend with the fact that, in playing performers, she often plays two separate but not entirely distinct roles nested within one another. This casting pattern has the effect of turning many of Monroe's performances into metaperformances. James Naremore explains:

> Film actors . . . must sometimes signal they *act persons who are acting*. In these moments . . . the drama becomes a metaperformance, imposing contrary demands on the players: the need to maintain a unified narrative image, a coherent persona, is matched by an equally strong need to exhibit dissonance or expressive incoherence within the characterization. Thus, we could say that realist acting amounts to an effort at sustaining opposing attitudes

toward the self, on the one hand trying to create the illusion of unified, individualized personality, but on the other suggesting that character is subject to division or dissolution into a variety of social roles.   (Naremore 72)

In two films noirs that came early in her rise to stardom, *Don't Bother to Knock* (1952) and *Niagara* (1953), Monroe plays deceptive femmes fatales who do not really maintain "coherent personas," but in all her subsequent roles of the 1950s, the split within her characters is largely external/social rather than internal/psychological. Indeed, in film after film, Monroe is called upon to embody characters who make their living as performers onstage, but who lead the rest of their lives offstage. In this way, Monroe's metaperformances often reflect on her own acting and the construction of her stardom.

By 1954, Monroe had become, as *Photoplay* noted with equal parts cliché and hyperbole, "an American institution as well-known and highly regarded as hot dogs or baseball" (Jane Corwin, "Orphan in Ermine," March 1954, 39). She was voted the top female box-office star for both 1953 and 1954 by movie exhibitors, though she was earning but a fraction of what most of her co-stars at Twentieth Century–Fox commanded, making her "probably the greatest bargain the studio ever had" (Custen 327). Monroe's work for Fox during the mid-1950s was disrupted by a series of contract disputes and a hiatus from filmmaking that lasted through most of 1955, during which time she relocated to New York, formed her own production company, and attended sessions of the Actors Studio. Monroe succeeded in negotiating a new contract, but her standoffs with Fox did relatively little in the way of realizing her oft-expressed ambition to "concentrate on dramatic roles and soft-pedal 'sexy ones'" ("Miss Monroe to Put Emphasis on Acting," *New York Herald Tribune*, 18 February 1953).[1]

Monroe's popularity spurred countless imitations, as Fox and several other studios attempted—with varying degrees of success—to produce their own ersatz Marilyns by molding various actors to the contours of Monroe's shapely blonde star image. Fox even fitted costumes Monroe had worn to such Marilyn substitutes and replacements as Sheree North, Corinne Calvet, Roseanne Arlen, Barbara Nichols, and Mamie Van Doren (Spoto 396n). After returning to Hollywood from New York, Monroe took on somewhat more ambitious roles in *Bus Stop* (1956), an adaptation of William Inge's critically acclaimed play, and opposite Laurence Olivier in *The Prince and the Showgirl* (1957), a farce dealing with political intrigue in pre–World War I Europe, before appearing in *Some Like It Hot* (1959), another film that revolves around role-playing—although relatively little by Monroe's character, Sugar Kane Kowalczyk.

After 1956, Jayne Mansfield temporarily took Monroe's place as Fox's "newest queen of Sweaterdom" ("Will Success Spoil Rock Hunter?," *New York Herald Tribune*, 12 September 1957). Her first film was *Illegal* (1955), an apparent takeoff on *The Asphalt Jungle* in which she "plays precisely the same sort of role" as Monroe in the earlier film (Bosley Crowther, "Sincere Flattery," *New York Times*, 29 October 1955, 12). Mansfield's breakthrough came that year not in film, but on the stage, as Rita Marlowe, an over-the-top caricature of Monroe, in George Axelrod's Broadway play *Will Success Spoil Rock Hunter?*—a role she reprised in the rather different film that was released under the same title a few years later. Much of Mansfield's publicity was reflexive inasmuch as it concerned her insatiable desire for publicity and the various stunts she had performed for the benefit of the media in order to put herself before the public. Press accounts of Mansfield inevitably turned to statistical verification—estimates not only of her measurements but also of the voluminous publicity she had generated (numbers of pictures published in the newspapers, lines of newspaper copy about her, etc.). Thus, Mansfield's very stardom implicitly acknowledged its construction through the media—a concept reinforced and reflected in her films by the star-making story *The Girl Can't Help It* (1956) and the ubiquitous paparazzi and fanatical fans of *Will Success Spoil Rock Hunter?* (1957).

Kim Novak was initially promoted as a replacement for Columbia's rebellious "love goddess" Rita Hayworth, and an answer to Monroe, "another starlet getting the 'blonde bombshell' studio buildup . . . another Marilyn Monroe" (Bob Willett, "Good Enough's Not Good Enough for Me," *Montreal Star Weekend Magazine*, 15 March 1957; see also Lippe). Billed as the "lavender blonde," Novak was initially cast in supporting roles similar to those of Monroe's early films. In the film noir *Pushover* (1954), Novak is a gangster's moll—like Monroe's character in *The Asphalt Jungle*. In the remarriage comedy *Phffft* (1954), she is the attractive blonde who keeps company with a divorcée—like Monroe's character in *Let's Make It Legal* (1951). Yet Novak rarely played showgirls. Even in her one such role during the 1950s, as a burlesque dancer in the musical *Pal Joey* (1957), Novak plays a rather different kind of showgirl character—one bubble-bath scene notwithstanding. She trades lines with the wise-cracking womanizer Joey (Frank Sinatra), cleverly rebuffs his initial advances, and stands up for herself when he changes her part in the show without asking her. Like Novak's other onscreen incarnations, she is assertive yet vulnerable, willing to express her emotions—even if it means an argument with an authority figure and/or the man she loves. Novak's characters express their own desires in addition to being objects of others' desires; men look at them, but these women also look back. By 1956, Novak had become a serious rival to Monroe in annual polls of top box-office stars. In 1957, she was featured on the cover of *Time* magazine. Novak's onscreen persona also involves role-playing—most famously as Madeleine Elster/Judy Barton in *Vertigo* (1958) and most reflexively as the eponymous 1910s and 1920s stage and screen actor in the forgotten biopic *Jeanne Eagels* (1957).

The films of Monroe, Mansfield, and Novak foreground reflexivity by referring the viewer both directly and indirectly to the persons and processes through which their films have been constructed. This kind of reflexivity hardly amounts to a Brechtian critique of institutional cinema (see Stam, Burgoyne, and Flitterman-Lewis 198–203), yet it can subtly disrupt the illusion of a film's fiction and characters without in any way alienating the spectator. This disruption is comparable to what Jane Feuer, in her consideration of late-studio-era musicals (a category that fits a number of Monroe's films), terms "critical reflexivity" (107–10). Reflexive Hollywood films like these, Feuer says, "leave behind a residue of deconstruction, which sometimes lingers long after the happy ending has passed into the deeper recesses of our memory" (107). This "residue of deconstruction" takes various forms in the films discussed below, all of which complicate our vision of these three stars.

★★★★★ Performance, Parody, and Persona

Reflexivity would become a defining feature of Marilyn Monroe's screen persona when she began starring as professional entertainers in 1953, but it is also attends a number of her earlier supporting roles. In her first speaking part, as the aspiring actor Miss Caswell—sarcastically described as "a graduate of the Copacabana School of Dramatic Arts"—in *All About Eve*, she is seated obliviously on the stairs during a party while her escort pontificates that theater and film actors' "greatest attraction to the public is their complete lack of resemblance to normal human beings." This backstage film's focus on actors reflects on the acting that went into the film—including an emerging persona that would come to be identified with Monroe.

A different kind of reflexivity ripples through Monroe's presence in *Clash by Night*, in which she plays the naïve young Peggy, who aspires to something beyond her job in a canning factory and a predictable future with her boyfriend in a small fishing town after she gets to know her boyfriend's more cynical older sister Mae (Barbara Stanwyck). In her last scene in the film, Peggy's boyfriend Joe (Keith Andes) confronts her, angrily calls her "blondie," and tells her that she must choose either to be like Mae or be with him. She chooses the latter and rushes into his arms in tears, but this heated confrontation is followed by a scene that takes place in the projection booth where Mae's lover Earl (Robert Ryan) works. Earl is peering through the small window, watching the film projected in the theater as he starts up one projector and shuts off the other in a changeover. This slightly jarring transition offers an eyeline match cut between the scenes and gives the impression that the projectionist has been watching the embrace between Monroe and Andes unspool on the screen—reminding us that we are watching a film and emphasizing the fictiveness of what we have just seen. In an earlier scene in the projection booth that begins with another such reel change, Earl removes a reel of film from one of the projectors and rewinds it as he misogynistically comments that the "celluloid angel" on the screen needs to be "cut up."

Monroe's first starring role, as Nell, a mentally unstable babysitter in *Don't Bother to Knock*, involves further degrees of role-playing since her character likes playacting and because this character's personality splits as the film progresses. Hired as a babysitter for the night, Nell tries on her charge's mother's clothes and jewelry as soon as she puts the girl to bed, cloaking herself in the accoutrements of a wealthier lifestyle she imagines could be hers through marriage. This role-playing becomes even more overt when neighbor Jed (Richard Widmark) observes her dancing through a window from across the courtyard and telephones the room. Realizing that she is being observed, she initially draws the blinds to prevent him from seeing her, but then coquettishly opens the shade. When he invites himself over, she concocts a fiction about herself and why she happens to be in the apartment, but must confess that she has been lying after the girl awakens and interrupts their flirtation. The revelation of her true identity is traumatic and she becomes convinced that Jed is the lover she lost in a tragic airplane crash several years earlier—a loss from which she has never recovered. She believes that if he leaves her, he will die, and endangers the girl while trying to prevent him from going away. The theme of selves performed for others to see is heightened by the spatial and temporal limitations of the film, which takes place entirely over the span of a single evening largely within the confines of several rooms in one residential hotel, making it into a chamber drama of sorts.

In *Home Town Story* (1951), *As Young as You Feel* (1951), and *Monkey Business*, Monroe plays attractive young secretaries who each discharge their office responsibilities and rebuff their co-workers' advances with varying degrees of success. Unlike the proficient and professional secretaries in the former two films, Miss Laurel's work in the boss's office at the Oxly Chemical Company in *Monkey Business* seems to consist largely of being leered at. "Anybody can type," shrugs Mr. Oxly as he and Dr. Fulton (Cary Grant) watch her sashay out of his office, both men conspicuously eyeing her posterior. Once Fulton has accidentally ingested a youth formula, he recognizes Miss Laurel instantly after seeing only her ankles beneath a sign. In her last scene in the film, Mr. Oxly chases Miss Laurel around the laboratory after also ingesting the formula, gleefully amusing himself by spraying her with water. As Laura Mulvey remarks, "With hindsight, she exists even then, on the edge between *acting* a part and *being* the living sex symbol" ("*Gentlemen*" 220).

Monkey Business marks the beginning of what Lois Banner describes as the "Marilyn persona" which "appeared full-blown" in *Gentlemen Prefer Blondes*: "a comic 'Marilyn' that was a masquerade of femininity and the 'feminine mystique' of the 1950s . . . a wiggling walk, jiggling breasts, childlike voice, and pouty lips, characteristics that confirmed 1950s femininity while burlesquing it" (7–8, 13). In his laudatory review of *Monkey Business*, Jacques Rivette glossed Monroe as a "monster of femininity" (127), but her monstrous impersonation of 1950s femininity took on a distinctly parodic quality with subsequent roles and also, as Banner notes, because Monroe performed the "Marilyn persona" in her public life offscreen (13–14). In *Gentlemen Prefer Blondes*, Monroe's character Lorelei Lee is constituted entirely as a performance. She performs several musical numbers onstage, but the film also suggests that her most ignorant offstage actions—asking for directions to "Europe, France" before boarding the ship, attempting to force a diamond tiara around her neck as if it were a necklace—are every bit as much of a performance as her famous rendition of "Diamonds Are a Girl's Best Friend." With her buxom figure and ostentatious costumes, she is continually being observed by other passengers on the ship—not least of all by the detective sent to photograph and tape-record her: a scenario that lends a performative quality to everything she does. The courtroom masquerade her best friend Dorothy Shaw (Jane Russell) performs in baby-doll voice and platinum wig near the end of the film only highlights the extent to which Monroe's Lorelei herself is a construction of costume and performance. The sense that she performs as vigorously offstage as onstage culminates when her future father-in-law comments that she is not so dumb, to which she responds, "I can be smart when it's important, but most men don't like it"—a line that Monroe supposedly suggested to director Howard Hawks (Spoto 229).

Several of Monroe's films foreground role-playing by emphasizing the transitions between onstage and offstage personas. As saloon singer Kay in the western *River of No Return* (1954), she sings and dances provocatively in two onstage numbers, but both these sequences are immediately followed by backstage scenes that show her behaving quite differently. Later, when she and farmer Matt Calder (Robert Mitchum) have fled with his son downriver on a raft, he confronts her: "What kind of an act is this?" She responds, "I'm a performer, didn't you know—songs and dances." At the end of the film, she casts her high-heeled pumps into the street, discarding the last vestiges of her stage persona as she rides away on Matt's buckboard to form a reconstituted nuclear family, complete in her transformation from torch singer and stripper to farmer's wife and mother. Like *Bus Stop, River of No Return* mostly suggests that there is a distinct split between the singer's onstage persona and her authentic offstage personality. But, like *Gentlemen Prefer Blondes*, one sees in *There's No Business Like Show Business* (1954) that the performer's performances do not take place exclusively onstage but extend offstage as well. After hat-check girl and aspiring actor Vicky (Monroe) performs an impromptu audition onstage to wild applause, she goes backstage to begin rehearsing how she will greet the producer who she hopes will cast her in a show, trying out different greetings before a mirror. The latter films suggest that the self is rehearsed, staged, and acted just as much in private as in public, carefully managing these private performances to achieve specific and desired results and to particular strategic ends.

★★★★★ The Monroe Fantasy

In the final scene of *The Seven Year Itch* (1955), Richard Sherman (Tom Ewell) receives an unexpected visit from family friend Tom MacKenzie (Sonny Tufts) while his wife and son are away on summer vacation in Maine. But he is not alone when MacKenzie shows up: the young woman from the upstairs apartment who spent the night in his bed is still there. Sherman gets agitated and, before MacKenzie can even discover his female guest, blurts out: "The blonde in the kitchen . . . Well, wouldn't you like to know. Maybe it's Marilyn Monroe." The joke, of course, is that the blonde in the kitchen, who enters the scene one minute later dressed only in a bathrobe (after MacKenzie has been fortuitously knocked unconscious), *is* Marilyn Monroe. This line of dialogue winks reflexively at the audience and punctures the film's fiction, which has already been stretched to a breaking point by Sherman's continual conversations with himself and a number of interpolated daydream sequences—devices borrowed from George Axelrod's play *The Seven Year Itch*, which was still playing on Broadway at the Fulton Theatre when the film opened.

As the cause of the eponymous irritation in *The Seven Year Itch*, Monroe is the ultimate embodiment of a married man's libidinous heterosexual fantasies, "less a woman than a product of the average middle-aged man's overactive imagination" (Lewis, "1955" 142). In the film, she appears initially as an impalpable fantasy, coming into view on the threshold of Sherman's vision (and ours) as a shadow silhouetted behind a curtain—the top of a head poking out from above a balcony—but emerges into sight in more evenly lit medium shots and close-ups that isolate her shapely torso, posterior, and smiling face. Her arrival at the doorstep of Sherman's apartment building coincides with the departure of his wife and triggers a series of fantasies in which he makes out with his secretary, a night nurse, and his wife's best friend in comically exaggerated scenes of passion, narrated matter-of-factly in voiceover by Ewell. These fantasies are induced not so much by the sensational paperback fiction that Sherman publishes as by movies. The torrid vignettes in which Sherman imagines his respective conquests are parodies of scenes from films like *From Here to Eternity* (1953), to which his wife (likewise imagined) remarks, "Lately, you've begun to imagine in CinemaScope, with stereophonic sound." Such "deliberate citations" of other films, "with the same frames, angles, and positions of the actors," led François Truffaut to conclude that *The Seven Year Itch* is "a filmed critique of films . . . estimable for its attempt at demystification" (160). Through the character of "The Girl," who performs in live television commercials, the film also points to the way that celebrity is constructed through the media. In a daydream sequence, we see her in the television studio performing in one of these commercials and then the immediate broadcasting of her face and her voice to faraway television sets.

The line about the "blonde in the kitchen" is absent from the play, of course, because on Broadway "The Girl" was played by the dark-haired Vanessa Brown and because in the play she is never in danger of being discovered, having slipped out of the apartment first thing in the morning to get to work at the television studio. Unlike the play, which hints that Sherman and "The Girl" have an affair during the night between Acts 2 and 3, in the film Sherman sleeps on the couch and their day-and-a-half flirtation is never physically consummated.

The film's ending has been frequently criticized—perhaps most severely by its director Billy Wilder (124, 176)—as an unfortunate concession to Hollywood censorship. As she descends in a nightgown through the boarded-over opening in the ceiling that once separated the two floors of the former duplex, accompanied by ethereal music, she clutches a hammer in one hand and a cup, toothbrush, and tube of toothpaste in the other. Tooth-

Marilyn Monroe on the set of *The Seven Year Itch* (Billy Wilder, Twentieth Century–Fox, 1955). Courtesy of Photofest.

paste is the very product she promotes in commercials on the "Dazzledent Toothpaste Hour," and when she reaches the bottom of the staircase, she says (in dialogue that could have been lifted from a hardware store commercial), "It was so easy: I just pulled out the nails," then raises her eyebrows coyly in a close-up shot that echoes her televised toothpaste pitch. By staging seduction with the tropes of a television commercial, the film mocks the mass media strategy of constructing consumer desire through sexually attractive models. "The Girl" is depicted in the film as an advertisement come to life, a walking commercial that is nearly as fleeting and immaterial as the mass-mediated fantasies with which she is associated. Yet with this ending "The Girl" remains a fantasy not only for the audience of the film, but also for Sherman, who is positioned as a spectator within the film— albeit a very talkative one—once his family goes off and he discovers the gorgeous model living above his head. We are even left with a sense that, in the end, "The Girl"—like Monroe herself—is hardly more palpable than any of Sherman's other overheated hallucinations. Thus, it is relevant that the most famous moment of the film, when Monroe's white skirt is lifted by a subway train passing beneath a sidewalk grating, takes place outside a movie theater where she and Sherman have just watched *The Creature from the Black Lagoon* (1954). One mass-mediated fantasy begets another.

★★★★★ A Star Is Manufactured

By the mid-1950s, Laura Mulvey points out, "Marilyn Monroe, with her all-American attributes and streamlined sexuality, came to epitomize in a single image . . . a brand of classless glamour, available to anyone using American cosmetics, nylons and peroxide" (*"Gentlemen"* 216). With her visible use of hair dye, cosmetics, and hosiery, Monroe's likeness was marketed as a product of consumer beauty products, yet this marketing scheme also implied that the likeness might itself be mass-produced. Jayne Mansfield's stardom took this logic to its ultimate conclusion. Hence, we have the apt description of her career as "a slickly and expertly manufactured article" (Alton Cook, "She Acts? It Doesn't Matter," *New York World-Telegram*, 14 September 1957). The publicity-hungry Mansfield also filled the temporary void left by Monroe's departure for New York, making "Miss Mansfield a darling of the United States press, which had such a hard time even getting to see Miss Monroe after she joined the New York Actors' Studio" (Richard Donovan, "She Will Do Anything for Publicity," *Saturday Evening Post*, 1 June 1957, 100). It was also noted at the time that Mansfield received "careful nurturing" from Fox in terms of film projects and co-stars (as Novak had at Columbia), "a benefit that was not extended to Marilyn Monroe, the other blond publicity phenomena of [the] decade" (Cook, "She Acts? It Doesn't Matter").

In *The Girl Can't Help It*, Mansfield is Jerri Jordan, the girlfriend of a powerful racketeer who hires alcoholic talent agent Tom Miller (Tom Ewell) to make her into a star in six weeks. Miller's initial "buildup" for Jerri's career consists of visits to a series of nightclubs, with well-timed trips to the powder room at each stop as she struts by the respective club owners in high heels and a red-sequined open-back strapless dress that shows off her hourglass figure in a plan that proposes potential stardom in almost entirely physical terms. For Truffaut, director Frank Tashlin had "solved the problem of satirical comedy and even criticism" in *The Girl Can't Help It*: "Rather than mock a subject with caricature, he exaggerates the very excesses of what he parodies" (Truffaut 152). The film's exaggerations include not only a send-up of hyperbolic rock 'n' roll performers like Little Richard, but also a take on what Tashlin termed the "immaturity of the American male . . . breast fetish" (in Bogdanovich, *Who the Devil Made It* 773). The breast fetish is exaggerated, parodied, and simultaneously exploited in a sequence that shows Jerri walking down the street in a form-fitting black dress that turns men's heads and (in Tashlinesque animated cartoon fashion) melts a large block of ice, causes a milk bottle to froth and boil over, and shatters the eyeglasses of a man who watches her walk up the stairs to Miller's apartment, where she strolls into his bedroom, supporting a bottle of milk against each of her breasts. Ed Sikov describes this sequence as "a deliberate frontal assault. Jayne's breasts may be objects of desire, but she uses them as weapons, defeating men by rendering them as helpless as nursing babies. . . . Here, Jerri Jordan is explicitly the fetishized figure of woman, so disruptive an image that it destroys whatever meager illusion of reality the film has maintained to this point" (217–18). Through such spectacular displays of Mansfield's singular body in motion, the film tends to collapse the distinction between character and actor. Mansfield's next film for Tashlin would go even further in reflecting the terms of her stardom and interrogating its mass mediation.

The play *Will Success Spoil Rock Hunter?* was Axelrod's autobiographically inspired follow-up to his hit play *The Seven Year Itch*. In it, a playwright struggles to write a worthy follow-up to a hit play and tussles with the Hollywood studio system while a hack fan magazine writer quickly obtains the love of a famous Hollywood sex symbol, Rita Marlowe, and an Oscar for best screenplay by selling his soul to the devil. Writer-director-producer Tashlin (in that order, he insisted [see Godard 61]) totally transformed Axelrod's farcical take on Hollywood and the plight of the successful playwright-cum-journeyman-screenwriter, however, into a broad satire on advertising, television, celebrity, and the American ethos of success, retaining little more than the play's title, the general setup of the first act (which turns up in a later scene of the film), the names of several characters, and Mansfield in the role of Rita Marlowe.

While the film version of *Will Success Spoil Rock Hunter?* is more of a satire on the advertising industry and its stranglehold on television, it also lampoons Hollywood stardom and mass-mediated celebrity through the

Jayne Mansfield starred with Tom Ewell in *The Girl Can't Help It* (Frank Tashlin, Twentieth Century–Fox, 1956). Courtesy of Photofest.

character of Rita, who plays a comparatively larger role in the film than in the play. Indeed, the film's credits sequence includes not only a series of faux television commercials, but also a pitch for Mansfield, "a talented and gorgeous star with a fabulous figure," made by Rock Hunter (Tony Randall) in direct address to the audience. In the play, Rita is a parody of Monroe (her name also invokes "Love Goddess" Rita Hayworth), but in the film, she is both a parody of Monroe and a caricature of Mansfield herself. As future novelist Philip Roth put it in his review of the film: "Rita Marlowe, I take it, is intended to be a caricature (if that is the right word) of Marilyn Monroe; as it turns out, Miss Mansfield's satire is a satire of Miss Mansfield: she quivers her hips, her breasts, her lips, and on and off produces an aria of screeches and whinnies" (Philip Roth, "Nymphs and Satyrs," *New Republic*, 14 October 1957, 21).

As Monroe had done in 1955, Rita comes to New York from Hollywood to form her own production company and to put some distance between herself and an ex-lover—in Monroe's case, former baseball star Joe Di-Maggio, whom she married and then divorced in 1954. Yet the film elides the distinction between the fictional Rita and movie star Mansfield by alluding to Rita's roles in such recent and forthcoming Mansfield films as

The Girl Can't Help It, The Wayward Bus (1957), and *Kiss Them for Me* (1957). Mansfield's real-life lover, bodybuilder Mickey Hargitay, plays Marlowe's bare-chested ex-lover, "TV jungle man" Bobo Branigansky, further prompting viewers to compare the film's onscreen story with what they knew of Mansfield's highly publicized private life.

We first see Rita on a television news broadcast that shows her at the airport leaving for New York and talking to reporters. She appears again on television when the airplane arrives in New York, and several of her subsequent appearances in the film foreground the television cameras and reporters that seem to follow her every move. The relentless publicity through which stardom is created becomes a source of a number of the film's gags. The morning after Hunter secures her product endorsement by pretending to be her boyfriend (in a ploy to make Branigansky jealous), the news breaks that the two are involved and he, too, is besieged by cameras and reporters. After fielding telephone calls from Hollywood and New York gossip columnists Louella Parsons and Earl Weaver, Hunter finds that live television crews have staked out his apartment. When Marlowe arrives and Hunter is unable to hear what she is saying, his friend and fellow adman tells him to "turn on the TV . . . any station, it's like when the President speaks." They realize that she is coming upstairs not by looking out the window but by watching her on the television set (on top of which is a framed portrait of Rita, put there by Hunter's niece, one of her most devoted fans). In this scene, as in the film, the mediated "reality" of television—on which manufactured celebrities act as linchpins for commercials, interviews, and gossip—overwhelms direct experience as the primary means by which people relate to the world, themselves, and one another.

☆☆☆☆★ The Star Looks Back

The *Time* magazine cover story about Kim Novak published just before the release of *Jeanne Eagels* emphasized that "Kim Novak herself was virtually invented, the first top-flight star ever made strictly to order for delivery when needed" by Columbia Pictures and Harry Cohn ("A Star Is Made," *Time*, 29 July 1957, 52). The story of Novak's creation was a consistent part of the discourse about the star, but this was not as unusual as *Time* made it out to be (see McLean, *Being* 198–205; see also Byars). In contrast, however, to the careers of Mansfield and, to a certain extent, of Monroe, Novak was given more opportunities to develop a nuanced and multi-dimensional star image that went far beyond her blonde hair and sex appeal. Novak's characters are often working women or business owners like Marjorie Oelrichs in *The Eddy Duchin Story* (1956), who was born into a wealthy family but prefers running her own interior design studio to a life of leisure, and Gillian Holroyd in *Bell, Book and Candle* (1958), who is proprietor of a shop selling primitive art and a part-time witch (see McLean, "Movies and Allegories of Ambivalence" 216–220). In a line from *Jeanne Eagels* that stands as commentary on her own screen roles, she says, "Don't think I'm just a dumb blonde."

Like Monroe, another so-called "dumb blonde," Novak was rarely taken seriously as an actor. An article published during the making of *Vertigo* derided her acting and her intelligence: "When Kim Novak is described as one of movietown's 'brightest' stars the reference is not necessarily to her acting ability or her I.Q." (Vernon Scott, 1957, unidentified clipping). George Sidney, who directed her in three films, compared her to the famous actor she played in *Jeanne Eagels*: like Eagels, Novak was relentlessly driven to the pursuit of acting, yet unable to articulate why she "gets to the studio ahead of time and puts her entire self into every little thing" (qtd. in Joe Hyams, "Unhappy Lot of the Movie Queens," *New York Herald Tribune*, 4 August 1957). Journalists came away a bit perplexed after interviews with the "moody" Novak, claiming (in seeming contradiction) both that she was not a talented actor and that she worked too hard. While the public was interested in Novak's rumored romances with (most controversially) Sammy Davis Jr. and Rafael Trujillo Jr., son of the Dominican dictator, she claimed: "My big love affair is my work. I don't have much time for anything else" (qtd. in Lee Belser, "Men, Says Moody Kim Novak, Must Always Make Jokes," *New York Journal-American*, 14 October 1957).

In *Picnic* (1955), Novak plays auburn-haired nineteen-year-old Madge Owens, the "prettiest girl" in a small Kansas town who is "so tired," she says, of "just being told I'm pretty" and "of only being looked at." While her mother encourages Madge to date Alan Benson (Cliff Robertson), a young man from a wealthy family, on the night of a fateful Labor Day picnic, she instead makes love with one of Alan's college friends, Hal Carter (William Holden), a muscular dropout who drifts into town on a freight train. While Alan can hardly believe that Madge is "real," telling her, "It doesn't matter whether you are or not. You're the most beautiful thing I've ever seen," Hal, who is also wowed by her beauty, treats her like a "real thing" and not just an image. It is this attitude, in part, which leads her to follow Hal to Tulsa when he hops another freight train out of town at the end of the film.

Picnic inverts narrative cinema's tendency to make women the objects of what Mulvey has described as the "male gaze" (*Visual* 19). In contrast to Mulvey's examples, *Picnic* foregrounds the way that women look at the frequently bare-chested Hal. Men talk about looking at women (and especially about looking at Madge) in *Picnic*, but the film consistently constructs Hal—rather than Madge—as the object of the gaze (see Byars; Cohan, *Masked Men* 168–82). Madge is introduced to viewers drying her hair while in a nightgown in medium shot, face and shoulders visible through an upstairs window. But in this sequence, she is entirely in the company of other women, who talk to her from the porch area below and barely glance in her direction. Hal and Madge meet when she emerges from the house fully dressed; the ensuing exchange of reverse shots highlights his sweaty torso as well as the way women look at it. Shots of Madge and the other women are generally in the third person, but the scene concludes in the first person with Madge looking back at Hal as she returns to the house and a point-of-view shot of him through the screen door.

The scene in which Hal goes swimming, diving, and frolicking in the pond as all the girls stare at him in his trunks is not unlike Monroe's appearance in a form-fitting one-piece bathing suit as Miss Laurel in *Monkey Business*, when she is ogled by a line of men standing next to the high-diving board. Though Hawks is known for his comic reversals of traditional gender roles, it is Joshua Logan's *Picnic* that makes Holden's muscular calves the fulcrum of a scene, just as *Monkey Business* uses Monroe's shapely legs as spectacle when she raises her dress to show Dr. Fulton that she is wearing the non-rip stocking prototype he invented. On the afternoon of the picnic, while the group sits among a cluster of trees, close-ups from the point of view of Miss Sidney (Rosalind Russell) of Hal's calves as he raises the leg of his trousers are intercut with shots of Madge and her younger sister Millie, who each gaze longingly in his direction, creating a shared, and distinctly female, point of view. As Hal gets up and goes over to stand by a tree, a full shot shows all the women present (including the elderly Mrs. Potts) turning to look at Hal. That this female point of view is highly sexual is confirmed not only by Hal's comment about the "very big foot" that fills his boots but also by the next shot, a close-up in which Miss Sidney, seated beside the tree on the ground, barely averts her eyes as she looks at his crotch, which is now rather close to her head. Men take pleasure in looking at women in *Picnic* (indeed, Madge's appearance draws Hal to her), but the film goes to great lengths to inscribe female visual pleasure into its very structure.

One of the most surprising inversions of Hollywood cinema's characteristically male point of view comes, ironically, just after Madge wins the annual beauty contest and floats down the river, newly crowned as the Queen of Neewollah, spotlight shining on her face. At the moment everyone is looking at her—a moment dedicated to admiring her physical attractiveness—Hal becomes the object of her gaze: he is seen standing on the landing in a moving camera shot that is singularly her point of view from the passing swan boat. She looks at Hal again from the bridge as he dances with her younger sister (in a high-angle point-of-view shot) and, attracted by what she sees, soon cuts in. Staring directly at him, she slinks onto the makeshift dance floor and begins dancing with him, first hand-in-hand with their eyes locked on one another, then clasped in a tight embrace that nearly brings their lips together. In this scene, Madge's vision prompts her actions and she starts to seduce Hal after some hesitant flirtation on both their parts.

If the sight of Hal ultimately provides the impetus for Madge to leave the small town she yearns to escape, visual pleasure is also fraught with problems in *Picnic*. The film never entirely departs from what Mulvey describes as the "masculine third person" (*Visual* 29), but its strategic recourse to female point of view and its story about the discontents of being looked at tend to deconstruct the pleasure one can take simply in gazing at Novak's screen image. Madge and Hal are both characters who have grown accustomed to being looked at. Madge is a beauty queen, always dressed in lovely, carefully fitted clothing appropriate for the occasion. Hal is an athlete, the star college football player adulated by his peers. (Hal was also an artist's model and even got a Hollywood screen test.) But, whereas the teenaged Madge has already grown tired of being looked at, the older Hal continues to make a spectacle of himself like an adolescent. Through much of the film, he invites others to look at him by speaking loudly, swinging his limbs wildly, and doing physical stunts. But in the film's climactic scene, he changes his attitude in an instant and begins to resent being the object of visual attention (especially from the opposite sex). From this point on, he flees everyone but Madge, drives off into the darkness, and tries to hide himself from sight after a violent confrontation with Alan and two police officers.[2]

Picnic explores both the limitations of the unreciprocated look as well as the erotic possibilities of the reciprocated look. But in the end, the film underscores the gap between image—whether visual, mental, or mechanically reproduced—and tactile reality. Early in the film, we see Madge's mirror image positioned between her and her mother while she tries on a party dress and her mother extols the luxuries a "girl as pretty" as she could have with Alan. As the ensuing conversation suggests, her mother, like others, is attuned to the erotic and economic possibilities of Madge's appearance—her image, an image that literally comes between her and her mother. Another image comes between them at the conclusion of the film. The morning after the picnic, her mother (Betty Field) picks up the newspaper to find a pixilated black-and-white photograph of Madge as the Queen of Neewollah, which we see through her point of view. In the very next shot, an over-the-shoulder shot from slightly further back, however, the newspaper is lowered to reveal Madge (in Technicolor) emerging from the house dressed in a skirt and jacket of the very same shade of blue as her party dress, on her way to catch the bus to Tulsa to be with Hal. As the newspaper drops out of the frame, Madge's image goes out of focus and then becomes clear and sharp. The mother drops the newspaper, setting aside the impoverished image, and rushes to grasp her daughter's arm as she finally recognizes the person behind the picture.

★★★★★ Reflecting on Acting

Like *Gun Crazy* (1950), *All About Eve* (which it was accused of imitating), and *Sunset Blvd.* (1950), *Jeanne Eagels* is set in the world of show business, spanning the carnival, Broadway theater, and silent-era filmmaking milieux seen in these other films. It is the most reflexive of Novak's 1950s films, detailing actor Jeanne Eagels's fictionalized rise from the lower rungs of American traveling entertainment to big roles on Broadway and in Hollywood. Eagels comes to the carnival as an entrant in a beauty contest and soon gets a job with the show, dancing the hula in a grass skirt, having knives thrown at her, and showing off her body as a "coochy dancer," but she aspires to act in *Becky Sharp* rather than performing a strip-tease for a tent full of hollering men. This becomes a possibility when the owner of the carnival, Sal Satori (Jeff Chandler), gets a concession on Coney Island, allowing Eagels to enter the tutelage of an accomplished New York acting coach, Madame Neilson (Agnes Moorhead). As an up-and-coming actor, she makes her biggest breakthrough by duplicitously outmaneuvering an older alcoholic actor, Elsie Desmond (Virginia Grey), for the role in the play *Rain* that makes her career. But, despite subsequent successes on stage and screen, Eagels is continually haunted by Desmond, whose comeback role she stole, and eventually becomes just like her: an aging has-been unable to work because of her drinking problem. In an ending that echoes *Sunset Blvd.*, she descends a staircase and approaches until her face nearly fills the screen—swooning from a fatal dose of pills swallowed in despair. Some measure of redemption is provided by the film's coda, which shows the recently deceased—and now immortal—Eagels onscreen, singing a song in the talkie "Forever Young" as Sal watches tearfully in a packed movie theater.

Earlier, Eagels is seen onstage in her most famous part, that of prostitute Sadie Thompson—recently played onscreen in *Miss Sadie Thompson* (1953) by Rita Hayworth. While more than one critic thought "allowing Miss Novak to essay one of Miss Eagels' more sultry stage moments" was "one of the [film's] serious mistakes" (Justin Gilbert, *New York Mirror*, 1 September 1957), this extended scene of dramatic stage action has the effect of putting Novak's subsequent scenes in the film into metaphorical quotation marks.

Eagels's temper tantrums and bouts of drunkenness strike one as doubly performed—at one level by the actor Novak, who plays Eagels, and at another level by the character Eagels, who manipulates others by playing an exaggerated, melodramatic version of herself during fits of anger and bouts of apparent drunkenness. This pattern of behavior starts when Eagels goes to visit Madame Neilson and becomes angry after she is initially refused acting lessons. Amused and unexpectedly impressed by Eagels's outburst, Neilson reframes her anger as a performance of anger and advises Eagels to repeat the line with less physical emphasis and "stop the bad dialogue" before accepting her as a client. In what we see of her stage acting, Eagels plays roles that foreground her sexuality—the "wiggle" that one critic of the film spotted in this scene ("The Screen: This, Too?," *New York Times*, 31 August 1957, 19)—just like the scantily clad parts she had played in the carnival. Offstage, however, she embodies the highly performative roles of the temperamental stage diva and unstable Hollywood star. Novak's acting further becomes a metaperformance in a scene at Paramount Pictures, where Eagels is acting in a silent film directed by Frank Borzage. A slate indicates that the film-within-a-film is being shot by cameraman Robert Planck (the cinematographer of *Jeanne Eagels*). As the cameraman cranks, Borzage (in a cameo) directs Eagels—in yet another role-within-a-role that emphasizes her as an object of male sexual attention—and her costar from a chair in front of the camera, flanked by a script girl and several on-set musicians. Shots of the director and cinematographer alternate with flickering, fast-motion footage of Eagels acting histrionically and at a slightly rapid clip—a cliché of silent screen acting depicted even more comically in *Singin' in the Rain* (1952).

★★★★★ Roles-within-Roles

Kim Novak's performances as Judy Barton, Madeleine Elster, and Carlotta Valdes in *Vertigo* are nested within one another like Russian dolls. These roles further multiply and reflect one another in dizzying fashion throughout the film when, at various points, she is Judy impersonating

In a publicity still for *Vertigo* (Alfred Hitchcock, Paramount, 1958), Kim Novak's two selves are on display. Courtesy of Photofest.

Madeleine acting as if she were Carlotta (and not just Carlotta, but the "sad Carlotta," as the owner of the Argosy Bookshop explains); Judy pretending not to have been the woman who impersonated Madeleine; and (in Scottie's most ecstatic moment) Judy playing herself playing Madeleine. It is a true tour de force, with these roles forming a veritable mise-en-abîme that shifts kaleidoscopically throughout the course of the film.

Like John "Scottie" Ferguson (James Stewart), we first get a good look at Madeleine (impersonated by Judy) as she strides forward purposefully through the crowded dining room of Ernie's Restaurant in a shimmering emerald dress. A sidelong glance and slight swallow betray that she is performing for Scottie, who is seated at the bar observing her. Indeed, she pauses for a moment when she comes nearest his stool, her face illuminated in profile as the light in the room brightens. She turns her head—ostensibly to look for her companion, but in fact confirming that Scottie sees her—and barely avoids making eye contact with Scottie, maintaining the "fourth wall" that separates her from her audience of one. She glances again in Scottie's direction to confirm that he is watching the next day at the flower shop, approaching the slightly open door through which he peeps and pausing momentarily—again she barely avoids eye contact with him—before turning to walk away. She performs this same sequence of actions later at the cemetery, pausing when she comes closest to Scottie while never looking directly at him, and then turns to walk down the path. These are examples of what Raymond Durgnat describes as one of the hallmarks of Novak's style, "a quick hesitation followed by an almost laborious deliberateness" (Durgnat 167). But, in these examples, what Durgnat terms "Kim's eternal hesitations" (168) have an added effect. The way that Novak (as Judy [as Madeleine]) holds her head and obliquely redirects her eyes signals that she is looking in Scottie's direction and simultaneously trying not to look at him—and at us, because many of these shots are from his point of view. Rather than returning his look, she goes on to play the role of spectator herself, sitting in front of the portrait of Carlotta as Scottie watches her stare at the painting. (Unlike Madeleine [Judy], the painting seems to look back.) She again plays the spectator being watched watching when she goes to the window of the McKittrick Hotel and looks out across the city. Much later, when we first see her as Judy walking down the street with three female companions, she comports herself differently and immediately makes eye contact with Scottie, returning his gaze and beginning her performance as Judy-pretending-not-to-have-impersonated-Madeleine.

Vertigo of course inverts the female gaze that figures so prominently in *Picnic*, with significant portions of the film structured around Scottie's point of view. Thus, for Mulvey, the film showcases cinema's general tendency toward exhibitionism, in which women "connote *to-be-looked-at-ness*," while at the same time its hero (James Stewart) reflexively "portrays the contradictions and tensions experienced by the spectator" (*Visual* 19, 23). Mulvey also notes that *Vertigo*—unlike *Rear Window* (1954)—explores the interface between scopophilia and performance (a vein of her argument—and her specific analysis of this film—that has not been discussed nearly as thoroughly): "She knows her part is to perform, and only by playing it through and then replaying it can she keep Scottie's erotic interest" (*Visual* 24). As such, *Vertigo* reflexively dramatizes the work of the film actor, who must repeatedly perform credible simulations of reality for viewers who are seldom, if ever, acknowledged as such. Even more to the point here, *Vertigo*, through Madeleine (Judy [Carlotta]), doubly enacts this scenario in a way that resembles the roles-within-roles of Novak, Monroe, and (to a much lesser extent) Mansfield.

Novak, the only one of these three actors to survive the 1960s (Mansfield died in an automobile accident in 1967), has come to understand *Vertigo* as a personal allegory for her career in Hollywood:

> When I read the lines, "I want you to love me for me," I just identified with it so much. . . . It was what I felt when I came to Hollywood as a young girl. You know, they want to make you over completely. They do your hair and makeup and it was always like I was fighting to show some of my real self. So I related to the resentment of being made over and to the need for approval and the desire to be loved. I really identified with the story because to me it was saying, Please, see who I am. Fall in love with me, not a fantasy.
>
> (qtd. in Auiler 25)

Professionally, Novak's pleas went unanswered (as did Monroe's), for in Hollywood, an actor's "real self" found little traction outside of the gossip columns. As director George Sidney so bluntly commented after the release of *Jeanne Eagels*, "Isn't it kind of hopeless anyway in being someone else? An actor is a projection of some one else's words—she's a character created with the help of a director" (qtd. in Hyams "Unhappy Lot of the Movie Queens").

As Sidney suggests, sentiments like Novak's feelings toward *Vertigo*, however heartfelt, are mostly rendered moot by the workings of the Hollywood image industries, which produce personas and performances that work to lodge themselves in memory and dominate the imagination. As in *Vertigo*, in the end it does not matter who Madeleine or Judy or Kim Novak really is. Like both Madeleine and Judy, Novak is doomed to climb the bell tower steps at the insistence of a frantic voyeur (as Novak had undoubtedly done numerous times in rehearsal on a Hollywood soundstage for director Alfred Hitchcock) every time *Vertigo* is screened—just as Monroe must inevitably descend the steps again and again extolling diamonds in *Gentlemen Prefer Blondes*. Recognizing these unforgettable moments as performances of performances and looking closely at the spiral of roles that spin out from the screen images of these three stars does not bring us any closer to their respective realities, but it does reveal some measure of the complexity and artistry crystallized in their films.

NOTES

I thank Kristie Falco, whose research turned up a number of useful sources cited in this chapter, and the College of Staten Island's Undergraduate Research Fellowship program, which funded her work. Thanks also to Murray Pomerance for his counsel and to Barton Palmer for his patience.

1. Unless indicated by the inclusion of page numbers, all citations from newspapers and magazines are from the Marilyn Monroe, Jayne Mansfield, and Kim Novak clipping files, New York Public Library for the Performing Arts.

2. The turning point of the film comes when Miss Sidney wants to see more of what she glimpsed earlier at the picnic and brazenly yanks up Hal's pants legs to expose his calves again while he and Madge are dancing. Intoxicated, she grabs Hal and starts dancing with him, but this uncomfortable embrace comes to an even more uncomfortable end when she tears part of Hal's shirt off as he tries to elude her clutches. "It's all his fault," she shouts, blaming Hal for "making eyes at Madge," but we realize that blame rests squarely with her for "making eyes" at the man she likens to a naked statue of a Roman gladiator and trying to act on an attraction she believes is reciprocal. This is a mistake her soon-to-be-husband Howard (Arthur O'Connell) did not make, telling Hal just a few minutes earlier while both men are looking at Madge (in lines borrowed more or less directly from the original play [see Inge 116]), "I look forward to seeing her every time I go over to the Owens' house, but I tell myself, 'Howard, old boy, you look all you want, but you couldn't touch her with a ten-foot pole.'" See also Cohan, *Masked Men* 168–82, for a discussion of the film's use of Holden's body as spectacle both onscreen and in *Picnic*'s advertising campaign.

6 ☆☆☆☆☆☆☆☆☆☆☆

Audrey Hepburn
The Film Star as Event

WILLIAM A. BROWN

Roland Barthes famously wrote that Audrey Hepburn's face is an event (while that of Greta Garbo is an idea) (56–57). This chapter expands on Barthes's perception in order to construct a theory of how Hepburn (the performer and the face) can be understood from the perspective of contemporary philosophies of the virtual. For, strange and perhaps unexpected though it may seem in a book about film stars, it appears that, particularly in the case of Hepburn, ideas of virtuality can enrich our understanding of this star—and vice versa.

First, however, we must understand how this "event" came about; that is, we must consider the circumstances that enabled Audrey Hepburn to

Courtesy of MovieStarNews.

emerge at the time that she did. Let us look at both the political and industrial contexts within which Hepburn's star ascended, as well as at Hepburn's biography and career.

In the 1950s Hollywood saw the breakup of the studio system (Welsch 11). The number of productions was shrinking (Rosen 316). Conversely, independent and overseas productions (as well as revenues from overseas markets) were on the rise (see Krämer 197). European production and distribution, together with the return of spectacle in Hollywood via new technologies, which were employed as a reaction against television, saw 1950s Hollywood cinema develop a strand that we might term "spectacular cosmopolitanism" (see Lev 3; Pomerance, "Introduction" 9).

If Hollywood was suffering, the American economy more generally was undergoing something of a consumerist boom: refrigerators and other modern conveniences (including television) were becoming commonplace (see Pomerance "Introduction") thanks to the development of the department store (see Anderson), and there was a renewed interest in clothes and fashion, industries that also found their way into Hollywood features. The postwar "refeminization" of fashion took its lead from Paris couturiers (Turim 213), with Christian Dior's 1947 New Look playing a particularly important role (214–15) and the "sweetheart line" being driven by associations to dance and ballet (223). As far as the relationship between fashion and cinema is concerned, the 1950s proved to strengthen the bond between these two industries. Charles Eckert has already written about the arrival of fashion designers in Hollywood, and how their work led to "a preference for 'modern films,' because of the opportunities they offered for product display and tie-ins" (38). Meanwhile, Charlotte Herzog has similarly analyzed the emergence of fashion shows in films, meaning that film and fashion (together with magazines, radio, and other media networks) became "mutually supporting channels of exploitation" (135). As a result, the fashion designer became an increasingly powerful figure in Hollywood (Gaines, "Costume" 199).

Further industrial/contextual factors enabled the emergence of Audrey Hepburn. The first of these, linked to the rise in consumerism, is the rise in tourism, particularly transatlantic tourism, something enabled by the introduction of regular and affordable transatlantic flights (see Endy 49–50). It is important to remember that the promotion of Europe as a tourist destination for Americans also has its roots in the complex mission to restructure Europe in the aftermath of World War II, a mission that has at its center the so-called Marshall Plan. As Endy (54) argues, the Marshall Plan, together with its Travel Development Section, encouraged Americans to spend money in Europe, thereby using nongovernmental money to help (Western) Europe's economies to recover from the war.

While analyses of cinema's effects on tourism have recently risen to prominence (see Grihault; Bolan and Williams), we can see cinema's role in the promotion of tourism taking place already in the 1950s—as the establishment of Disneyland in 1955 testifies.[1] However, Hollywood's role in the promotion of American tourism was not confined to just domestic tourism—as with Disneyland—but also played a major role in the promotion of American tourism in Europe. As explained, Hollywood began at this time to make films set in Europe for several reasons. First, there was the desire to exploit growing markets in Europe; Italy, in particular, saw cinema expand in the 1950s (see Krämer; Smith, meanwhile, speaks of Hollywood's attempts to muscle in on the French market; for a look at Hollywood in Spain, see Rosendorff "El Caudillo"; Rosendorff "'Hollywood'"). Second, the studios wanted to maximize profits from the theatrical chains that they still owned in Europe; a prime method of achieving this was to make films set there. Third, though perhaps less important, various Hollywood talents, not wishing to become prey to the House Un-American Activities Committee (HUAC), left the United States for Europe in the 1950s (a prime example being Gene Kelly; see Wollen 51).

Typically, film historians argue that the "Americanization" of Europe that took place as a result of these moves was aggressive and calculating on the part of Hollywood (see, *inter alia*, Jarvie "Postwar"; Jarvie "Free Trade"; Trumpbour *Selling*). Smith goes so far as to call this a "Disneyfication" of Europe, in particular of Rome and Paris in terms of how they were depicted onscreen (51). However, one might also interpret this trend as a "Europeanization" of Hollywood, something that Smith (43) equally suggests in her analysis of *Sabrina* (1954), in which the Larrabee family is understood as trying to model itself on the European paradigm of the aristocracy. This counter-trend (Europe influencing Hollywood) is emphasized by the wealth of talented European filmmakers (Douglas Sirk, Billy Wilder, among others) that had fled Europe for Hollywood during the war and who not only looked back fondly upon their homeland(s) but also brought to Hollywood a European sensibility (Gibbs 77). Whether "Disneyfying" Europe, being "Europeanized," or both, it is worth remembering that Hollywood was working not just for itself during this period, but also for the American economy and for the Marshall Plan, and thus for a Western Europe undergoing reconstruction as a whole (see Jameson 60).

To refine our understanding of this relationship between Hollywood and Europe, we can analyze shifts in stars and the star system in the 1950s, and how stardom ties in with fashion in cinema. Marjorie Rosen might see the 1950s as dominated by the "Mammary Woman," as typified by Marilyn Monroe and Jane Russell, but, in opposition to the "mammarians," Rosen also sees the rise of the waif. Rebecca Bell-Metereau identifies this "alternative" type of female star as "continental," and includes among their number Jean Simmons, Audrey Hepburn, Leslie Caron, Grace Kelly, and Deborah Kerr (93; see also Smith 32).

Barry King says that for actresses of this period, "the ideal ingénue should be aged between 18 and 22, 5 feet 3 inches to 5 feet 7 inches tall, possess a well-proportioned body and an exceptionally beautiful and interesting face" (176). This type, so often characterized as gamine-like, is indeed an intriguing alternative to Monroe and company, and does suggest a shift in taste among American audiences toward a more "European" look, even if, as Smith also points out, male leads tended at this time to be more rugged and "American" (with exceptions being Louis Jourdan and perhaps Cary Grant), an "Americanness" that suggests American males conquering European females (Americanization) as opposed to the other way around (Europeanization) (32).

The rise of the gamine star is also linked to fashion and the clothes she wears (Gaines, "Costume" 182). After the arrival of the French New Look, however, fashion designers do play an increasingly important role in the creation of stars, whose status as star is "constructed as much by publicity releases and women's page fashion features as by their performances" (Gaines, "Costume" 198). Thomas Harris confirms this when he writes that Paramount, in particular, promoted its stars with gimmicks, such as a publicity campaign in advance of the star's screen appearance, a "discovery," and glamorous pictures in print media (41–42). Family background and the actor's backstory also helped build this star image—as did the association between fashion and the star offscreen as well as on (Gaines, "Costume" 200). Having established a complex and intertwined set of circumstances that led to Hollywood's interest in Europe, in European fashion, and in European starlets in the 1950s, we can now turn our attention to Audrey Hepburn herself, in order to see precisely how it was that she (almost miraculously) emerged as a star.

★★★★★ A Gamine against the Grain

Audrey Hepburn was born Audrey Kathleen Ruston to an Anglo-Irish father and a Dutch baroness mother in Belgium on 4 May 1929. Growing up in the Netherlands during World War II, she underwent extreme hardships while under Nazi occupation, surviving on very little food, raising money and running errands for the Dutch Resistance, and witnessing first-hand the Battle of Arnhem. After the war, Hepburn moved to London, where she studied ballet under Marie Rambert. Unable to make it as a professional ballerina, Hepburn took to the stage and appeared in films, gaining small parts in review shows and movies such as *Monte Carlo Baby* (1951), *The Lavender Hill Mob* (1951), and *Nous irons à Monte Carlo* (1952). When filming in Monte Carlo, she was "discovered" by French novelist and playwright Colette, who insisted that Hepburn star in the title role of the Broadway version of her play *Gigi*. Hepburn played Gigi to great acclaim, before making her first major film as Princess Ann in *Roman Holiday* (1953), for which she won the Academy Award for Best Actress. Her other starring 1950s roles were in *Sabrina, War and Peace* (1956), *Funny Face* (1957), *Love in the Afternoon* (1957), *Green Mansions* (1959), and *The Nun's Story* (1959).[2]

In these films, Hepburn emerges as having an ambiguous nationality. While various audiences (American, Dutch, British) laid claim to her as "theirs" (Spoto 243; Krämer 201), other commentators have seen Hepburn as being neither American nor European (see Spoto 242–43), as securely European (Welsch 26; Wilson 31; Phillips and Vincendeau 12), and as *both* European, predominantly French-European, and American (Handyside "'Paris'"; Moseley, "Audrey Hepburn" 294). What "nationality" Hepburn is or was is not as important, however, as the very ambiguity surrounding this issue, for, as we shall see, her very lack of identifiable origin is what allows this actress, who made eighteen films in Europe and eleven in Hollywood, to arrive as an "event," as if fully formed and from out of nowhere.

Matching the ambiguity of Hepburn's nationality is her ambiguous gender. Commentators have often described her as boyish or a tomboy (Wilson, "Gamine" 31; Haskell, *From Reverence* 268; Haskell, "Our Fair" 10) and as combining masculine and feminine qualities (Welsch 319–20). Lizzie Francke and Elizabeth Wilson, in writing of Hepburn as a "gamine against the grain," recount how George Cukor had even intended to have Hepburn play Peter Pan in a movie that never ultimately saw daylight (31).

Writers have definitely picked up on Hepburn's difference from the other female stars, such as Marilyn Monroe, Jane Russell, Grace Kelly, and Elizabeth Taylor, who were working in Hollywood at the time (see Rosen 302–03; Welsch 319; Bogdanovich, "Last Innocent" 126; Clarke Keogh 14). In fact, Rosen describes Hepburn as "one of the decade's most intriguing and individualistic heroines" (302). This sense of individuality, of uniqueness, and of independence is important, as Hepburn refused to be molded by her studio, Paramount, in the same way that other stars were molded by theirs (Welsch 291). An example of Hepburn's refusal to be shaped by Hollywood can be seen in her defiance of Paramount publicist Arthur Wilde, who thought she should have her bust padded (see Spoto 72).

This "independence" is matched by many of her 1950s film roles, in which Hepburn often plays a European (*Roman Holiday*, *War and Peace*, *Love in the Afternoon*, *The Nun's Story*). When Hepburn's characters are American, often they have European ancestry and/or live in or spend time in Europe, notably Paris (see *Sabrina*, *Funny Face*). Her outsider status is also marked in *Green Mansions*, in which she is South American (Venezuelan?). As Francke puts it, "her gamine appeal could be translated into exotic otherness" (31). Furthermore, her independence is reinforced by the sense that none of Hepburn's characters ever has to work. In a manner that ties Hepburn's screen persona to the expanding tourism industry of the 1950s (particularly tourism by Americans in Europe), Hepburn is associated both with not working and, more positively, with holidays.

Her first appearance is, of course, in *Roman Holiday*, the story of a princess who takes a day off work. In *Sabrina*, the principal character does not do the work of a servant (even though her father and friends are of this class), but goes away to Paris to study and, eventually, to "live." In *Funny Face*, Jo Stockton is not long working in a bookshop before being flown to Paris, where she spends much of her time refusing to do the modeling work she is supposed to be doing. Hepburn does little or no identifiable work in *Love in the Afternoon*; in fact, the only films where she does do work in the 1950s are *War and Peace* and *The Nun's Story*, in which Hepburn becomes a Florence Nightingale figure, helping the wounded and the sick in Russia and the Congo, respectively. In other words, if Hepburn is to do work, it is not going to be work ostensibly for profit, but charity work to help others.

Other features that made Hepburn seemingly the ideal star for the time include her height and appearance. In accordance with Barry King's "recipe" for 1950s female stardom, Hepburn was 5 feet 6½ inches tall and had an exceptionally interesting face (later to be described as a *Funny Face*). Although only slightly older than the twenty-two-year-old Princess Ann when she starred in *Roman Holiday* (she was twenty-four), it has been noted by Gaylyn Studlar that Hepburn typically played characters younger than herself (173). A trained ballerina, Hepburn enjoyed a publicity buildup of the type described above (she was a Paramount actress, after all), although she benefited also from the fact that her "discovery" was supposedly genuine (thanks to Colette) as opposed to a media concoction. Given her wartime childhood, Hepburn's backstory was also of immediate interest to fans, while her rapid association with Hubert de Givenchy made of Hepburn the

The asexual appeal of Hepburn suited her for the lead role in *The Nun's Story* (Fred Zinne-mann, Warner Bros., 1959). Courtesy of MovieStarNews.

archetypal star, dressed by the *couturier* both onscreen (from *Sabrina* onward) and off: "This made Hepburn even more exotic as an international star—to be dressed by a Paris designer was unusual" (Wilson 40). Given that she sported a "European" appearance and sensibility at a time when Hollywood was expanding aggressively into Europe, and that she was acceptable as an American, Hepburn arrived as a star with all the assets desired by 1950s Hollywood. No wonder she could consider herself fully formed and so reject the advice of Arthur Wilde. Perhaps it was for this reason that Billy Wilder said, "You cannot duplicate her or take her out of her era" (qtd. in Spoto 86).

Furthermore, her wartime childhood, reflected in Hepburn's perennial thinness (see Dyer "Never"), makes the star a reminder that World War II, which devastated so much of Europe and cost so many lives around the world, was a war worth fighting. Beautiful but bony, dressed in her smart clothes, and exuding *joie de vivre* (Rosen 302), Hepburn seemed an innocent saved from the atrocities of war. As Simon Brett wrote in 1964, "She incarnates all that is worth fighting for" (10). Perhaps it is for this reason that Dina Smith equates Hepburn with Paris, itself an "international gamin" that was in need of a makeover after the war (27). We shall discuss shortly what scholars term the Cinderella narrative of Hepburn's films (Studlar; Smith; Moseley *Growing* and "Dress"), but it is perhaps worth suggesting that Hepburn's "European" frailty attracts older, American men (they can "save" her; she wishes to be "saved"; see Welsch 316–19).

Audrey Hepburn will always be associated with fashion, in particular the *haute couture* of Hubert de Givenchy. As Stanley Donen says, "Audrey was always more about fashion than movies or acting" (qtd. in Studlar 159). Pam Cook writes that clothes separate the body from the outside world, and that, through this demarcation of public from private space, they expose our vulnerability (43). Fashion, more than simple "clothes," makes this exposure worse, since fashion "dictates an identity" imposed upon us by public pressure and social convention. Fashion thus "oppresses" women, who must use it to conform to a certain image of attractiveness. In terms of the function of clothes and fashion within cinema, Cook continues by explaining that dress must be an "exterior indicator of the inner self," meaning that the clothes that an actor wears must reveal their inner persona or must fit the actor's role, a system that breaks down the division between interior and exterior (52).

In Hepburn's films, we can see how clothes do function as self-expression in the face of social pressure, and we can see how the clothes "fit the actor's role" (so much so that, as Smith puts it, "Hepburn's body becomes the clothes she wears" [43]): when Sabrina arrives at the Larrabees' ball after her time in Paris, she is wearing a white chiffon dress with floral embroidery, a dress that is set apart from the other guests' New Look style gowns by "the dark tasselled trim and dark lining that round off the train, the weight of the fabric apparent as Hepburn moves, and the fact that it creases" (Bruzzi 15). That Sabrina is set apart from the other guests by her costume suggests that the dress functions as "self-expression," but, given the formality of the occasion and the class subtext of the film (Sabrina is the daughter of a mere chauffeur; she arguably does not belong in the world of the Larrabees), it can also be understood only in response to "social pressure" (in contrast to but dependent on the other guests at the ball). That said, since the film deals with Sabrina's emergence or metamorphosis from bare-footed girl into beautiful woman (a Cinderella narrative), the dress also fits the actor's role, though it draws a lot of attention and is therefore "spectacular" (see Bruzzi 15–18).

However, Hepburn and Sabrina's clothes function beyond the diegesis. Bruzzi and Studlar both identify *Sabrina* as a key film in changing the relationship between high fashion (especially Parisian *haute couture*) and stars, between high fashion and cinema as a whole; and, more generally, they see it as changing the role of fashion in society, a change dependent as much on Hepburn as on the clothes themselves: "Hepburn's persona brought high fashion down to earth and made it emotionally accessible to young, middle-class women" (Studlar 168). Rachel Moseley similarly comments: "In acting as both social armour and signifying system, clothes, through Hepburn, act both to distinguish the star and her female admirers, but also to connect them to the social, offering them power and protection simultaneously" ("Dress" 111–17).

In other words, fans of Hepburn mimic the "Audrey style" (see Clarke Keogh) in order to assert their own individuality, a paradoxical individuality, since it is inspired by Hepburn—together with Givenchy and, perhaps, Paramount costume designer Edith Head, and an individuality that can be seen as a response to social pressure but which also offers a rapprochement between the individual and her social role.

Studlar argues that the Hepburn look became so widespread that women felt pressured to conform to her image: the Hepburn look came to be associated with social pressure, not freedom from it (169). However, even though fans of Hepburn felt that they might not be as beautiful as the star, they still felt that Hepburn offered hope and inspiration, and freedom from Rosen's "Mammary Woman," as Haskell (*From Reverence*), Francke and Wilson ("Gamine"), and the women in Moseley ("Dress") all testify. In fact, Hepburn can be seen as opening up a specifically feminine space in the lives of women in the 1950s and onward (see Bruzzi xix).

This is not just femininity as defined by males (who supposedly want the Mammary Woman), but a femininity that has space for Haskell's tomboy (that is, a femininity that can include some masculinity), a gamine/elfin look that has only its own, feminine interests at heart, and that persists even when "encased in *haute couture*" (Wilson 38). "Fashion is thus an exclusory device, an interloper into the traditionally male-orientated relationship between the viewer (male or female) and the female image" (Bruzzi 24).

Hepburn's haircut is equally important in the transformation that she undergoes in her films, as she metamorphoses from little girl to independent woman. Spoto has pointed out that the cutting of hair forms a central scene in both *Roman Holiday* and *The Nun's Story* (129), while Molly Haskell has theorized that "the [short] haircut is a rite of passage—a liberation from the childhood of being told what to do, but at the same time a break from traditional femininity" ("Our Fair" 12). And the bobbed or tied-back hair is certainly a part of the "Hepburn look," a look that shifts emphasis from Hepburn's head to, more specifically, her face with its boyish features. Yann Tobin describes how Disney took Hepburn's silhouette as the inspiration for the title character in *Sleeping Beauty* (1959), while also explaining her influence on the presentational style of the diva Maria Callas ("Audrey" 56). Similarly, Patty Fox writes that Hepburn inspired Jacqueline Kennedy's appearance during the buildup to her husband's presidential campaign in the late 1950s (115).

We now turn our attention more fully to Roland Barthes's description of Hepburn's face as an *event*.

★★★★★ The Hepburn Event

According to complexity theory (for a gentle introduction, see Steven Johnson), an event, or singularity, is a spontaneous emergence of novelty. It is spontaneous not because it has no cause, but because its cause is, as per chaos theory, attributable not to any single factor but to a multiplicity of factors. The event is therefore closely linked to the notion of emergence, which has similarly received scholarly and popular interest in recent times (see Johnson). Within the discourse of recent continental and North American philosophy, the event can also be understood through the concepts of virtuality and actuality. The virtual is pure potential: it is all that is possible. The actual, meanwhile, is that which "is," that which has "come from" the virtual. The virtual, therefore, is a catalyst for change: when the virtual comes into contact with the actual (infinite potential/virtual changes are realized as one actual change), this is a moment of affect, a moment of inspiration, an event, a singularity, a moment when something new emerges. Contrary to intuition, the virtual is no less real than the actual, even if we as humans can see only the actual. Without the virtual (potential, possibility of change), the actual would not exist (see Massumi).

In *Funny Face* (Stanley Donen, Paramount, 1957), Hepburn's large-eyed expressive face was as beautiful as it was funny. Courtesy of MovieStarNews.

A complex of factors (postwar Europe, the Marshall Plan, television, consumerism, fashion, the star system) played a part in the seeming inevitability of Audrey Hepburn's rise to stardom. That Barthes describes Hepburn as an *event* is therefore apt, since the fact that we cannot identify a single cause for her emergence (since it appears almost random), but instead must identify a confluence of diverse causes, suggests that she is precisely an event, a singularity that is novel (albeit rooted in a complex history of causes), and a catalyst/inspiration for change. There is a sense, therefore, in which Hepburn is a virtual star as well as being a flesh and blood/actual human being.

Peter Bogdanovich remarks that everyone fell in love with Audrey Hepburn immediately ("Last Innocent" 126). To fall in love is arguably the ultimate affect or inspiration that anyone can offer us and, if we are to take Bogdanovich at his word, this therefore reinforces Hepburn's perceived novelty and her association with the virtual, even if she emerged eventfully from a complex array of causes. What Bogdanovich perceives as Hepburn's "wholeness" (she arrives fully grown, a virtual character from a Botticelli painting) is matched by her association with holidays: wholeness here becomes holiness. It seems no coincidence that her wholeness/holiness should lead Hepburn twice to play a nun (*The Nun's Story* and, later, in *Robin and Marian* [1976]), as well as to play an angel in her final film (*Always* [1989]). That Hepburn in fact renounces her pious calling in *The Nun's Story* is discussed later, but, as far as Hepburn's star persona is concerned, wholeness and holiness seem intimately linked to her status as *event* (arriving whole, as if virtual, as if from nowhere).

If Hepburn gives the impression of emerging without an identifiable cause (because the reasons for her emergence are multiple and diffuse), then she emerges as a seeming *spectacle*. The spectacular nature of her dress in *Sabrina*, precisely at the moment of her emergence into society, has already been discussed. But tied to this sense of Hepburn as event is her status as spectacle, especially because spectacular cinema, within film studies discourse, is so often contrasted with cause-and-effect driven narrative cinema, precisely because spectacular cinema is given no *narrative reason*. Rachel Moseley (*Growing*) interestingly observes how Hepburn is often depicted on thresholds (41) and as "in-between" (47). These two concepts are important since the very ambiguity of Audrey Hepburn (her in-betweenness) is also a key factor in her spectacular nature, in her emergence as a virtual film star. The reason for this is that ambiguity defines the virtual; if the virtual is potential, or infinite possibility, then it is also indefinable and ambiguous. Moseley writes that the Cinderella type so often incarnated by Hepburn is "the fulfilment of an earlier, unexpressed *potential*: she has grown up and *emerged* into the world" ("Dress" 117; my emphasis).

However, in addition to the ambiguity of Hepburn, there is also a sense in which she seems to embody not one thing or the other, but both or all things at once. Again, this is an important idea in our understanding of

Hepburn as a virtual star who is also an actual person. For, as the virtual becomes actual—at the moment of emergence/of coming into being/of transformation/of metamorphosis/of becoming—then so, too, can the virtual and the actual be seen to coexist at the same time. Richard Dyer speaks of how film stars resolve ideological contradictions; but here Hepburn resolves not only these kinds of distinctions (European and American identity, for example) but others as well. Simon Brett says that "like many another classic heroine, she is 'all things to all men'" (11) before explaining that in *Green Mansions* she is able to be both animal and human (a reconciliation reinforced by the common descriptions of Hepburn as a doe or a gazelle). Others see her reconciling the contradictions between savagery and refinement (Trumpbour, "Politique" 101), between intelligence and sexiness (Wilson 37), between intelligence and non-intelligence (Viviani 57), and between dream and real life (Tobin, "Jeunesse" 54–55). Some writers, indeed, mistake Hepburn's onscreen life for her offscreen life (see Gilbert Guez, "Audrey Hepburn," *Cinémonde,* 25 September 1962, 19). To a certain extent, the confusion is understandable. We need only recall that Hepburn was dressed by Hubert de Givenchy in real life as well as onscreen to begin to understand ambiguity surrounding what of Hepburn is "real" and what is not. The confusion is increased further when we consider that Hepburn was as "holy" offscreen as she was on: she worked as a goodwill ambassador for UNICEF in the later years of her life (although, paradoxically, that we know this is dependent on its being mediatized, on its taking place *on*screen).

I take a different approach to this issue. Immanence is a concept that is closely tied to virtuality, for that which is immanent is in the world but not of the world (Massumi 33). As such, pure immanence is the potential for change. It is full of possibility, it is of the virtual realm. It is intriguing that the notion of being in the world but not of the world is a concept tied to many religious sermons regarding Christian piety, regarding that concept we have already seen associated with Hepburn: holiness. However, Hepburn, as Sabrina, has famously said that she has learnt to be *both* in the world *and* of the world. This is something affirmed by many of Hepburn's roles: not only do men fall in love with her, but Hepburn as an actress (whether "good" or not) also plays characters that fall in love back. Hepburn is not one for scenes of nudity, but she is a character with an aggressive sexuality: Sabrina is on a mission to ensnare David Larrabee (William Holden); Princess Ann (*Roman Holiday*) and Jo Stockton (*Funny Face*) are independent enough not to do what they are supposed to be doing (for a while at least); and Sister Luke in *The Nun's Story* (and later Maid Marian in

In all her "romantic pairings" (here with William Holden in *Sabrina* [Billy Wilder, Paramount, 1954]), Hepburn is the object of fantasy and impossible longings. Courtesy of MovieStarNews.

Robin and Marian) significantly gives up her "holy" calling in order to be more earthly. In other words, Hepburn may signify virtuality, but she is also actual. As such, knowing of Hepburn's "faults" as a real person or her limitations as an actress only goes to reaffirm her status as an "event," since she embodies both virtuality and actuality, another seeming contradiction that with Hepburn appears no contradiction at all.

Virtuality is apposite as a concept to describe Hepburn, for it also connotes her virtue (Hepburn as nun; Hepburn in real life as resistance messenger and UNICEF goodwill ambassador), as well as her boyishness. We have already mentioned her androgyny, but we might add that she can be sexually aggressive (a "masculine" trait), as well as the fact that her characters often have male names (Sister Luke, "Jo(e)"—in both *Funny Face* and *Two for the Road* [1967]). And yet, as a spectacular female, Hepburn is also utterly feminine/feminized. If Mary Ann Doane argues that femininity can be a masquerade, then in the case of Hepburn, it is ambiguous to the point of indiscernible: it is both a masquerade (virtual) and really *her* (actual). In writing of Sally Potter's *Orlando* (1992), Stella Bruzzi says that "in a sense androgyny that is both abstract and real elides these differences. . . . The abstract and the real become the same" (198). In Hepburn, the virtual and the actual also become the same.

Perhaps Hepburn's ultimate combination of both virtual and actual, of star and person—a combination that only enhances her "star" status—is reflected in the endings of her films. As Moseley has pointed out, the wedding in *Funny Face* is the only one in her career, and even that is a fantasy musical number ("Dress" 111). Her romance with Linus Larrabee (Humphrey Bogart) seems unconvincing and we have already sensed that Sabrina will *not* be accepted by Linus's mother, Maude (Nella Walker). Princess Ann gives up her holiday to return to her duty as princess. And *The Nun's Story* ends with Sister Luke (now Gabrielle van der Mal once again) stepping uncertainly out of the convent and onto the streets of Brussels.

These unhappy—or not so obviously happy—endings are complemented by the unsatisfying brevity of Hepburn's career. There are a number of reasons for her early "retirement" from acting, including her decision to concentrate on her family, the fact that post-1960s moviemaking practices no longer suited her (Spoto 216), her fear that she was becoming too old for audiences' tastes (Rosen 370), and the idea that, because of the large number of actors seeking work, there was less need for *acting* and more a demand for actors who more or less readily resembled the role to be played (King 178–79). Writing of *Breakfast at Tiffany's* (1961) in 1962, Herbert Feinstein already perceived Hepburn to have outstayed her welcome: "As H. L. Mencken pointed out, one earlier talented and sexy dancer, Valentino, was spared this sort of sad, grand delusion by his death just past thirty" (66). Although Hepburn did not die until 1993, she started to make fewer films and went into early retirement, choosing instead to lead a "real" life (become actual) rather than to persist as a star (remain virtual), a decision that again reaffirms her as singularity, as event, because of the very brevity of her career.

Sacrifice is a key theme of *A Nun's Story*, but it can also be understood as a key theme of Hepburn's career. Not only does Gabrielle van der Mal sacrifice a normal life for the life of a nun, but she also and subsequently learns to sacrifice her holiness for earthiness. The film at once sees Hepburn sacrifice her star persona (no Givenchy here) while also reaffirming it (Hepburn does have a significant haircut; she is the nun who is singled out in spite of the ethos that none should be). In fact, here Hepburn does seem both to act (her star persona "disappears," as Corliss would put it) and also to be a star (her persona is also, simultaneously, paradoxically, on display). As Jean-Luc Nancy points out, a sacrifice is to make something sacred, to set something apart. And images, as Nancy says, are apart: they are from heaven, they are sacred. To become a star (to become part of the heavens; to become light; to become an image; to become cinema; to become virtual) is to undergo a sacrifice of one's actual self. Yet Hepburn, in cutting her career far shorter than it need have been, also sacrificed her star status, her virtual persona, in order to lead an actual life, a decision that only adds to the "perfection" of Hepburn's stardom, as do her comebacks, as if Hepburn could cross the line between actual (being a real person) and virtual (being a star) whenever she wanted. The unhappy ending, choosing to be unhappy: this can be the greatest sign of freedom and independence that there is. Perhaps this is what makes Hepburn truly unique.

If Hepburn herself is an "event" in the sense I have been developing the concept here, her face (its importance recognized by Barthes) also incorporates the themes of emergence, of virtuality and of the potential for change. The iconic image from *Funny Face* is of Jo's eyes, lips, and nostrils removed from her face and turned into a 2-D Richard Avedon/Dick Avery (Fred Astaire) photo. In the same way that an event emerges from a confluence of causes, in such a way that the event provokes something *new* (that is, the result is greater than the sum of its parts), so does this photo of Jo/Hepburn remind us that she is more than just eyes, lips, and nose. (Hepburn is reported as finding her individual body parts unattractive; but from these unattractive parts *emerges* something truly beautiful.) In his discussion of faces, Richard Rushton writes that "the face is . . . *potential*—it is of the order of the possible and the *virtual* (as Deleuze claims in the wake of Bergson). It is the face that opens up the world as an experience of possibility; it is the very conception out of which worlds are born" (225). For Rushton, the face "reshapes the world so that we think or feel the world differently" (224). It hardly seems likely that all faces possess such potentiality, but certainly it is such a face that Hepburn seems to have. In the screen narratives in which she starred, the other characters reacted strongly to that face, and so have fans and scholars, male and female alike. One reason seems to be that her face can be read as a catalyst for change, as an inspiration, as the embodiment of a potential and possible world, of the virtual itself. But Hepburn's face is also an actual face. With her almost impossible face, from which beauty emerges in spite of the "funniness" of its parts, Hepburn reconciles star and person. She is unique in showing the perfection of imperfection. In and through Hepburn, we do not so much see a beautiful thing as learn to see the beauty in all things. In this respect, Audrey Hepburn, as star-person, is cinema itself.

NOTES

1. Endy (242) lists the following films as promoting Paris as a tourist destination during the 1950s: *An American in Paris* (1951), *April in Paris* (1952), *Lovely to Look At* (1952), *Gentlemen Prefer Blondes* (1953), *Ma and Pa Kettle on Vacation* (1953), *The French Line* (1954), *The Last Time I Saw Paris* (1954), *Sabrina* (1954), *To Paris with Love* (1954), *To Catch a Thief* (1955), *Silk Stockings* (1957), *French Can-Can* (1955), *Funny Face* (1957), *Paris Holiday* (1957), *Gigi* (1958), and *Perfect Furlough* (1959). With regard to Rome, we might list *Roman Holiday*, together with Jean Negulesco's *Three Coins in a Fountain* (1954), among others.

2. In the 1960s, she took parts in *The Unforgiven* (1960), *Breakfast at Tiffany's* (1961), *The Children's Hour* (1961), *Charade* (1963), *Paris—When It Sizzles* (1964), *My Fair Lady* (1964), *How to Steal a Million* (1966), *Two for the Road* (1967), and *Wait Until Dark* (1967). Hepburn then "retired" from acting until 1976, when she reappeared as Maid Marian in Richard Lester's *Robin and Marian* (1976) before acting in *Bloodline* (1979) and *They All Laughed* (1981). Finally, Hepburn appeared as an angel, Hap, in Steven Spielberg's *Always* (1989) before passing away from cancer on 20 January 1993.

7 ☆☆☆☆☆☆☆☆☆☆

Doris Day
and Rock Hudson
The Girl Next Door
and the Brawny He-Man

FOSTER HIRSCH

"Doris Day" and "Rock Hudson" are movie star monikers from another era that sound glossy and superficial. Could actors with such silly manufactured labels ever have expected to be taken seriously? In addition, their thunderous popularity places them under suspicion, artistically speaking: in the 1950s the two stars were box office champions with millions of fans for whom they could do no wrong. Over a half-century after

---

Courtesy of MovieStarNews.

the peak of their fame, Day and Hudson are still widely regarded less as genuine actors than as appealing personalities. Day is the wholesome, upbeat girl next door, Hudson the stoic, brawny all-American male.

Born in 1924 in Cincinnati, Ohio, as Doris Mary Anne Kappelhoff, Doris Day seemed to embody the epitome of homespun virtue from the American heartland. She was the sister, daughter, best friend, girlfriend, wife, or mother many viewers wished they had. She may have been prettier, blonder, more talented than any girl next door was ever likely to be, but still she seemed accessible, a type easy to recognize and to identify with. Born in 1925 in Winnetka, Illinois, as Roy Harold Scherer Jr., Rock Hudson was equally homegrown and, despite his improbably good looks, equally "average." (Before he became Rock Hudson, he adopted the last name of his stepfather and was known as Roy Fitzgerald.)

If Doris Day became a virtual synonym for an unthreatening, immaculate American femininity, Rock Hudson represented her male counterpart. His sex appeal was as safe as hers, and for all his allure he exuded a humility and good nature that dissolved the envy of males and triggered the maternal instincts of many women. In appearing to play to type, the two actors conformed to the traditional Hollywood formula for stardom in which versatility is regarded as an all but useless skill and even a possible threat to popular acceptance. Actors in the studio era typically became stars because they could play a particular role or could project a quality better than anyone else did at the time. Often, screen icons like Spencer Tracy, Gary Cooper, Humphrey Bogart, and James Stewart, praised for sincerity and naturalness, were commonly thought to be acting "themselves," or at least inventing personae that were close to who they really were in the real world.

Metropolitan critics in the 1950s by and large didn't care for the unsophisticated types that Doris Day and Rock Hudson incarnated, and they tended as well to discount the performers' skill in projecting those types. The exceptional popularity of the two actors, however, was based not only on their personalities and good looks, their dazzling white teeth, and prize-winning smiles, but also on their apparent ease in projecting "themselves." They looked comfortable onscreen. Their ability to speak and move in natural ways in front of the camera, however, demanded a mastery of technique both performers cleverly disguised. Rarely did either of them allow their fans to catch them at work, employing the tricks of their trade. Like all top-of-the-line movie stars, Day and Hudson knew, through instinct, training, and experience, how to act without appearing to. Yet their ability to banish traces of their craft prompted the frequent, curious response that they weren't really actors at all. But while critics and fans accepted Day and Hudson as more or less carbon copies of Doris Anne Kappelhoff and Roy Fitzgerald, the actors, acutely aware of how much the reality of their own lives differed from their fabricated star images, had the last laugh. To sustain the public roles that had been created for them, both stars knew exactly how much performing was involved.

"I'm not the All-American Virgin Queen," Day claimed in her memoir, anxious to separate herself from her movie-star alter ego. "This image I've got—oh, how I *dis*like that word 'image'—it's not me, not at all who I am. It has nothing to do with the life I've had" (4). Cheery Doris Day may have brought happiness to many fans but very little to the performer herself. The only role the real Doris claimed to have wanted was as a fulfilled wife and mother, goals that her unsought success as a big-band singer and then as a movie star seemed to thwart. Day had four failed marriages. Her first husband, Al Jorden, a pathologically jealous jazz trombonist, beat her.[1] Her third husband and her longtime manager, Martin Melcher, left her indebted for millions. For most of his life she had a distant relationship with her son Terry Melcher, her only child, who died in 2004 at age sixty-two (for further details see Kaufman; Santopietro).

As soon as she paid off her debts, the actress abandoned the role she felt she had been forced to perform for twenty-five years. Eighty-six at the time of this writing, Doris Day has not made a movie appearance in over three decades, and no amount of persuasion from producers or the public could possibly bring her back. The actress has made it clear that her retirement from the screen is final—beyond negotiation. However, she has remained in the public eye through her unflagging support for animal rights. And her friendship with Rock Hudson continued until the very public and tragic end of the star's life from AIDS in 1985.

When Roy Fitzgerald, a fun-loving gay man, appeared onscreen as he-man Rock Hudson, Hollywood's Platonic version of a regular guy, the actor was conducting a high-wire masquerade. If the mask slipped, he would be exposed, and in 1950s America his career as a top star would be shattered. However, unlike Doris Anne Kappelhoff, Fitzgerald relished being a movie star, and to preserve his status he entered into a marriage of convenience in 1955 with Phyllis Gates, a secretary in the office of his agent, Henry Willson. The personal costs of his offstage performance must have been steep—the marriage dissolved acrimoniously within eighteen months, although divorce proceedings were not finalized until 1958. Yet the marriage accomplished what it was supposed to: it gave Rock Hudson an extended run (see Oppenheimer and Vitek for further details).

Friendly and easygoing, a practical joker with a wicked sense of humor, Rock Hudson was among the most beloved actors in Hollywood, and his popularity ensured protection. Many colleagues knew he was gay but agreed to remain silent. Throughout his career Hudson was open with friends and co-workers, but even in the 1980s he was not comfortable about coming out, figuring, probably correctly, that to do so might cause the demolition of "Rock Hudson." When it was announced in Paris in July 1985 that he had AIDS, his secret was finally revealed. "I've always been a private person," he wrote in the foreword to his memoir, *Rock Hudson: His Story.* "I've never let the public know what I really think. Now that's changed—there's a lot I want to say and not too much time left. I want the truth to be told, because it sure as hell hasn't been told before" (n.p.).

In the real world, then, Rock Hudson was not a ladies' man, just as Doris Day was hardly the optimistic "eternal virgin" her name connotes to the present. Throughout their careers they were each enacting a charade, in effect appearing in drag in roles that had been constructed for them by the studios to which they were under contract. Day was at Warner Bros. from 1948 to 1954; Hudson was at Universal-International for much longer, from 1949 to 1965. Day often resented the way her studio handled her career, but in the end she did as she was told. Hudson was a more pliant employee, for the most part grateful for the treatment he received. And indeed, he was far better cared for at his studio than Day was at hers. Universal specialized in the kinds of films—westerns, melodramas, lightweight adventures, and romances—that provided appropriate showcases for the actor. On the other hand, the music department at Warner Bros., to which Day was assigned, was distinctly second-rate, with none of the luster of the directors, singers, dancers, choreographers, composers, and designers under contract to MGM, the studio that made arguably the best musicals in Hollywood history.

☆☆☆☆☆ The Girl Next Door

Following her peripatetic career as a big-band singer noted for her husky tone, her relaxed phrasing, and her refreshing appearance—even in smoke-filled nightclubs she exuded robust good health—Doris Day was signed by Warner Bros. to a standard seven-year contract. Though she had never had an acting lesson, her handling of lyrics revealed an actor's instincts. The prospect of acting in movies, however, had only one attraction for the singer: filming would relieve her of having to perform for live audiences. The camera, intervening between her and the public, offered a kind of shelter, the comfort of distance. (Indeed, once she began her film career Day never again made in-person appearances as a singer.)

Without the benefit of any apprenticeship, Day was cast in a leading role in her first film, *Romance on the High Seas* (1948), a breezy, haphazardly constructed musical comedy typical of the studio's dim track record in the genre. Although some Warner Bros. executives had expressed doubt about the novice's ability to carry a film, Michael Curtiz, a volatile, foreign-born director enamored of Day's all-American aura and convinced of her potential, threatened to walk off the job if she was not hired.

However, in casting her as a tough chorus girl who becomes a star—a part in the mold of Ginger Rogers and Betty Grable—he misjudged her. Although Day, to be sure, had a common touch—there were coarse tones in her speaking voice that were to plague her throughout her career—she had a softer, more genteel side that Curtiz had overlooked. He also did not protect her visually. Her eyes and nose and her round face (Day notably lacked the prominent cheekbones that often seem to be a prerequisite for Hollywood stardom) looked puffy. Despite the slipshod presentation, audiences responded warmly. In *It's a Great Feeling* (1949), a send-up of the star-is-born formula, the studio misused her again. She plays another commoner, Judy Adams, a rube from Gurkee's Corners, Wisconsin, who works as a waitress in the studio commissary and is eager to break into movies. The character is frequently the object of ridicule. No matter how often her goal for stardom is derailed, Judy/Doris remains upbeat. Judy's big chance arrives when she is made over into a French music hall star named Yvonne Amour and (mis)cast in the title role of a new vehicle, *Mademoiselle Fifi*. Of course, Judy Adams masquerading as Yvonne Amour is inept to a surreal degree. Throughout the film, fully fledged Warner Bros. stars of the time—Joan Crawford, Gary Cooper, Edward G. Robinson— make cameo appearances in which they parody themselves. The old-timers could afford to indulge in self-mockery, but at this early point in her career, before her own stardom was secure, Doris Day could not. It's only in the finale, when she sings a ballad in a casual, straightforward style, that Doris Day emerges. Her talent is recognized at last and *Mademoiselle Fifi* is replaced with a story in which Judy Adams can play "herself."

Once the studio realized who "Doris Day" was, she was cast in vehicles that for the most part were tepid imitations of the kind of material produced with far greater finesse at MGM. In *Tea for Two* (1950), for instance, a feeble reworking of *No, No, Nanette*, she is an unlikely heiress in the Roaring Twenties. *On Moonlight Bay* (1951), a folk musical based on characters created by Booth Tarkington, is an attempt to evoke the nostalgic Americana of MGM's peerless *Meet Me in St. Louis* (1944). Day, however, is on home ground as a baseball-playing tomboy who falls in love with the boy next door and becomes progressively feminized. She's cozy and reassuring, but like many of her projects the film is not fully conceived as a musical: there are no original songs and the musical numbers have only a sketchy link to the characters or the story. In *April in Paris* (1953) she is another tough cookie (never a comfortable fit for the performer), chorus girl Ethel Jackson, aka Dynamite Jackson, chosen by mistake to represent America at the Paris Theatre Festival.

The deficiencies of Day's Warner Bros. catalogue are not due entirely to studio mismanagement, however. To be sure, the films are superficial; but so is the actress. Day has a masked, self-protective quality that sometimes corrupts her perky charm. She often seems to be holding something back, as if fearful of letting the audience know who she really is. In many of her ephemeral vehicles she is occasionally guilty of the charges leveled against her by her detractors: she is bland and boring. It may be that for the woman herself, the persona provided a cover that she was reluctant, or unable, to shed or to move too far beyond. Nonetheless, in her three sturdiest Warner Bros. films Day departs successfully from formula.

In *Young Man with a Horn* (1950), an atmospheric, hard-boiled semi-biography of self-destructive jazz musician Bix Beiderbecke (here called Rick Martin), Day is sympathetic big-band singer Jo Jordan who loves and loses the title character (Kirk Douglas). As Jo, Day is enacting a close self-approximation and gives what may well be her most authentic musical performance on film. She sings four songs, at different stages of her character's career. In the first, a swing number, Day's stage comportment suggests why she could have been a big-band singer despite her fear of live performance. Since the band rather than the singer is the main attraction, Jo is the equivalent of another instrument, expected to blend in with the sound of the band. After she sings, Jo takes a seat onstage, out of the spotlight, as the band continues playing. Later, she performs in a recording studio and as a headliner in a swank supper club. Day sings jazz and swing standards in creamy tones and in the intimate style that had helped to make her a big-band star.

The following year, as she was emerging as one of the studio's most popular attractions, Day was cast in a non-singing role. *Storm Warning* (1951), an exposé of the Ku Klux Klan set in an unnamed southern town, is the kind of hard-hitting social drama the studio had been specializing in since the early 1930s. (Stripped of the Klan overlay, the story is a bargain-basement version of Tennessee Williams's *A Streetcar Named Desire*, released

Doris Day's ability to portray characters other than the "girl next door" was rarely exploited. Here she offers a witty and appealing impersonation of *Calamity Jane* (David Butler, Warner Bros., 1953). Courtesy of Photofest.

by Warner Bros. in the same year.) Day appears as Lucy Rice, a naïve bowl-ing alley waitress with a predatory, steamy husband, Hank (Steve Cochran). When Lucy's cosmopolitan, hard-as-nails sister Marsha (Ginger Rogers) comes to visit, she witnesses Klan member Hank commit a murder. As Hank and Marsha square off, Lucy looks searchingly and with increasing concern from one to the other. Day, deglamorized and with a splotchy complexion, never for a moment seems on the verge of breaking into song. In an under-written role she is alert and vibrant and establishes beyond any doubt her viability as a straight actress.

In *Storm Warning* and *Young Man with a Horn*, Doris Day is restrained, partially erased. In *Calamity Jane* (1953), the only decent musical during her studio years, she whoops it up. As the bumptious title character, Day speaks (and sings) in a broad hillbilly accent, dresses in buckskin, and walks with a masculine swagger. After she falls for Wild Bill Hickok (Howard Keel), Calamity hesitantly learns how to dress and move in feminine ways. The concept of femininity as a masquerade that has to be acquired was daring for the time, and in context the movie's hit song, "Secret Love," has decided homoerotic overtones. But the film handles its potentially subversive subject matter with a light touch.

Warner Bros. predictably returned Day to business-as-usual vehicles for the remainder of her contract. In the impoverished *Lucky Me* (1954), she plays a character on the lowest rung of the show business ladder, a chorus girl who is part of a failed vaudeville team. Even a made-to-order score by Broadway composer Jule Styne, working way under par, does not elevate the project. In *Young at Heart* (1954), Day's last film at the studio, she is trapped in a vapid ingénue role as one of three blonde daughters—Dad (Robert Keith) is a music teacher—in an all-American family living on the kind of idyllic suburban street found only in movies. The family's white-bread composure is disrupted by a rough-and-tumble piano player from the other side of the tracks (Frank Sinatra) who bridges class barriers because he plays the same kind of music the family does. It's typical of the film's undernourished musical program that Day and Sinatra sing together only briefly, and only at the end.

When she was finally liberated from Warner Bros., Doris Day was determined to prove how ill-used she had been as a contract player. And with four strong performances in a row she hit her stride at last. In *Love Me or Leave Me* (1955), *The Man Who Knew Too Much* (1956), *Julie* (1956), and *The Pajama Game* (1957), she remains true to her "image" while expanding her range. In MGM's *Love Me or Leave Me*, she is Ruth Etting, a singer of the 1920s who had a sweet though far from distinctive sound and who (for good reason) would be forgotten except for this film. A plain-looking woman with a startlingly flat speaking voice, Etting had a brief vogue in Broadway revues and an even briefer film career in primitive short subjects in which she was cast as commoners waiting to be made over. It was her colorful private life that made her story worth telling: the singer had a possessive mobster boyfriend, Moe Snyder. Although James Cagney plays Snyder with scene-stealing energy, Day holds her own, banishing the smiles, the bounce, and the good cheer of her earlier musicals. Instead of emerging as a specific, fully developed character, however, Day's Etting is a generalized figure, a sullen dime-a-dance floozy with conventional show business aspirations. And with a contemporary bubble-cut hairstyle and her apparent discomfort in period clothes and makeup, the actress does not project the image of a character from an earlier time. Nonetheless, read as a dark version of her own persona—her Ruth Etting is Doris Day in a glum, bitter mood, no doubt drawing on memories of her marriage to her abusive first husband—her performance reveals undeniable commitment. Charles Vidor, her director, was no better than those she had had at Warner Bros.

In her next film, however, Alfred Hitchcock's *The Man Who Knew Too Much*, she worked (at Paramount) with the only great director she was ever to have. Because Day herself was aware that she was operating in a higher stratosphere, she grew worried when Hitchcock never said anything to her. Was he displeased with her work? Did he intend to replace her? She became so agitated that she did something she had never done before: she confronted her director, who assured her that his silence indicated approval. He said he didn't have to speak to her because she was playing the role just as he wanted it played.

As always, Hitchcock had cast shrewdly. Playing an American abroad, a former singer named Jo (the same name as her character in *Young Man with a Horn*) now retired and married to a physician from Indiana (James Stewart), the actress offers one of the most penetrating versions of "Doris Day." Act one is set in Morocco; act two in London. The exotic and unfamiliar backgrounds reframe the star and cause us to view her in a new way. She's especially vivid in the Moroccan scenes where she's a wary innocent recoiling from strange food, smells, and sights. Slyly, Hitchcock undermines the character because for all her vigilance Jo, with nearly fatal consequences, is wrong in her assessments of the several foreigners she encounters. Like her husband, who it turns out does not know too much, Jo knows far too little of the world beyond her own.

A quintessentially American couple, Day and Stewart converse in the intimate tones of partners attuned to one another. The finest acting moment in Day's career takes place in a scene in which her husband informs her that their young son has been kidnapped. As the sedative he has given her kicks in, Day conveys Jo's anguish in symphonically diminishing waves. There can be no doubt that Hitchcock upgraded "Doris Day." But is there a hint of condescension in the fact that the role has been made to order for her, as if she would not have been capable of playing a character further removed from home base? James Stewart is also not permitted to stray far from his popular image. The result, for Stewart, is one of his tamest performances—his character, like Day's, doesn't have the moral ambiguity and complexity that mark Hitchcock's richest work. But her firm performance in a straightforward role in a second-level Hitchcock thriller proved Day was a better actress than she had ever been given credit for at Warner Bros.

In *Julie*, a sub-Hitchcockian suspense drama directed for MGM by the overlooked Andrew L. Stone, who in the 1950s made a series of taut, swift noir films shot on location in a semi-documentary style, Day plays a woman on the run from a psychopathic husband (Louis Jourdan, wonderfully sinister). Fleeing for her life, Julie has no time for a song. And dressing down and wearing almost no makeup, the actress looks as "real" as she had in *Storm Warning*. Her resourceful character, managing to persevere against terrific odds, may reveal more about Day herself than any other of her films. In the (famously preposterous) climax, Julie without any prior experience flies a plane into a safe landing. Yet how many other top female stars of the 1950s could have projected the kind of competence needed for the job while also, as Day does, compelling her audience to suspend their disbelief?

Back at Warner Bros. as union leader Babe in *The Pajama Game*, set in a pajama factory in which workers go on strike, Day is equally level-headed. And, as in her three previous hits, she once again (to a carefully controlled degree) plays with her image, lining her trademark jauntiness with darker tones. Beneath Babe's sunny exterior are hints of a prickly ice maiden. In her strongest musical (it was the only time in her career when she had a director, Stanley Donen, who knew how to make the genre work on film), Day performs with verve. She approaches the songs in a crisp, straight-ahead manner that reflects Babe's assertiveness, transforming lyrics, as needed, into declaration or inner monologue.

After four home runs in a row, Day stumbled with a batch of disposable comedies including *Teacher's Pet* (1958), *It Happened to Jane* (1959), and, worst of all, *Tunnel of Love* (1958), an unwatchable stage-bound farce about the difficulties of a suburban couple trying to have a child. At this point, at a time when Day needed to be re-presented, she had the good luck to find a studio, Universal-International; a property, a light comedy of seduction called *Pillow Talk*; and a compatible co-star, Rock Hudson, who was able to launch her to a new level of popularity.

☆☆☆☆☆ The Brawny He-Man

Rock Hudson was discovered in the late 1940s by the influential agent Henry Willson, who specialized in spotting, grooming, promoting, and often seducing handsome young men. The names that Willson gave his protégés—in addition to Rock, he christened Tab Hunter, Rory Calhoun, Guy Madison, Chad Everett, Race Gentry, and Troy Donahue, among numerous others—were intended to suggest rigorous heterosexuality; but insiders knew otherwise. At a time when homosexual desire could neither be named nor openly expressed onscreen, Willson had to operate covertly, but for gay viewers the films that featured his stable of youngsters were bewitching double texts layered with innuendo.

When Willson signed Roy Fitzgerald he was taking a big chance. The young man, a truck driver with a spotty education, had no apparent gifts besides his blazing good looks. His voice was squeaky and high-pitched. He spoke haltingly, in simple sentences laced with errors in grammar and pronunciation. He was gawky. In meetings with producers he was known to trip over himself and then to giggle nervously. And he had no discernible acting skill whatsoever. "You don't know anything, do you?" Willson asked the neophyte soon after they met; "I don't know nothing," Roy admitted (qtd. in Hofler 15). Yet Willson, a cunning judge of the market, was convinced Roy could be transformed into a movie star, a Hollywood Prince Charming. He paid for lessons to lower the young man's voice and improve his diction, and sent him to classes where the awkward young man learned how to move with "masculine" grace and control. When he felt his client was ready, Willson signed him to a standard seven-year contract at Universal: the studio's program of modestly budgeted, formulaic genre films seemed a promising environment for the untried youngster.

In Rock Hudson's first appearances, however, the training he had received barely showed. It was obvious, in the way he played minor roles in second features, that the wooden new actor with the trick name had been hired only because of his looks. Typically, as a good-natured gambler in *Bend of the River* (1952), Hudson is merely decorative, an object to be looked at, and other characters comment on his face and physique. Hudson for the most part is confined to the sidelines, watching as co-stars James Stewart and Arthur Kennedy do all the acting.

When he graduated to leading roles in lighter-than-air program pictures, Hudson still didn't seem to grasp what it took to create the semblance of a human being on film. In *The Golden Blade* (1953), an Arabian Nights extravaganza (and as Arabian as Grandma Moses), he plays a swashbuckling action hero. In a role requiring the kind of exuberant physicality that had made Douglas Fairbanks a silent-screen star, Hudson seems ill at ease in his body and expresses little relish for derring-do or for romance. His radiant smile, however, counts for a lot. As a reluctant Civil War soldier in *Gun Fury* (1953), pursuing his fiancée who has been abducted by southern renegades, he is equally pallid, unable to convey a sense of his character's troubled past or of the "fury" promised in the title. Again, all the "acting" is handled by others, in this instance Lee Marvin, Neville Brand, and Phil Carey as the southern looters.

It's likely that Hudson's career would have expired in the second feature unit of Universal-International if not for the fateful intervention of the studio's unlikely resident auteur, Douglas Sirk, a stage-trained European intellectual with a skeptical take on American movies and American life. Himself a victim of the studio system, Sirk was regularly assigned scripts he was too smart for; but often, through his masterful and sometimes sly use of mise-en-scène, he was able to redeem ordinary material.

Sirk sensed possibilities in Hudson, and to try him out he cast him in a few bread-and-butter roles. In *Has Anybody Seen My Gal?* (1952), a sub-par period piece set in the 1920s, Hudson appears modestly as a soda jerk, a social outsider engaged to the boss's daughter and rejected after her family becomes suddenly wealthy. As directed by Sirk, who clearly understood the actor's fundamentally sweet nature as well as his solitary air, Hudson is notably relaxed.

In Sirk's *Taza, Son of Cochise* (1954), Hudson plays a peace-loving Indian wearing dark makeup that would offend contemporary standards of political correctness. Moreover, at this point in his career he lacked the vocal authority, the diction, or the princely carriage required for the role. But once again Sirk, fully aware of the sexual masquerade of "Rock Hudson," cast the actor as an outsider. Dressed in Indian regalia (in which he appears topless) and in the uniform of an American soldier, Taza has a split identity: he is both "red" and "white," one of "us" as well as one of "them." Under Sirk's watch, Rock Hudson received gold-plated on-the-job training. And when Sirk offered him the demanding leading role of Bob Merrick in *Magnificent Obsession* (1954), a four-handkerchief tearjerker, the actor was ready. In the beginning of the film he is a spoiled, careless playboy who regards the world as his oyster. Indirectly, Merrick is responsible for the death of a prominent physician as well as the blindness of the man's widow, Helen Phillips (Jane Wyman). Chastened, Merrick becomes a distinguished doctor capable of restoring the sight of the widow, with whom he falls in love.

In an astonishing, star-is-born performance Hudson has the ease, simplicity, and naturalness essential for all good film acting, and he is in command of a voice that has a soothing, deep-toned resonance that was not noticeable in his apprentice period. He creates an inner life for his character. As Merrick begins to redeem himself, Hudson has a soulful expression in his eyes and a spiritual gravitas neither forced nor maudlin. Sirk, then coming into his own as a master of overloaded melodramas second to none, gilds the trashy, outrageous material with symphonic touches: the swelling tones of Frank Skinner's score; the intensely oversaturated colors of Russell Metty's cinematography; moist visual set pieces encrusted with pseudo-religious overtones. There may be ironic touches in Sirk's magisterial manipulations, but the actors play it straight. Like his co-star, Hudson remains subdued and unshakably sincere. For all the strikes against his being taken seriously—his name, his appearance, his no-talent early per-

Rock Hudson and Jane Wyman in one of the decade's most complex melodramas, *Magnificent Obsession* (Douglas Sirk, Universal, 1955). Courtesy of Photofest.

formances—Rock Hudson is consecrated in *Magnificent Obsession* as a debonair leading man who can also act.

From the beginning of his career, however, Hudson was often a curiously hesitant romantic partner, and in *Magnificent Obsession*, a saga of medical misfortunes, his character's courtship of Helen Phillips is distinctly secondary. But in Sirk's *All That Heaven Allows* (1955), the actor's problematic status as a screen lover becomes the focus of the film. As gardener Ron Kirby, a virile, pure, Thoreau-like man of nature, Hudson plays another outsider, a character who lives on an isolated farm and seems closer to trees and to forest animals than to other humans. When he comes to town, his sex appeal is disruptive, a potential threat to the social stability of a narrow-minded New England community. Ron falls in love with recent widow Cary Scott (Jane Wyman again), a mature, conservative matron with an androgynous name. The differences in age and class between the matron and the gardener unnerve Cary's country club friends as well as her grown son and daughter, who want her to marry a nonsexual man of her own station. To ensure a happy ending for the unlikely pair, the he-man of the forest has to be desexualized, which happens after an accident (of the kind that often besets characters in Sirk's delirious melodramas). Ron is bedridden, his upright, competent manliness compromised for the moment. As he lies flat on his back, Ron becomes at last a safe partner for Cary, and the couple is reconfigured as mother and son.

As in *Magnificent Obsession*, Hudson and Wyman perform in a hushed style that attains a quasi-mystical aura. Their director, cognizant that he is working with cheesy, old-fashioned material, endows the story with compositional touches such as his use of reflected surfaces and of frames within the frame that admirers have come to label the Sirkian "system." Sirk's enhancements, along with the skill of his actors, convert kitsch into enduring film art.

In both *Written on the Wind* (1956) and *The Tarnished Angels* (1957), Sirk cast Hudson as a solitary onlooker who stands by as other characters slip into emotional and sexual maelstroms. In *Written on the Wind*, Hudson plays the sturdily named Mitch Wayne, a man from a poor family—his father lives in a rustic cabin—who is the lifelong best friend to Kyle Hadley (Robert Stack), the son of one of the richest oil men in Texas. "Nearly" impotent (he is unable to give his wife a child), and a disappointment to his father, who prefers steady, reliable Mitch, Kyle cracks up, drinking himself into oblivion and driving his red sports car at death-defying speed. But in quieter ways Mitch suffers a crisis of masculinity, too. When Kyle's promiscuous sister Marylee (Dorothy Malone) comes on to him, he visibly cringes. And Mitch's abstinence is so strict that he also fends off Kyle's restless wife, for whom he claims an attraction. Hudson depicts the character's inner wounds through sorrowful, searching eyes and loaded silences.

Casting Rock Hudson as a character who seems resistant to heterosexuality may supply subtextual ripples, but the conceit is more than an in-house aside: Mitch's sexual withholding is central to the story. Marylee alone in her room in a hot pink negligee and enflamed by Mitch's rejections performs a masturbatory mambo to a record turned up to ear-splitting volume; as he races up the stairs to silence her, her father suffers a fatal heart attack. At the end, with both her father and brother dead, Marylee, rebellious no longer and dressed in funereal colors, assumes her place as head of the family empire as she fondles a model of a thrusting oil derrick, a phallic substitute for the terminally unavailable Mitch.

In *The Tarnished Angels*, Hudson is Burke Devlin, a hard-drinking journalist drawn to a group of daredevil barnstormers who race planes for a living. To the journalist, the manic, self-destructive flyers, Roger and La Verne Shumann (Robert Stack and Dorothy Malone), lead lives that seem more vital than his own, despite the fact that they are more than a little in love with death. This time Hudson's character is drawn to Malone's, but in the end, after the death of her husband in an accident, La Verne goes off with another man. A professional failure, fired from his job, as well as a sexual loser, the tearful, self-lacerating journalist is a character conceived against the grain of "Rock Hudson." Yet at this point in his career the actor was fully able to meet the acting challenge Sirk had given him.

In *Battle Hymn* (1957), Sirk again cast Hudson in a complex role, real-life Korean War hero Colonel Dean Hess, a man with a past he doesn't want fellow soldiers to discover: he's a minister in torment about having bombed a German orphanage. Hess has yet another problem: he's a married man (his pregnant wife is at home) who seems not to notice that a beautiful Eurasian nurse he works alongside (Anna Kashfi) is falling in love with him. He's more animated with, and more alert to the needs of, a fellow soldier who dies in his arms. Although he had a turbulent inner life riddled with contradiction, Hess was responsible for the rescue of hundreds of Korean orphans, and Hudson, with his post–*Magnificent Obsession* assurance, evokes the innate dignity of a man of destiny.

Douglas Sirk's transformation of Hudson from bumbling novice to confident leading man elevated the actor to a room at the top. George Stevens, impressed by the actor's richly understated performances in Sirk's melodramas, cast him in the demanding leading role in *Giant* (1956). As Jordan "Bick" Benedict Jr., patriarch of a Texas dynasty who is gradually liberated by his outspoken wife (Elizabeth Taylor) from outmoded convictions, Hudson performs in the lean style he had learned working with Sirk. With no fuss, he subtly limns his character's gradual shifts in attitude from autocrat to democrat. And as Benedict ages, Hudson alters the character's walk and body language. In contrast, James Dean as Benedict's business and romantic rival Jett Rink does a great deal of "great" acting. With carefully worked out gestures, tics, pauses, rapt gazes, and convoluted posturing, Dean gives an intricate, tortured performance. Offstage, Hudson and Dean did not get along. Hudson was suspicious of Dean's Method-based, Actors Studio intensity; Dean was dismissive of Hudson's movie star image and of his on-the-job actor training. Yet in their own individual styles—Hudson's minimalist approach as opposed to Dean's illuminated psychological realism—both are brilliant. And both deservedly earned Best Actor Oscar nominations.

Giant gave Rock Hudson the kind of credibility that Sirk's melodramas at the time could not. It is only in historical retrospect that the Sirk/Hudson films, still suspect to some historians, have been parsed and praised; in the 1950s their box office success was rarely accompanied by critical approval.

With the legitimacy conferred by his Oscar nomination, Hudson was given two major dramatic roles in 1957. In *Something of Value*, he plays Peter, a moderate British landholder in Kenya during the Mau-Mau uprising. The lone American in the cast, he does not try for a British accent, and his unwillingness to do so is initially jarring. His apparent refusal of "acting" is reinforced in his scenes opposite Sidney Poitier, who as Peter's lifelong friend Kimani speaks in a lilting African rhythm. But Hudson's naturalism, his reassuring voice, and his decency provide the stature that Peter must have. A glance suffused with both love and horror that his character gives Kimani during a climactic struggle reveals the incisive, economical style that had become Hudson's signature.

In *A Farewell to Arms* Hudson is the victim of producer David O. Selznick's misguided tribute to his then wife, Jennifer Jones, hopelessly beyond her depth as British nurse Catherine Barkley, who falls for an American soldier, Lt. Frederick Henry, in Italy during World War I. Hudson has the appropriate qualities for Hemingway's hero: vulnerable masculinity; grace under fire; an aura of moral integrity. When the character struggles with his decision to leave the army, or when he weeps over Catherine's death during childbirth, Hudson performs with at least a semblance of emotional depth. But he cannot possibly find his footing in scenes played with his blurry, vacant co-star.

☆☆☆☆★ **Intersection**

By the time Rock Hudson's career intersected Doris Day's in 1959, he was both a major celebrity and an increasingly, though far from universally, respected actor. In 1959, Day was still a popular personality, but she needed a hit far more than her co-star did. And in *Pillow Talk*, a blockbuster about two sparring Manhattanites who share a telephone line and who of course end up as a couple, she found it. This performance earned Day her only Oscar nomination. But the film in fact is a stronger showcase for Hudson, who for the first time revealed an unsuspected gift for light comedy.

Day plays Jan Morrow, an unmarried interior decorator by turns brittle, romantic, indignant, sentimental, prissy, and energetic. Other than the character's chic metropolitan style, in short, the role added no new elements to "Doris Day." Playing Brad Allen, a swaggering Broadway composer with drop-dead sex appeal who takes on the persona of Rex Stetson, an innocent country boy from Texas, Hudson has the more visible acting challenge. In one delicious scene, Rex pretends to be gay, and Hudson thereby affords in-the-know viewers with the Pirandellian spectacle of a

Hudson and Day exploited their gifts for sexual farce in a famous series of fifties films, here in *Pillow Talk* (Michael Gordon, Universal, 1959). Courtesy of Photofest.

gay actor playing a straight character who pretends to be gay in order to seduce a resistant straight woman. Since the composer conducts his elaborate masquerade in order to conquer the career woman, the premise might invite charges of chauvinism. But Hudson's deft self-mockery as he lightly sends up his performance in *Giant*, as well as his he-man image and Day's ebullience, surely defuses any possible feminist objections. The stars' evident delight in each other's company—onscreen and off, Day and Hudson were crazy about each other—is palpable and helps to turn what could have been a queasy sex farce into a light-as-air story of comic seduction tailor-made for the end of an age of innocence.

Perhaps not so surprisingly, *Pillow Talk* marked the beginning of a downward turn in the careers of both performers. In the 1950s, their celebrity had widespread cultural implications: Doris Day and Rock Hudson were familiar yet idealized versions of personality types that audiences in the Eisenhower era felt comfortable with. In the tumultuous cultural shifts of the 1960s, however, the stars began to seem increasingly old-fashioned. Under the misguided management of Martin Melcher, Day appeared in forgettable confections during the last eight years of her film career (her last film, *With Six You Get Eggroll*, was released in 1968). She began to seem like a specialized star on the order of Elvis Presley or Jerry Lewis, turning out vehicles for undiscriminating fans. When she rejected the role of Mrs. Robinson in *The Graduate* in 1967, her doom was inevitable. She was clearly by then a back number—yesterday's movie star.

For a number of reasons, "Rock Hudson" survived longer than "Doris Day" (his last film, *The Ambassador*, was released in 1984). Hudson's persona had more "give," was less confining, than was Day's. And besides, the actor enjoyed his public role, whereas Day had always at some level regretted hers. Also, then as now, it is easier for a man to grow old on film than it is for a woman. In the 1960s and beyond, Hudson continued to appear in light comedies, routine westerns, and war films, and in mediocre television series that exploited his convivial manner. His one major dramatic role was in *Seconds* (1966), a pretentious, hollow horror film in which he was again to have played a double role, a dead-at-heart conservative banker who is reborn as a free-thinking bachelor painter. Since Hudson backed out of playing the banker (John Randolph took the part), he killed any chance of either expanding his range or delivering a virtuoso turn.

Doris Day and Rock Hudson were authentic movie stars with public images that made them famous and at the same time "troubled" their artistic legacies. Like most stars, they could operate at full tilt only within a limited range; but as actors they were far shrewder than their reputations suggest. Their standing, however, is not equal. Because Hudson had the good fortune to have Douglas Sirk as his mentor, he appeared in four or five melodramas that are among the finest films of their kind ever made in America; these treasures, along with his appearance in *Giant*, assure him a permanent place in film history. Day, certainly no less talented than Hudson, did not have a champion like Sirk to guide her, and with the possible exception of *The Man Who Knew Too Much* she did not appear in a single film that has passed the test of time at the same level as Hudson's strongest work. Her still large and enthusiastic fan base surely appreciates Day more than her movies, whereas Rock Hudson is admired for his performances in cherished films. Enough time has passed since their 1950s heyday for the careers and the iconographies of the two stars to be reevaluated. More than fifty years ago, Doris Day and Rock Hudson forged powerful connections to many moviegoers; yet to fair-minded viewers they still have something to say.

NOTES

1. Day was married to Jorden from 1941 to 1943, to George Weidler from 1946 to 1949, to Melcher from 1951 to his death in 1968, and to Barry Comden from 1976 to 1981.

8 ☆☆☆☆☆☆☆☆☆☆
Marlon Brando
Actor, Star, Liar

SUSAN WHITE

It is one of Hollywood's deep ironies that a man who hated stardom, and professed himself to be in it for the money on most pictures, became one of the most admired star personae to emerge from the last days of the studio system. But Brando's perceived failures as an actor were also regarded as a violation of the contract made with his audience. His insistence on describing acting as fakery and as "sickly" (Manso 116), as well as his disrespect for his own talent and for those fooled by the artifice of Hollywood (Manso 633–34), gave him the dubious prestige of a disinterested genius.

What has been called Brando's "rogue personality" first came to public attention when his star began to rise on New York's theatrical scene (Hatch

---

Courtesy of MovieStarNews.

50). In 1976, Pauline Kael described her first view of Brando, while he was performing in *Truckline Café*:

> We all know that movie actors often merge with their roles in a way that stage actors don't, quite, but Brando did it even on the stage. I was in New York when he played his famous small role in *Truckline Café* in 1946; arriving late at a performance, and seated in the center of the second row, I looked up and saw what I thought was an actor having a seizure onstage. Embarrassed for him, I lowered my eyes and it wasn't until the young man who'd brought me grabbed my arm and said, "Watch this guy!" that I realized he was *acting*.
>
> (Kael 57)

Kael's confusion and her escort's excitement anticipate the range of responses to Brando's style reiterated throughout his film career. On the laudatory side, critic Steve Vineberg describes Brando's "uncanny absorption" in this role, and his ability to give a "new vitality" to the old strategy of "playing a subtext at odds with the text" (Vineberg 155) in his stage and screen performances of *A Streetcar Named Desire* (1951). Vineberg praises his ability to "[tear] apart the conventional music of a line of dialogue, discovering a way for scripted words to express the tension in an inarticulate man between what flies out of his mouth and what he can't find words for" (155). This unconventional approach to dialogue, which sometimes annoyed other actors who waited in vain for their cues, was often perceived as "mumbling." Associated with the painful inarticulacy of oppressed masculinity, his diction was certainly appreciated by the New York intelligentsia, who thought they heard the "genuine" man breaking through the muttering. The general public, however, seems to have regarded Brando's mumbling with amused suspicion.

The film adaptation of *Streetcar*, in which Brando bares his muscular chest, also inspired both discomfort and arousal: "The Age of the Chest" was born at this moment, according to *Playboy* writer Richard Armour (qtd. in Cohan, *Masked* 167). Brando was aware of the impact he had made in *Streetcar* both on Broadway and onscreen, and, as he metamorphosed into a film actor, he was cautious about accepting film roles that focused on his potential for brutality. Even, or perhaps especially, in the roles where he played a brutal, inarticulate working-class man, Brando was cinematically treated as an erotic object. He was lit as if he were a woman. Not since Valentino had male eroticism in film ignited such public debate.

Brando's betwixt and between status as actor and as sex object was reflected powerfully in the many roles he played between 1946 and 1960. The 1950s rebel (whether Brando, James Dean, or, more subtly, Montgomery Clift) was advertised as using Method acting to project outward his (for it was almost exclusively male) inner angst. By the 1940s, "the Method" had become a lucrative brand name—and like "independent" cinema in the early twenty-first century, the New York–based Actors Studio became a repository, even a factory, bringing the aura of genuine emotion to films that would become mainstream hits or otherwise impact mainstream film style. But even Brando's status as a Method actor has produced doubt, although he became virtually the poster boy for this acting style. (A casual survey of books on Method acting reveals that many of them index Brando's name more often than that of any other actor.) In a crucial essay on Brando's performance in *On the Waterfront* (1954), a pivotal film in the development of Brando's image as Method actor and for which he won his first Academy Award, James Naremore comments:

> Brando's emotionality and slight abstractedness has something in common with the Method's valuation of expression over rhetoric—an essentially romantic attitude that reaches its ultimate form in what Strasberg called the "private moment." In the Actors Studio, Strasberg frequently requested professional actors to imagine or relive an experience for themselves alone, ignoring their audience. . . . It gave Hollywood acting an emotionalism not seen since the days of Griffith, but it reversed Griffith's priorities, viewing characters in somewhat clinical rather than purely moral terms and (in its first stages at least) centering on male rather than female stars.   (202–03)

Just how did Brando deviate from the Method—as conceived by the Actors Studio or by the general public? One might answer that question by examining the acting philosophy of one of Brando's most important mentors in both the Method and other acting techniques—Stella Adler—who studied with Stanislavski and worked for many years with the Group Theater, where the Method was formulated. The Method as Adler conceived and practiced it differed profoundly from that of the Actors Studio's most famous director, Lee Strasberg, who took over in 1951, when Brando was still a young actor. Whereas Strasberg interpreted Stanislavski's system using the technique of "substitution"—substituting personal memories for those of the play's character—Adler's approach was more textual and less focused on "affective memory." Elia Kazan, another of Brando's most important mentors and a founding member of the Actors Studio in 1947, shared the approaches of both Adler and Strasberg, although his relationship with the latter was fraught with conflict (see Hirsch). This question of influence is crucial to understanding Brando's acting style. As Naremore puts it,

> Even though the Studio was often associated with a new American style, its work was easily assimilated into the mainstream of expressive-realist acting, and its specific achievements are difficult to assess. Brando and Marilyn

Monroe are often singled out as two of the Studio's "pupils," but they barely qualify. Brando was trained chiefly at Erwin Piscator's Dramatic Workshop, where he encountered both Lewis and Strasberg, but where he also learned about Brecht.   (198)

Bertolt Brecht's theater is associated with the actor's self-conscious distancing from his or her role. It is a form of anti-realism or anti-naturalism that draws on ideologies in conflict with the romantic/realistic idealism of the Method. Naremore's comment about Brando's exposure to Brechtian acting styles is important in that it allows for the possibility of regarding Brando's performances as self-conscious and technical, rather than as spontaneous outbursts from the heart. Oddly enough, the seemingly authentic emotions displayed by the Method actor were closely associated (as in *On the Waterfront*) with the political movements of the period, although Brechtian "distanciated" acting is a more sustained form of political theater than is the Method.

This conflict between acting as pure and highly self-conscious technique versus acting as spontaneous outburst is an ancient one. More perhaps than almost any other star, Brando found himself in the middle of the conflict, as his acting style began to deviate from the projected interiority that audiences expected of him. The kind of theatricality that emerges at the end of the decade in *Mutiny on the Bounty* (1962) and even in many of Brando's earlier roles has traditionally been placed by critics at the opposite end of the spectrum from the received ideas regarding "natural" performances associated with the Method. This dichotomy between an actor's self-conscious awareness of his technique versus the immersion or absorption in a role is a rewriting of an old conflict in the Western perception of theater, which certainly goes back to Plato's condemnation of mimeticism in theater and has been perhaps most aptly articulated by the eighteenth-century French *philosophe* Denis Diderot. In an essay that continues to influence critics and theorists to this day, Diderot articulates what he terms the "actor's paradox," namely, that actors who feel the emotions of the characters they portray are much less able to move audiences than are actors who approach their craft without emotion but focus instead on consistency and technique (see Fried). Diderot found that the actors of his day who used improvisation and spontaneity could not sustain performances. Interestingly, the Russian filmmaker and theorist V. I. Pudovkin discusses a similar "actor's paradox," stressing the need for the actor to construct an organic persona:

> The image the actor builds as his work develops, on the one hand is constructed out of himself as a person with given individual characteristics and on the other is conditioned by the interaction of this personal element and

the intention in general of the play. The final object of the actor and his performance is to convey to the spectator a real person, or at least a person who could conceivably exist in reality. But at the same time . . . when he walks on the stage, nothing within him is destroyed. If he be a nice man acting a villain, he still remains a nice man acting a villain. Hence the creation of the image must be effected not by mere mechanical portrayal of qualities alien to him, but by the subjugation and adaptation of the qualities innate in him.

(Pudovkin 36)

Often considered a "naturalist," Pudovkin actually advocates the "subjugation" of the actor's innate qualities so that a sense of absorption in the role can be tempered by technique. Similarly, the anti-naturalists, including Brecht, are not interested in the actor as in any sense living out his role. As Jeremy Butler suggests, "Brecht demands that the spectator be alienated from the performance. He or she should recognize the work behind the theatrical illusion of reality and remain distant from the characters" (66–67).

Clearly, the dichotomies set up in the various polemics regarding acting styles are resolved according to their historical context. What is read by audiences as either realistic or anti-realistic depends upon the theatrical or cinematic norms they have internalized. Naremore describes how the elocutionary control familiar to audiences in the nineteenth century was undermined by new forms of expressiveness made possible by the developing cinema. Many actors who flourished after Lillian Gish's performance in *True Heart Susie* (1919), as after Marlon Brando's work in the 1950s, used a range of subtle facial expressions that conveyed an impression of "realism" to their audiences: Paul Muni, James Cagney, Edward G. Robinson, James Stewart, and Irene Dunne are among the "Classical Hollywood" actors who stand out in this respect. The arrival of the Method as the new realism, the new reflection of authenticity within the studio context, is as much a postwar ideological phenomenon as a new style of expression in cinema.

The rhetoric of authenticity surrounding Brando's "best" performances is almost overwhelming—and even rather disturbing. It comes as no surprise that some postmodern, modernist, materialist, and deconstructive critics have distanced themselves from describing any form of acting as "realistic." "Realism" in acting comes burdened with the double sins of essentialism (assuming that there is an essential reality to be captured by actors) and empiricism (assuming that the "authentic" emotions called forth by certain actors can be scientifically measured and verified by means of semiotic analysis, studies of the brain, facial expressions, and so on). But instead of rejecting the notion of realistic acting entirely, we might instead examine what makes certain forms of acting seem "realistic" to critics and audiences. How else are we to know why Brando was regarded as a revolutionary? Vineberg praises the performances in *On the Waterfront*, where Brando "gave voice to the tentative, intuitive emotional gropings of all the young men in America who felt betrayed or misunderstood by the adult world," and in *The Wild One* (1953), in which Brando "embod[ied] the new, restless force in the youth of the Eisenhower era . . . and defined 'cool' and 'hot' for an entire generation" (161). Brando biographer Peter Manso describes "the actor's concentration, his attention to the smallest detail" (362). *On the Waterfront* inspires the highest order of praise: "The inner coherence of the performance was staggering, so free of false notes that Kazan wound up calling it 'the finest thing ever done by an American film actor.' For Malden it was 'genius'" (Manso 368).

Brando's physical relaxation, facial expressiveness, and diction, and his work with props, are among the most eulogized aspects of his performances. His first film, *The Men* (1950), in which he plays a war-wounded paraplegic, already demonstrates these characteristics and the pitfalls that Hollywood will present to the actor. It's a self-consciously Method performance, relying for its realism on Brando's work with wounded veterans in the Birmingham Veteran's Hospital in Southern California, where he lived for a time before filming began. That the physically powerful and sexually potent Brando is paralyzed from the waist down in the role of Bud Wilcheck is an interesting challenge for the actor—but it's also a gimmick of the kind that will continue to make Brando's work look overly self-serious in later films. The film suffers from a wandering focus and from poor chemistry between Brando and Teresa Wright, his love interest. Age may have been a factor: Wright already seems stiff at thirty-two, while Brando, only six years younger, sizzles (after some awkward early scenes). Wright's prudish persona in itself may not have presented a problem, in that Brando came to specialize in starring opposite demure young women, who worked as foils to his latent sexual aggression. But her body language seems defensive in response to his physicality—she exudes not shyness but disapproval—which in some ways furthers the plot but diminishes her work with Brando. The self-consciousness of Brando's early scenes doesn't lend itself to a Brechtian interpretation—anything of that nature is covered over with the gluey earnestness of the "socially responsible" film.

Sexual aggression is anything but latent in his next role, possibly to this day the most celebrated work of his career. In the breakthrough screen performance as Stanley Kowalski in *A Streetcar Named Desire*, Brando was said to bring unusual sensuality, hints of barely concealed violence, and a surprising sense of play to the role. A close reading of some of Brando's facial

Marlon Brando as Stanley Kowalski in *A Streetcar Named Desire* (Elia Kazan, Warner Bros., 1951). Digital frame enlargement.

expressions and bodily postures captured by the film may give us a sense of what was perceived as subtle and realistic acting during the early 1950s.

In a scene early in the film, Stanley appears in the apartment doorway and looks at his wife Stella (Kim Hunter) and sister-in-law Blanche (Vivien Leigh), undercutting the physical tension he brings into the room with a broad, even goofy, smile that wrinkles his cheeks and forehead. But then his expression suddenly changes in a manner that is not revealed to the other characters. This downcast look, emphasizing the hooded eyes and parted lips, suggests the character's "inner life" (for it is not the face he has prepared for the faces he meets), and it evokes the aura of a private realm into which the unacknowledged spectator alone is invited. Back lighting emphasizes the contrast between Brando's muscular body (which is not bent forward or stooped) and his melancholy, abstracted facial expression. The implication is clear. Kowalski will be "misunderstood" by all those who do not have a chance to gaze upon every facet of his expressiveness. Later in the film, he commits what should be an unforgivable act of violence and family betrayal—raping his wife's sister as the wife lies in the hospital after giving birth to their first child—but the finale leaves open the question of whether his wife Stella will forgive and forget, even though the rape has pushed Blanche over the edge into a full mental breakdown. Our horror at Stella's likely connivance at her husband's transgression is mitigated by both his intoxicating sexuality and the glimpses we have had (and that we assume Stella has had as well) into the soul of a confused man-child. As she does earlier in the film after Stanley beats her, it seems that Stella will always answer the anguished, bewildered crying out of her name (probably Brando's most memorable cinematic moment). Stella is interpolated as a sexual subject by her husband's desperate sexual neediness, whose reflex is an intensely flattering worshipping of her as an erotic object.

Brando continued to work with Kazan, taking the title role of *Viva Zapata!* in 1952. *Zapata* is a biopic of Mexican revolutionary Emiliano Zapata and yet another entry in the earnest socially conscious films favored by Brando (and Kazan) through the 1950s. Brando's technique is superb: he brings to the role the kind of actorly mimeticism, somewhat dependent on externals like makeup, seen before him in the work of Paul Muni and afterward in that of Meryl Streep, both great imitators. Here Brando is in costume, and for the viewer used to his less disguised initial screen and stage performances, the weirdness of his brownface and mustache is offset by his extraordinary absorption: at many junctures in the film he projects, even as he embodies, the paradox of flamboyant concentration. *Zapata* is the first film where Brando's work with animals produces remarkable results, giving his style a "present-ness" to which audiences responded well when the film was released. Already ironclad in his ability to lock gazes with other actors, Brando is even more mesmerizing when looking into the eyes of an animal unselfconsciously returning the gaze. The actor holds a pig as comfortably as a farmer would, picks goo from the eye of his white stallion, plays with puppies, poses nonchalantly with a goat—business that settles the character firmly in the physical world of peasant life, an essential aspect of his character. Similarly, this confidence of touch also appears in moments when Brando singles out a part of a human body for special attention. The abstracted quality noted by Naremore and others is purposefully deployed when he caresses the arm of the woman he loves (Jean Peters) as if it is the first time he has seen a woman's arm, and he is lost in wonderment at its delicacy.

★★★★★ Shades of Theatricality

In 1953, Brando appeared in two films that furthered his career in radically different ways: Joseph L. Mankiewicz's *Julius Caesar*; and the soon-to-be iconic *The Wild One*. Agreeing to appear as Marc Antony was a calculated move on the part of Brando, who was eager to leave behind his typecasting as a working-class brute (Manso 321–23). Like Zapata, this would be another role he would play *en costume*. Particularly because it was a Shakespeare property, Brando would need technical prowess if the performance was to be brought off credibly. Not surprisingly, Brando was nervous about taking on the Bard alongside British stage veterans James Mason and John Gielgud. At the same time, MGM producer Dore Schary was more than reluctant to cast Brando in the role and only agreed after hearing a taped performance in which Brando (his identity deliberately withheld from Schary) was heard delivering Antony's funeral oration with clarity and precision. Mankiewicz encouraged him to play the role straight, in every sense of the word, and Brando asked Gielgud to coach him. To Gielgud's delight, the younger man took his hints seriously and the resulting eloquence Brando achieved in the role of Marc Antony put to rest any notion that he was an inarticulate mumbler. But the film also required Brando to present the very image of Roman nobility. Mankiewicz declared that "it's not stripping his skin but just *becoming*, and I'm not even hinting at any of this Stanislavskian shit of Mr. Strasberg's. . . . With that statue, it was just two silent looks . . . like a passage of exquisite music" (Manso 329). Brando's "Method" is to emulate as closely as possible the corporeal language of the great Shakespeareans. He plays (becomes?) a Shakespearean actor with complete conviction.

With the success of *Julius Caesar*, Brando took on a Stanley Kramer project, to be directed by Laslo Benedek, whose potential for a critique of social institutions intrigued him. *The Wild One* is a film about rebellion, based in some sense on an actual incident. Censorship and other factors blighted the production, however, rendering it as cartoonish as *Julius Caesar* was stately. Perhaps Brando's iconicity in the film devolves to some extent upon his cartoon-biker look. He again deploys props, once for the purposes of seduction. In both *The Wild One* and, later, *On the Waterfront* (1954), the props help the Brando character woo a timid young girl. The "hood" he plays in *The Wild One*, Johnny Strabler, is both more playful and more aggressive than Terry Malloy in *On the Waterfront*.

Sucking on a bottle of beer, Johnny watches the coin with which he teases the girl, Kathie (Mary Murphy), who, raised in a small town, has obviously never met anyone like him. Kathie becomes a spectator whose virginity is ravished by Brando's gaze, while her body language shows her slowly opening to him. He looks at her with mock seriousness, deviating from his focus on the prop, and ends the little sequence with an overtly comical mug. Here Brando's facial muscles are relaxed, with the exception of his canted eyebrows and rounded lips. The effect is that of a comic mask,

In *The Wild One* (Laslo Benedek, Columbia, 1953), Brando proves seductive with the local barmaid (Mary Murphy). Digital frame enlargement.

revealing its wearer as a self-conscious ironist. *The Wild One*, intellectually disappointing perhaps, proved monumentally influential, especially for adolescent and young adult filmgoers as it redefined masculine coolness for the postwar generation. The butchering job effected by the editing brought out the film's potential iconicity at the expense of more subtle social engagement, despite the indirectness with which Brando's sexual magnetism is conveyed.

The complexity of Brando's changing facial expressions and work with props reaches an apogee in *On the Waterfront*. Naremore's reading of Brando's performance as Terry Malloy bears quoting at length:

> Brando helps the central dynamic of the film succeed by letting us see the play of conflicts in his behavior. He gives an ambiguous significance to all the objects he touches—for example, in one scene he angrily brandishes a pistol and then cradles it sadly against his cheek, converting it suddenly from a phallus into a breast (206). . . . The same naturalistic rhetoric and the same feeling of power and nobility hidden beneath a vulnerable, inarticulate surface, help to account for Brando's impact in the celebrated taxicab scene, which encapsulates the film's major themes in a single, virtually self-contained, episode and forever establishes one definition of the method.   (208)

The strong "through line" establishing the "dramatic purpose" of Terry's brother Charlie (Rod Steiger)—making sure that his brother doesn't testify before a federal crime commission—leads to conflicting behaviors revealing Charlie's dual loyalties in the cab scene. Is he willing to kill his brother to protect the mob and himself? Naremore notes that Steiger "undergoes a variety of quick, apparently spontaneous changes as the scene progresses: at first he smiles nervously, trying to be paternalistic and manipulative; when this fails, he becomes by turns abusive, threatening and distraught" (208).

By contrast, Brando operates from a fairly secure position, largely *reacting* to events. Wise to Steiger's patronizing attitude, he tolerates everything until the scene provides him with what one contemporary manual of Stanislavskian acting calls a "beat change"—a sudden reversal of the action, motivated by the character's discovery of new information. When Terry realizes that Charlie is "taking him for a ride," a close-up marks his shocked response. Painfully and almost gently, he begins lecturing his brother, charging him with having betrayed their relationships years before. His quiet speech leads to a climactic moment of recognition, and the scene ends in silence as each man contemplates what has happened.

When Charlie pulls a gun, Terry allows the emotional impact of the moment to well up and express itself through impassioned gentleness. He smiles ironically, while his eyes, whose lids are permanently swollen from years of abuse in the ring, are those of a reproachful lover, sad and languid. With great delicacy he reaches for the gun, softly, fractionally pushing it aside, another phallus become not a breast but an ineffectual emblem of tarnished manhood, a reminder of the brotherhood that Terry's words also evoke: "You was my brother, Charlie. You shoulda looked out for me a little bit."

Terry's smile gradually becomes more tender and more ironic, his right eye registering anger while his left eye holds a steady and probing gaze into the eyes of his traitorous brother. But then, Brando again deploys the strategy of the hooded, downcast gaze, his hand touching the gun imploringly, balletically. Taken out of context, the image could certainly be interpreted as representing something like sexual foreplay. Brando was so adept at performing gender, as Judith Butler might put it, that he is able to give power to his performance of heterosexual masculine despair by drawing on the very qualities that in 1950s America would be thought to contradict traditional masculinity: incestuous homoeroticism, passivity, delicacy. The feminizing mimetic skill would play a major role in turning Brando's public against him. It's no surprise that emotionality displayed by male Method actors, who called on "affective memory" to construct a character, brought

In one of the decade's most memorable scenes, from Elia Kazan's *On the Waterfront* (Columbia, 1954), Brando gently chastises his brother Charlie (Rod Steiger) for not having properly taken care of him. Digital frame enlargement.

them dangerously close to the feminine, and often triggered the reassuring balance of ultra-masculine (usually violent) moments. Often, and at the peril of ending their careers, gay or bisexual actors, like Montgomery Clift and Brando (who once jokingly described himself as "trisexual"), proved able to bring forth the socially marginal aspects of their sexual identities in their acting. *Mad Magazine* parodied Brando's already parodic performance in *The Wild One*, dubbing him "Marlon Branflakes"—a name that the actor apparently liked, since he used it humorously for the rest of his life. In the Turner Classic Movies's biographical documentary *Brando*, Johnny Depp describes Brando's habit of making late-night phone calls using assumed names such as the one *Mad* gave him.

Another memorable scene from *Waterfront* highlights Brando's ability to use props as a means of both breaching and reinforcing his distance from other characters, and to challenge gender roles. One hallmark of Method acting is the performer's spontaneity, especially a willingness to improvise. Often accounts of the production of Brando's films differ as to who was responsible for suggesting an improvisational moment (rendering it not entirely improvisational, of course; Brando's reaction to Steiger pulling a gun in the celebrated taxi scene, often cited as an illustration of Brando's genius with props, may have been inspired by advice given him by his friend Carlo Fiore, who was on the set [Higham 143]). The "authorship" of such moments matters only insofar as popular conceptions of Method acting value authentic emotional response over intellectualization or outside influence. Both Kazan and Brando laid claim to the idea of using one of the gloves of his love interest Edie Doyle (Eva Marie Saint) as a motivational force in one of the film's early scenes in which Terry and Edie get to know each other in a children's playground.

Sitting on a swing, Terry plays with and then puts on the glove. To me, one of the most powerful things about Brando's use of the prop here is the fact that he scarcely looks at it even as he pulls it on. We are pulled bodily into his gesture. One senses that this is not an unconscious action (especially if, as Kazan claimed, the glove was Terry's "way of holding her" [Naremore 193]), but it is keeping her from walking away from a man whose political ties and sexual magnetism frighten and overwhelm her. His supreme confidence in negotiating the physical realm offsets his character's sense of awkwardness as he attempts to engage the delicate, convent-raised, and very innocent young woman. Saint, by contrast, looks down at her scarf in a self-conscious way, burying her gaze in its folds.

Brando's scandalous sexuality, found by audiences to be so repugnant or troubling in his later films, is anchored in *On the Waterfront* by a suitably heterosexual plot. But the actor plays his feminine side close to the edge. Some of the film's success flowed from Brando's ability to project a sexual openness that seems to know no gender. Although audiences, then as now, were more comfortable with subtext than with plots explicitly dealing with homosexual passion, the wild popularity of Brando's style indicates a desire on the part of the viewing public to see self-contained masculinity break down into feminine tenderness and reach across the void to touch another lonely man. At the same time, viewers felt reassured when a female chaperone deflects sexual desire away from potential male partners.

There may be a number of ways in which we could try to understand Brando's "rhetoric of naturalism" as a historical phenomenon. One of those approaches might explore the empirical aspects of facial expression. By way of a beginning, we might look at how Brando's smiles work within the historical and narrative context of the films under discussion, using Paul Ekman's work in the "Facial Clues to Deceit" in *Telling Lies* to characterize each facial expression. For example, the broad smile Brando uses at the beginning of the *Streetcar* sequence analyzed above can be described empirically according to Ekman's system as a "Chaplin smile," one of the fifty different smiles his research has categorized. The Chaplin smile is unusual because it is produced by a muscle that most people can't move deliberately, and so "it is a supercilious smile that smiles at smiling" (Ekman 156).

Ekman's description of the Chaplin smile happens to fit perfectly both the physiognomic and contextual elements of Kowalski's broad grin. Brando was certainly able consciously to manipulate facial muscles over which most people have no conscious control (at least according to my experiments in the mirror and other casual surveys), and it so happens that the spectator has been given inside information about Stanley's "true" feelings about Blanche's intrusion into his married life. His smile is supercilious and, in conjunction with his aggressively displayed muscular torso and his familiar S-curved slouch, becomes rather frightening. The whole reads as deceitful. Interestingly, Ekman describes the Method actor as a particular case in which the detection of lies, or the reading of behaviors as playacting or genuine, becomes very difficult. The liar could also use the Stanislavski technique, and if so there should be no signs that the performance is false, because, in a sense, it would not be. The reliable facial muscles would appear in such a liar's false expression because the liar feels the false emotion. The line between false and true becomes fuzzy when emotions are produced by the Stanislavski technique (Ekman 140).

While any look at Brando's early films reveals that his version of the Method was heavily stylized, there seems to be evidence that this kind of "absorbed" acting style, as culturally specific as it may be, draws on the material basis of emotion in a way that excites a sense of "truth-telling" in the spectator. When, in addition, this "truth" is valorized artistically, the emotional investment in the actor-as-truth-teller is powerfully annealed. Brando's control over his facial and bodily movements—whether by happenstance, through biology, or through training—gave him an enormous strength in a world that demanded a certain visible evidence of "truth" from its young male actors. That he provided few facial clues to deceit was the heart of Brando's talent and what made that talent both frightening and controversial. In his later films, Brando worked the fuzzy area between truth and lie in a way that became more and more menacing to his public.

It may be that a "new" acting style simply incorporates expressions, movements of muscles, not emphasized in earlier "realistic" acting. Realism may depend, then, upon approximating some subcategory of so-called universally recognized expressions. The authors of "Components and Recognition of Facial Expression" describe "the simultaneity of facial movement": "the expressions of happiness fear, anger, surprise, and sadness include at least two facial movements occurring simultaneously" (Gosselin, Kirouac, and Doré 245). Brando's "realism," as dated and culturally specific as it may now seem to film spectators, is founded upon that simultaneity and evolution of expression in "microsequences," broken down into what scientists using the Facial Acting Coding System call "action units" (see Banninger-Huber). An actor who provides, through his ability to reproduce emotion-driven facial expressions, action units with microscopic accuracy conveys to audiences something that looks like a startling new level of realism, and collapses the difference between real and fictive emotion. Without the context of the proscenium, we might actually be induced to believe the lie of a simulated emotion.

This is powerful and dangerous magic when held in the hands of the thespian. We want him to startle us with his naked and authentic emotion, but we must also be able to identify what he is doing as "technique," or his acting ability is derogated as too easy. But if that technique is so excellent as to be almost foolproof, the actor must show himself to be a worthy guardian of the magic. Brando's offscreen pranks, his mercurial relationships, his provocative use of male and female qualities to seduce his audience, his alignment in the public eye with social changes seen as dubious by many, all made him suspect in the eyes of a predominantly conservative 1950s America. Brando the sacred actor easily slips into the role of the con artist.

That "con" began in earnest with *Desiree* (1954), a potboiler adapted from the popular novel of the same name. Darryl F. Zanuck forced Brando to fulfill his contract by taking the role of Napoleon Bonaparte in the film—after the actor literally ran away from the proposed production of *The Egyptians* (released as *The Egyptian* in 1954). The mimetic skill foregrounded in *Julius Caesar* is massively abused by Brando in his depiction of Napoleon, under the directorship of the uninspiring Henry Koster. The posturings are a bit too painterly, the enunciations ostentatiously precious, the whole humorless and yet inappropriately hilarious. One has to admire Brando's willingness to destroy the film, to show the lie of the imitation, to act, as he put it more than once in his career, with his makeup.

★★★★★ **Years of Excess**

From 1955 through 1958, Brando continued on what many consider to have been a downhill slide. His rebellion against Hollywood becomes more entrenched in *Guys and Dolls* (1955), *The Teahouse of the August Moon* (1956), *Sayonara* (1957), and *The Young Lions* (1958). *Guys and Dolls* paired Brando with Frank Sinatra, who already disliked the man who had (Sinatra believed) stolen the part of Terry Malloy from him. Goldwyn intended this film, adapted from the popular Broadway musical, to bring in a lot of money—and this required big names, no matter how ill assorted. Stefan Kanfer notes that Brando was not ready for a "big-league musical":

> Marlon had taken some choreography classes as a newcomer in Manhattan, but had never sung anywhere except in the shower. All that would be taken care of, he was assured. His character would be built up, dance lessons would be furnished. MGM's vocal coach, Leon Ceparo, was the best in the business. Ceparo, however, would be conned by Brando's ability to ape the mannerisms of others.   (139)

Kanfer's account of the production is revealing. All the buzzwords used to condemn "cheap" mimeticism are pulled into the service of describing Brando as a bad singer and mediocre dancer. His ability to emote on cue becomes, in the biographer's eye, a suspicious and superficial kind of artistic cheating. Similarly, *Time*'s characterization of the film as "false to the original feeling" (qtd. in Kanfer 140) provides a concise summary of its anti-mimeticism. There are "real" feelings beneath the surface that can be expressed in a "true" or "false" manner. And there is no doubt in Kanfer's mind about which of these alternatives Brando had now chosen.

Thus we enter the era of the accent. With *The Teahouse of the August Moon* (1957), a film that Brando wanted very much to make, the actor indulged his growing political liberalism by supporting the making of a post–World War II Japanese occupation story that dramatized how the American military had been outsmarted. Just named the number one box-office star in America, Brando was able to convince MGM to adapt the Broadway show. (Dore Shary commented, "If he had wanted to play Little Eva, I would have let him.") The closely studied imitation of a Japanese speaking flawed English is painful to watch in the twenty-first century, and to some contemporary critics was painfully "synthetic" (Bosley Crowther), as was the conspicuous makeup and shiny black wig. The frenetic miming, the urge to disappear beneath the skin of an "other," pays a dubious, perhaps unintended homage to the stereotypical cleverness of "Orientals." And yet, despite what some critics have said, the smattering of Japanese essayed by Brando is well pronounced; the effort is "sincere." Enormously ironic is the fact that at the same time that he was making *Teahouse*, Brando fell in love with Anna Kashfi, an olive-skinned Hollywood starlet who claimed to be Anglo-Indian. Almost all of Brando's serious affairs, and most of his dalliances, were with women of color, whether Asian, Latin, or Pacific Islander. But Kashfi, too, was a mime: she was in fact born Joanna Mary O'Callaghan, the daughter of Franco-British parents. It was only after the birth of their son, Christian, that Brando discovered her ruse. Theirs would be a long and stormy relationship, bringing happiness to no one involved. Like the problematic relationship of an imitation to its "original," the lie would often enter in and dominate Brando's life.

Against his better judgment, Brando signed on for another Asian-interest film, *Sayonara*, which proved too close to the gloomy and condescending *Madame Butterfly* for the actor's comfort. Warner Bros. gave Brando license to change the script (a license soon revoked), and Joshua Logan directed. Brando decided to play the character as a southerner—not the case in the Broadway version. Logan was happy with this, as it brought an American civil rights dimension to the story about postwar Japanese women who marry American soldiers. Stefan Kanfer describes Brando's "instincts" in this film as "playing him false" (149), an interesting variation on the *actor* playing his *own instincts* false that was the common refrain of Brando criticism. Despite these problems, the role is a preparation, I think, for the much more "profound" and (agonizingly) thoughtful southern military man in *Reflections in a Golden Eye* in the following decade. Both characters evince an overcoming of normativity (racism, homophobia), but it's the later, less liberally recuperable character that makes an interesting statement about the performance of sexuality.

Brando's next "accented" performance in the 1950s was as the German officer in *The Young Lions* (1958), in which he starred opposite one of his chief Method rivals, Montgomery Clift. Brando's approach to the role directly contradicts novelist Irwin Shaw's vision of Christian Diestl as an unreconstructed Nazi. Brando makes Diestl a solid, moody, cultural relativist tragically drawn into the Nazi war machine. The *New Yorker* wrote that Brando had turned Diestl into "a poor young mixed-skier who wishes he didn't have to go around shooting people" (Kanfer 159). Clift, in contrast, was widely lauded. Many have hypothesized that Brando's disgust with the Academy Awards came out of his lack of recognition for both *Sayonara* and *The Young Lions*. "Marlon now made a point of denigrating the whole idea of prizes; as he put it, 'I never believed that the accomplishment was worth more than the effort.' This cool, ironic statement veiled his true feelings" (Kanfer 153). What's striking in Kanfer's assessment is the persistence of the surface-depth metaphor: the Method actor's tragedy is that his "true feelings" must be covered over. Another lie.

As a coda to the discussion presented here of Brando's engagement with the enactment of masculinity, we might briefly consider his performance in a film that lies beyond the purview of this volume. No doubt, Brando's play with gender and sexuality as moveable feasts reaches its apotheosis in John Huston's *Reflections in a Golden Eye* (1967), adapted from Carson McCullers's novel. His closeted gay character, Major Weldon Penderton, is undoubtedly unsympathetic, but *Golden Eye* may nonetheless be his best film. The deliberate mismatch between lusty heterosexual Leonora Penderton (Elizabeth Taylor) and Penderton, her husband, produces as much discomforting tension as the casting in the more baroque and celebrated *Who's Afraid of Virginia Woolf?* Brando deploys subtle, contradictory, remarkable facial expressions to reveal the conflicts in the character, who is aware of the trap of conventionality surrounding, and the unforgiving nature of, his own "difference." The film was not a success, presumably because it unrelentingly exposed the core of heterosexual masculinity as an empty confection, an inauthentic act. As Judith Butler hypothesizes:

> If heterosexuality is an impossible imitation of itself, an imitation that performatively constitutes itself as the original, then the imitative parody of "heterosexuality"—when and where it exists in gay cultures—is always and only an imitation of an imitation, a copy of a copy, for which there is no original. Put in yet a different way, the parodic or imitative effect of gay identities works neither to copy not to emulate heterosexuality, but rather, to expose heterosexuality as an incessant and *panicked* imitation of its own naturalized idealization. . . . [Naturalized heterosexuality] can become an occasion for a subversive and proliferating parody of gender norms in which the very claim to originality and to the real is shown to be the effect of a certain kind of naturalized gender mime.   (Butler 308)

In the film, Brando's character is shown *practicing* both hetero- and homosexual behaviors, the most famous scene of which was later imitated by Martin Scorsese in *Taxi Driver* (1975). Both Travis Bickle and Penderton posture in front of a mirror, rehearsing different versions of masculinity— for Travis, it's the phallic macho man he wishes to approximate. Penderton seems to be rehearsing a civil and intimate conversation between lovers— that this lover would be a man is indicated by his secret viewing of photos of Greek statues (the Apollo Belvedere), and by the desiring looks Penderton gives Private L. G. Williams (Robert Forster), a beautiful young soldier who has a habit of riding through the woods naked, as it happens just where his superior officer can see and come to desire him. At the end of the film, the major is deceived into believing that his beloved also desires him, as Williams slips surreptitiously into the house the major shares with Leonora. But, to Penderton's horror, the soldier proceeds to the wife's bedroom: he is, after all, heterosexual—or else simply cruel in his constant self-presentation as erotic spectacle. The emptiness and rage, as well as the posture of helpless longing that transmogrifies into jealous rage, all serve to disturb, to uproot the masculine self sought, usually in vain, beneath Brando's surface for the preceding decade. If homosexuality, queerness, are distressing artifice, so, too, is heterosexuality—its "lie" has the same source in Brando's mercurial acting as does the brutality and rage of Stanley Kowalski. As Penderton thinks he is awaiting his lover, he smoothes down his thinning hair and pulls in his flabby chin. Brando's face seems frozen in its vulnerability and desire. He looks like a little boy waiting for a haircut, a recruit taking a chewing out, or, more provocatively, a virginal young girl. All are truth, yet all are lies. Perhaps we have come to know Brando after all.

9 ☆☆☆☆☆☆☆☆☆☆☆

Jerry Lewis
From Hamlet to Clown

FRANK KRUTNIK

A star for six decades, Jerry Lewis has enjoyed phenomenal success in cabaret, in cinema, on television, and on Broadway. In the United States, he maintains a place in the national consciousness, courtesy of his activities as chairman, presenter, and symbolic figurehead of the annual Labor Day telethon for the Muscular Dystrophy Association, an organization he has fervently supported since the 1950s. Apart from his connection with the MDA, Lewis has also become part of the texture of everyday life because of his association with "the French," a long-established and pervasive truism of popular cultural mythology. Hardly a week goes by without someone somewhere cracking wise about his status as a French folly. These Lewis quips have persisted for over forty years because they immediately

Courtesy of MovieStarNews.

and resolutely affirm the superiority of commonsense Americanism over the idiotic pretensions of French (intellectual) culture. As David Thomson observes, "Few things are held against the whole of France more fiercely than the French love of Lewis" (443). Dana Polan argues that the dismissive attitude toward Jerry Lewis has become an article of faith among American critics and intellectuals, who present their dislike of Lewis and what he does as "a natural commonsensical, automatic reaction that is categorically beyond debate." For example, Polan cites critic John Simon's assertion that Lewis's work represents "the kind of low, infantile, witless farce that does not interest me in the least" (qtd. in Polan 46).

Although the merits of Lewis's self-directed films have been hotly debated, comparatively little attention has been paid to the highly successful 1950s films that made possible his move into film directing with *The Bellboy* (1960). In partnership with Dean Martin, and subsequently as a solo performer, Jerry Lewis was one of the top box-office stars of the decade. This chapter examines his career as a fifties film star, considering not just what he did but also what he came to mean as a signifier of otherness incarnate. Lewis was a challenging and enigmatic figure long before the French got their hands on him. With the recent DVD release of many of his films and television shows, and with the publication of several books evaluating his career, it is now possible to think beyond the tired debates and prejudices that have hitherto impeded effective consideration of this unique, and uniquely complex, performer, star, and filmmaker.[1]

★★★★★ The Handsome Man and the Monkey

Jerry Lewis was a creature of American show business. Through the 1920s and 1930s, his father, Danny Lewis, peddled songs and comedy in small-time vaudeville and the Jewish resorts of the "Borscht Belt," accompanied by his wife, Rae, on piano. The parents' showbiz ambitions clearly infected their son, as Jerry made a precocious debut before an audience in 1932 at the age of six, singing "Brother, Can You Spare a Dime?" at a fireman's benefit in the Catskills (Levy 15). Five years later, Lewis had devised the routine that would service his showbiz aspirations for a time—a "dumb act" in which he acted out outrageously exaggerated mimes to phonographic records (Lewis and Kaplan 9). Lewis honed his performance during vacations in the Catskills until he quit school at sixteen to try his luck as a professional. Bookings were intermittent, but after confidence-building gigs at burlesque houses, hospitals, military dances, and nightclubs he managed to attract the services of a sharp Broadway agent, Abner J. Greshler.

Lewis first met Dean Martin in August 1944 when they were signed as individual attractions at New York's Glass Hat Club. Martin was the headliner, while Lewis played his record act and served as master of ceremonies. Lewis was immediately entranced by the crooner's exquisitely self-possessed masculine cool. Nine years older, Martin had led a far more boisterous life. He had been a prizefighter and a croupier in gambling joints, and was well versed in high jinks and womanizing. When they next shared a bill eighteen months later, at Manhattan's Havana-Madrid club, the two men began intruding playfully into one another's sets. "He would kibitz while I was on," Lewis recalls, "and I'd kibitz when he was on, never knowing what we were gonna do ultimately" (Tosches 84–93, 56–86, 126). These improvisations developed into a regular closing spot for the show. Reunited three months later at Atlantic City's 500 Club, Dean Martin and Jerry Lewis replayed their impromptu shtick, with sensational results. They were soon the talk of the Boardwalk, playing to packed houses every night (Tosches 140). Sensing a lucrative opportunity, Greshler hijacked Martin from his agent, Lou Perry, and launched the two entertainers as an officially billed team at Philadelphia's Latin Casino in September 1946 (Levy 76). Over the next few months Martin and Lewis worked increasingly prestigious club and theater gigs across the East and Midwest. Greshler also hired the services of renowned publicist George B. Evans, who cultivated their image as "freewheeling, fun-loving guys whose act was merely an extension of their everyday personalities and antics" (Tosches 145, 149).

On his own, Greshler claimed, Lewis had been "a scared kid with a high squeaky voice. He was afraid to talk, to express himself, and that was why he had been crazy to do a record act. He didn't have to speak. The record did it for him" (Gehman 106). With Martin, Lewis found a living replacement for these phonographic voices. Latching onto him as both a straight man and a front man, Lewis designed his comic persona as an inversion of everything the handsome man stood for. Against Martin's vocal and bodily control, Lewis pitted a strangulated voice, a body riven with discoordination, and a fervently excessive and directionless energy. A key feature of their club act is that Martin is "verbally or acoustically shanghaied into serving as a hapless foil for the strident and nonsensical but compelling antics of Lewis" (Gladwyn Hill, "The Borscht Belt's Latest Gift to the Movies," *New York Times*, 18 September 1949, 2:5). The handsome man's initial resistance ultimately gives way to an embrace, and he both consents to and participates in the carnivalesque two-man show.

Manic, edgy, risky, and dangerous, Martin and Lewis broke with the decorous professionalism of showbiz entertainment. Instead of simply run-

Dean Martin and Jerry Lewis live it up. Courtesy of BFI Stills.

ning through their routines, they "make live" with one another, igniting a vertiginous process of exchange and reversal that dissolves boundaries and differences. Lewis constantly craves attention, but he needs Martin there to legitimate his actions. The audience needs him, too, as an alibi and pretext for enjoying Lewis's bewitching excess.

Martin and Lewis's volatile and protean interaction served up a charismatic and complexly shaded spectacle of male abandon and male togetherness. By showcasing a range of emotional and guardedly erotic intensities between men, the team presented an intimate yet highly public alternative to the heterosexual affirmation that gripped America upon its return to a civilian order. As Lewis suggests, "I don't think that act, or those two people, would have meant one tenth of what they were had it happened ten years before" (JAS Productions). This was by no means a strictly private affair, for audiences looked on longingly as they watched these special friends put on their show—competing playfully against one another, having fun, being together, and loving it.

Colluding and colliding together, Martin and Lewis offered an unusually diverse palette of masculine identities and potentialities. They were able to do so because they operated under the protective cloak of comedy, which permitted all manner of deviations and subversions. In an era in which the normalization of gender identities and sexual roles was a particularly pressing obsession (May 98–113), Martin and Lewis set in motion a teasing negotiation that was analogous to heterosexual amorous comedy. The fact that earlier screwball romances were remade as Martin and Lewis vehicles—*Nothing Sacred* (1937), with Carole Lombard and Fredric March, became *Living It Up* (1954); *The Major and the Minor* (1942), with Ginger Rogers and Ray Milland, was reworked as *You're Never Too Young* (1955)—cannot simply be explained away as studio parsimony. There is some recognition here of the *appropriateness* of these prickly love stories to this particular male partnership, to what it did and what it meant, as well as to Lewis's radical departures from orthodox manhood (for he was cast in the erstwhile female roles).

Lewis repeatedly jeopardized the innocence of their intimacy with his strident departures from heteromasculine norms. A *Variety* review of one of their shows at the Paramount Theater, in support of *My Friend Irma* (1949), warned that "Lewis can get away with the nance stuff in a café—but not in a family theater" ("Paramount N.Y.," *Variety*, 5 October 1949, 5). In 1953, Robert Kass was alarmed by Lewis's imitations of "prancing imbeciles and mincing homosexuals" (122), and Bosley Crowther's *New York Times* review of *Money from Home* (1954) similarly complained that "Mr. Lewis runs too much to effeminacy, which is neither very funny nor very tasteful. Mr. Martin stands discreetly to one side" (27 February 1954, 11). The spectacle of feminization made Lewis the grotesque doppelgänger of Martin's self-assured, self-consistent masculine ideal. Ed Sikov argues that Lewis served the 1950s as "a jester in a court of sexual panic," his "anxiety-filled protogay characters" both displaying and displacing the specter of homosexuality:

> By incarnating the kind of subversive homosexual desire that could not be overtly expressed let alone fulfilled (hence its sheer repetition), and by doubly subverting this desire by making it seem, as Lewis's character puts it in *Artists and Models* [1955], "retarded," Lewis could express the (for want of a better word) homoeroticism that could no longer be denied on the screen but could scarcely be stated forthrightly in this era of officially-sanctioned gay-bashing. . . . He is the hysterical manifestation of his culture's failed repression— imminent sexual criticism incarnate.   (Sikov 190)

In a climate of tyrannical homosexual prejudice, Lewis's grotesquely affirmative buddy comedy translated fear into the uneasy embrace of laughter. But what needs to be added to the equation is the degree to which Lewis's hysterical assertion-denial of homosexual desire—his impersonation, as Sikov puts it, of a "gay icon from Hell" (185)—coincided with a *celebration* of his relationship with Martin. Lewis may have been grotesque, but Martin and Lewis were not.

☆☆★★★ Hollywood, and Bust

With the sizzling success of their cabaret work, Martin and Lewis found themselves hotly pursued by movie producers and by the radio and television networks. By the early 1950s, they were showbiz stars of the highest magnitude, having achieved so swiftly the pervasive cross-media celebrity that earlier entertainers had taken decades to build. Their films, TV shows, and live appearances were hits, their photographs adorned the covers of *Life* and *Look* magazines, they were on the radio, they released phonographic records (together and singly), and they even had their own monthly DC Comics book ("The Adventures of Dean Martin and Jerry Lewis"). In an era of nervous conformity, Martin and Lewis made it possible for diverse audiences—nightclub sophisticates, family television viewers, teenagers—to embrace a wild and bewitching liveness. Among their juvenile fans, Martin and Lewis inspired an intensity of cult hysteria usually reserved for pop idols like the young Frank Sinatra, Johnny Ray, and Elvis Presley.

Their television work was especially successful and today provides the best record of what Martin and Lewis could offer as a live act (see Balio; Spigel; Boddy; Anderson *Hollywood*). They hit it big in the clubs just as television was beginning to take off as a viable entertainment medium after its wartime hiatus. For two years, they did guest shots on such variety shows as "Toast of the Town" (1948), "The Texaco Star Theater" (1948), "The Bob

Hope Show" (1952), "Welcome Aboard" (1948), "Saturday Night Revue" (1953), and "Broadway Open House" (1950) before hosting the first of twenty-eight contributions to NBC's "The Colgate Comedy Hour" in September 1950. Playing against Ed Sullivan in Sunday night prime time, the "Comedy Hour" was a variety show with rotating hosts—initially, Eddie Cantor, Martin and Lewis, Fred Allen, and Bobby Clark. The team worked on all five seasons of the "Comedy Hour," drawing such ecstatic reviews and high ratings that they frequently beat Sullivan, pulling almost half the national audience (Levy 138). The pace would sometimes flag, but the trade reviews suggest that Martin and Lewis—fondly referred to as "madcap revelers," "the zanies," "the daffiness boys," and "madmen of the megacycles"—maintained a remarkably high standard. Where most variety programs featured a serial host and various specialist performers—singers, comics, dancers, etc.—Martin and Lewis did just about everything themselves on these sixty-minute programs. An all-purpose two-man revue, they could deliver songs, dancing, patter, and slapstick without the need of guest stars or lavish production values. As manic, dynamic, and seemingly unmediated as their nightclub performances, the "Comedy Hour" shows amply demonstrated the team's explosive telekinesis.

Martin and Lewis's screen vehicles of the 1950s were certainly lucrative enterprises: *Sailor Beware* (1952), their most profitable venture, cost less than $750,000 to make and took in $27 million worldwide (Tosches 272). Hal Wallis allegedly had a mercenary attitude toward his comic cash-cows, warning writer Ed Simmons, "A Martin and Lewis picture costs a half-million, and it's guaranteed to make three million with a simple formula: Jerry's an idiot, Dean is a straight leading man who sings a couple of songs and gets the girl. That's it, don't fuck with it, go back to the typewriter" (Levy 104). Martin was certainly the most notable casualty of Wallis's formulaic production regime. Whereas he would join Lewis's madcap disruptions in their live shows, the films established a more straightforward division of labor between handsome man and monkey. The story material chosen for the team reveals Wallis's opportunism, with many of the Martin and Lewis vehicles deriving from retooled properties. *My Friend Irma* (1949) and its sequel *My Friend Irma Goes West* (1950) were based on the radio program; *Scared Stiff* (1953) remade Bob Hope's *The Ghost Breakers* (1940); and *Sailor Beware* and *Artists and Models* were based on Broadway plays. And, like many comics before them, they served time in a haunted house (*Scared Stiff*), at the circus (*3 Ring Circus* [1954]), out West (*Pardners* [1956]), at the racetrack (*Money from Home*), on the road (*Hollywood or Bust* [1956]), and in the armed forces (*At War with the Army* [1950], *Sailor Beware*, *Jumping Jacks* [1952], *You're Never Too Young*).

The films find different ways of balancing the competing demands of story and entertainment spectacle. At one extreme, *That's My Boy* (1951) has a relatively serious-minded story that anticipates such melodramas of masculine crisis as *Rebel Without a Cause* (1955), *Tea and Sympathy* (1956), and *Home from the Hill* (1960). The film's plot deals with questions of how to be a man, and how to be a man among men, with Lewis playing a characteristic psychoneurotic weakling cowed by a hyper-athletic father but finding solace in the sheltering embrace of Martin's gentle and manly buddy. Whereas a dramatically articulated Oedipal paradigm motivates *That's My Boy*'s scenes of comic disruption, the frame stories of Martin and Lewis's service comedies *At War with the Army*, *Sailor Beware*, and *Jumping Jacks* provide a loose linking structure for scenes of performance. Whatever role that narrative plays, however, the films' partnership discourse reverberates with a knowing awareness of Dean Martin and Jerry Lewis's identity as a team, and of the distinctive buddy relationship they played out across an array of contemporary media. The opening of *The Caddy* (1953) expresses this most clearly, when it documents the appearance of popular (fictional) entertainers Joe Anthony (Martin) and Harvey Miller (Lewis) at New York's Paramount Theatre with the aid of newsreel footage depicting the hordes of teenage fans that jammed the streets when (the real-life) Martin and Lewis played there in 1951.

The Stooge (1952) offers the most dramatically sustained exploration of the two-man relationship, with its intermingling of affection and hostility, togetherness and difference, independence and interdependence. This sober showbiz chronicle offers Dean Martin an unusually prominent role as a swell-headed crooner, Bill Miller, who fails to appreciate or acknowledge how much he owes to his partner, Ted Rogers. Miller's egotism damages his relationships with his agent, his wife, and the devoted Ted, whom he treats as a hireling rather than an equal. Firing Ted in a fit of drunken and egotistical pique, Miller decides to go it alone. He learns his lesson, however, when he flops miserably at his first solo show and abases himself before the audience with a repentant speech:

> I'm only half an act. The fella that made the act work is a little guy by the name of Ted Rogers, and he isn't here tonight. I can play an accordion and sing a song, but I need that spark, that something, the chemistry that makes two men a successful team. I've bored you, and I've imposed upon you. I've done an injustice to an audience. This is the biggest sin in show business, to be a ham. I humbly apologize.

But all is not lost. From a box by the stage, Ted calls out, "Who's your little Whozis"—the cue for a song—and clambers down onto the stage. The two men glide into a trademark routine to commemorate their reconciliation: Martin follows Lewis's lead; Lewis breaks into a manic solo dance; and they close the number in harmonious, interlocking togetherness.

The film affirms that with the entertainment team of Miller and Rogers, as with Martin and Lewis, neither man can attain fulfillment on his own. While the extended melodrama of *The Stooge* is hardly typical of their screen fare, the Martin and Lewis films routinely articulate similar tensions. Divisions are invariably resolved through partnership routines like that which wraps up *The Stooge*. These run the gamut from the playful skirmishing of the opening "What Would You Do Without Me?" number in *The Caddy*, to the more tender intimacies of the dressing room scene in *Scared Stiff* or the campfire sequence in *Pardners*. Such two-man performances remind us that, no matter what else they may do in the film—with, without, or to one another—*this* is the reality of Martin and Lewis. They belong together. The diffident Martin figure may at times wish to rid himself of the demanding monkey that clings to his very straight back, but he must ultimately accept that they are destined to be, as the theme song of *Pardners* expresses, "the greatest pardners, buddies, and pals."

☆☆☆☆★ A Man in Trouble

Bosley Crowther predicted in his review of *The Caddy* that "Mr. Martin, for his pretty singing and his romancing, rates the usual nod. But Mr. Lewis is slowly taking over. Just give him a couple more years" (*New York Times*, 18 September 1953, 16). He would soon be proved right. The promise of their union coexisted with a strong awareness that the competition between the two men, and between their distinctive talents, always threatened to rend the partnership asunder. When the end came in 1956, with Martin's inevitable revolt, the masquerade was over. News of Dean Martin's dissatisfaction began to filter into the public arena during the troubled production of *3 Ring Circus*. Lewis reported: "During the filming Dean kept blowing his top at me and everyone else, saying he was fed up to the ears playing a stooge. It got pretty hairy. There were days when I thought Dean would ditch the whole package. . . . It developed into psychological warfare for the balance of the picture" (Lewis and Gluck 185–86). They patched things up on this occasion, but the relationship was clearly on a downward spiral. Reported schisms and excited rumor-mongering made it difficult for audiences to believe that their freewheeling, fun-loving act was grounded in authentic feeling. They could still rip it up onstage, but backstage tensions intensified as Martin and Lewis fell increasingly out of love with one another. And, as they did so, the dynamic tension that had always fueled their success took on a new, more melodramatic character that would haunt Lewis's work and image for several years.

Martin was especially jaded by the team's films. On the set of *You're Never Too Young*, for example, he snapped at director Norman Taurog: "Why the hell should I come in on time? There's not a damn thing for me to do" (Gehman 146). His discontentment is frequently blamed on Lewis's growing ambitions as both a filmmaker and a sentimental clown. After the breakup of the team, Martin reputedly quipped: "The two worst things that happened to Jerry were taking a good picture with a Brownie and reading a book about Chaplin" (Levy 218). However, Martin was also doing well as a solo recording artist. After numerous releases on Capitol Records from 1948, he struck gold with his 1953 waxing of "That's Amore," from *The Caddy*, which was a massive popular hit in the United States and Britain (Tosches 233). In May 1956, on the set of *Hollywood or Bust*, their last film together, Martin allegedly delivered the killer punch, when he told Lewis: "You can talk about love all you want. To me, you're nothing but a dollar sign" (Lewis and Gluck 203). The partners agreed to go their separate ways.

The acrimonious fallout would plague them through subsequent years as each man struggled to escape the shadow of a shared past. After a faltering start with the misfire of his first solo venture, *Ten Thousand Bedrooms* (1957), Martin eventually proved his mettle as both an entertainer and a screen actor—with heavyweight character parts in such films as *The Young Lions* (1958), *Rio Bravo* (1959), and *Career* (1959). Only after parting from Lewis was he able to realize his potential as an iconic handsome man. Hollywood sex comedies like *Who Was That Lady?* (1960), *All in a Night's Work* (1961), and *Who's Been Sleeping in My Bed?* (1963) exploited Martin's suave allure, while his Rat Pack frolics with new buddy Frank Sinatra ensured him a niche in the headlines. NBC's highly popular "The Dean Martin Show" ran for nine seasons, from 1965 to 1973, and he simultaneously meandered through a series of throwaway cinematic adventures as Donald Hamilton's playboy spy Matt Helm. Through the 1960s, Martin limited himself progressively to an extremely lucrative persona as a casually inebriated yet sharp-humored swinger. Even though his solo work increasingly parodied his image as the handsome man, at least it was the organ grinder rather than the monkey who ran the show.

Lewis's debut as a solo artist came a mere two weeks after the demise of the partnership, when he filled in for a laryngitis-ridden Judy Garland at Las Vegas's Frontier Casino. His hour-long set was received with great enthusiasm, especially his closing version of the old Al Jolson song "Rock-a-Bye

Your Baby (With a Dixie Melody)" (Lewis and Gluck 208–09). Within weeks, Lewis recorded the song and several other numbers at his own expense and sold the material to Decca Records. The resulting album, *Jerry Lewis Just Sings*, appeared in November 1956, with "Rock-a-Bye Your Baby" as the single. Both discs charted: the single reached the Top Ten and stayed in the Top Forty for fifteen weeks, amassing sales of almost 1.5 million. The LP peaked at number three on the album charts and sold strongly for a further five months, outperforming all of Dean Martin's previous releases (Levy 216). Lewis could now have confidence in his own voice instead of relying on that of his erstwhile partner.

Instead of plugging in another straight man, Lewis chose to diversify what he could offer audiences. As one *Variety* TV reviewer put it, Lewis seemingly aimed to prove himself "a one-man cavalcade of show biz—one who has inherited the mantle of Al Jolson, Danny Kaye, Charlie Chaplin and some of the greats who have preceded him" ("The Jerry Lewis Show," *Variety*, 13 November 1957). It was a dream he worked furiously hard to realize. In the final months of 1956, for example, he not only made his first self-produced solo film, *The Delicate Delinquent* (1957), but also performed at numerous charity benefits, did guest shots on popular TV programs like "What's My Line" (1950) and "The Steve Allen Show" (1956), and headlined a lavish three-week engagement at the Sands Hotel, Las Vegas (Levy 217–31). *Variety* warned that the new Lewis unveiled at the Sands was by no means the much-loved Jerry of old:

> Those who see him here will be seeing a much different Lewis, now more the suave comedian than the goof; a straight singer rather than the off-key, screeching zany; a more often dignified entertainer rather than the most often mugging, eccentric bouncing clown. It takes some doing to get used to the new Lewis, just as obviously it will take some doing on Lewis' part before he himself becomes accustomed to his 'new' stage personality and finds the best in it.   ("Jerry Lewis," *Variety*, 5 December 1956, 73)

The flamboyance of Lewis's multifaceted drive for success would alienate many critics, reviewers, and observers. While he could win over popular audiences, the new Lewis who rose with such untimely haste from the ashes of the beloved entertainment team met with a remarkably hostile reception from cultural tastemakers. Attacks on his aspirations and abilities were to become commonplace in the press long before "the French" staked their claim to him. The opposition grew more vocal as Lewis explored territories barred to the simple funnyman of old. By the end of the decade he was not just one of the best beloved of American entertainers; he was also just about the most reviled.

Provoking particular ire was the increasing prominence in his film and television work of what Dean Martin sarcastically derided as "Chaplin shit" (Levy 160). "After years of such meaningless, nonsensical humor," Lewis told Bill Davidson in 1957, "we had just about run the gamut of things we could do. I firmly believe that you cannot 'sustain' with a pie in the face as well as you can with a puppy on your lap—that the best comedian is a man in trouble, a tragic figure, as Charlie Chaplin was" ("I've Always Been Scared," *Look*, 5 February 1957, 57–58). Films such as *The Caddy*, *Scared Stiff*, *The Stooge*, and *Living It Up* had teased with the Lewis figure's status as a harassed misfit, but the team's partnership dynamic had always trammeled the poignancy. Unshackled from his quarrelsome partner, Lewis was free to use his familiar Idiot/Kid figure to develop a more extended treatment of the comic misfit as a beleaguered outcast questing for recognition and acceptance. This mode of self-representation was by no means restricted to Lewis's professional performance. As part of his post-Martin PR makeover, Lewis disseminated his own biographical narrative of "Jerry Lewis," which portrayed him as a man in trouble who was trying to compensate for his personal traumas, and his fear of love withdrawn, by winning the reassuring love of others. He contextualized the traumatic breakup of Martin and Lewis within a bionarrative of abandonment that stretched back to the lonely childhood he experienced while his parents pursued their showbiz dreams.

Lewis fleshed out this biographical narrative in an article he wrote with journalist Bill Davidson shortly after the partnership folded. A nine-page cover feature in the February 1957 issue of *Look*, "I've Always Been Scared," exposes a bruised sensitivity cowering in the shadow of the manic clown. "All my life," Lewis declares, "I've been afraid of being alone" (51). In a story he would repeat with ever more emotive embellishment, Lewis portrays himself as a pathetic outsider who deploys the mask of comedy as a protective shield. Seeking love and acceptance via the showbiz success his father never attained, Lewis is compelled to win the substitute gratifications of applause and laughter: "If I could make people laugh, I thought, they'd like me and let me be with them" (54). This bionarrative defined Lewis's rebirth from the ashes of the blistering partnership not as a triumphant act of self-assertion but as a more desperate attempt to eradicate the nagging absence at the heart of his being.

What is at issue in the Davidson interview is not truth but myth. Like any star or celebrity, "Jerry Lewis" is more than simply a person. He constitutes a publicly circulated aggregation of signs that bears a shifting and unstable relationship to the private individual who embodies them. As a discursive construct, "Jerry Lewis" exceeds the control of Jerry Lewis (*né* Levitch). The dramatic ending of Martin and Lewis's much-loved partnership inevitably generated competing and contending representations of Lewis and his motives. The warmly receptive public relations exercises provided him with a chance to stake his own claim to the meaning of his star image, and to offer his own rationale for "Jerry Lewis." The psychological narrative articulated by these articles highlights the degree to which Lewis's star image occupied a very different constellation from the carefree zany of old. Whereas earlier publicity stressed the congruence between the onstage and offstage selves of Martin and Lewis, Lewis's solo career instituted a strategic opposition between the "real" man alone and the onscreen comic misfit. "It may be," offers *Look* magazine, "that audiences are drawn to him because they see or sense the real Jerry, the lonely man of many complexes" ("Always in a Crowd—Always Alone," 23 December 1958, 83–84).

☆☆☆★★ I'm a Nowhere

Jerry Lewis's move into film directing did not happen overnight but was the result of years of learning and experimentation. He demonstrated an almost obsessive fascination with moviemaking soon after arriving in Hollywood. In 1949, he opened his own camera shop in Hollywood (Marx 110–11). He also equipped his home with 16 mm film technology and made a series of ambitious home movies in the early 1950s with such Hollywood cronies as Martin, Tony Curtis, Janet Leigh, Shelley Winters, Van Johnson, and Jeff Chandler (Marx 156–57). "We did the pictures for fun," Leigh recalls, "but you could see that Jerry was learning all the time—how to direct actors, how to set up a scene, etc." (in Neibaur and Okuda 9). Lewis also demanded greater input into his Hollywood films, which did not please either Hal Wallis or hardened studio professionals like Norman Taurog. The director of six Martin and Lewis pictures and two of Lewis's solo films, Taurog told biographer Arthur Marx:

> In the beginning, he was a doll. He listened, did what I told him to do, and didn't bother anyone. Then one day I noticed him looking through the camera between takes and starting to make suggestions to Lyle Gregg, our cameraman, on things he had no business making suggestions about: how high a crane to put the camera on, for example, or what kind of lens to use. . . . I used to tell him, "For God's sake, Jerry, why do you want to waste your energy doing things other people are getting paid for? Nobody goes to a Martin and Lewis movie because you directed a scene or because you told the cameraman what to do. They go because it says on the marquee—Jerry Lewis in so and so; not Jerry Lewis, cameraman. Save your energy for acting."   (Marx 172)

Although Wallis opposed his star's meddlesome ambitions, he made several concessions—allowing him screen credits for material in *Sailor Beware* and *Money from Home* and permitting him a say in the choice of production staff (Tosches 240, 268–70). It was only after he finished with Dean Martin, however, that Lewis could begin to realize his cinematic ambitions. *The Delicate Delinquent* showed he meant business, as he not only starred in the film but also produced it for York Pictures (Levy 209). The following year he produced and starred in *Rock-a-Bye Baby* and *The Geisha Boy* (both 1958), which were also box office hits.

It was a period of transition and self-definition not just for Lewis but also for Hollywood's cinema industry as well. Geared toward the manufacture of a large number of films for a mass heterogeneous audience, the studio system was not so viable in the transformed postwar entertainment market. It was groping for new audiences and new directions in the wake of a drastic decline in attendances and the government-enforced dismantling of vertical integration. To meet the new economic imperatives, the studios reduced their armies of technical staff and contract players and sourced their films increasingly from independent outfits, to whom they offered financing and distribution deals in return. Through the 1950s, the Hollywood studios moved toward a more flexible package-unit system, in which films were assembled as specialized combinations of saleable elements (such as story, stars, director, and spectacular effects) (Bordwell, Staiger, and Thompson 330–35). In this environment, stars not only attained new importance as box office attractions, but were also liberated from studio ownership.

Paramount's initial doubts about Lewis's viability as a solo attraction were banished by the commercial success of *The Delicate Delinquent*. He proved that he was still a major asset for the company and one of the few sure-fire stars at the box office. By 1958, Lewis was the only major star remaining under exclusive contract to Paramount (Eames 225), and the studio was unwilling to lose their hot property to a competitor. When his contract came up for renewal in June 1959, he was offered $10 million for fourteen films over a seven-year period (Murray Schumach, "$10,000,000 Pact for Jerry Lewis," *New York Times*, 8 June 1959, 32). As Paramount's publicity office boasted, it was the largest price a Hollywood company had ever paid for a performer's services. The deal may have gone against the prevailing trend of stars avoiding long-term commitments to studios, but it granted Lewis the creative autonomy he desired. Under the new contract, half the films would be owned by Lewis, the other half by a combined interest of the newly formed Jerry Lewis Productions and Paramount Pictures, which would distribute the films (Levy 239). The contract granted Lewis the power to choose his producers and directors, paving the way for the self-directed films that were to provoke so much controversy in the 1960s.

Lewis starred in six films before the release of his first self-directed venture, half of them contractual obligations he owed Hal Wallis (Levy 209).[2] As James Neibaur and Ted Okuda suggest, Lewis is unusually restrained in the Wallis movies: he "plays it straight . . . in an effort to get laughs out of the material" (141). *The Sad Sack* (1957) and *Don't Give Up the Ship* (1959), a farce of sexual frustration, returned the comedian to the safe territory of the armed services, a context he had milked dry with Dean Martin in the early 1950s. *Visit to a Small Planet* (1960), his third Wallis film, also subjugates Lewis to the script, but this reworking of Gore Vidal's satirical Broadway play offers a more productive setting for the Lewis figure's characteristic otherness. As an extraterrestrial who chooses to vacation in the strange world of small-town America, Lewis is an explicitly and agreeably alien presence.

Lewis's own productions were more ambitious. Unlike the Wallis films, *The Delicate Delinquent, Rock-a-Bye Baby,* and *The Geisha Boy* all deal explicitly with the questions of self-definition found in the *Look* magazine and other mass-market articles about Lewis. As such, they also anticipate the autobiographical convolutions of the self-directed films. *The Delicate Delinquent* was, like *The Sad Sack*, initially conceived as a Martin and Lewis project (Levy 199). In the final months of the partnership, Lewis was eager to make a film based on the classical legend of Damon and Pythias, hoping its story of self-sacrificing male friendship would help heal the breach with Martin (Marx 196–97). The crooner allegedly took exception to the idea of playing a cop and refused the film. Written and directed by Lewis's friend Don McGuire, *The Delicate Delinquent* received a strategic makeover to showcase Lewis as a solo attraction. Although actor Darren McGavin substitutes for the absent Martin, he lacks the complex history Lewis shared with the handsome man.

At the height of his success with Dean Martin, Robert Kass suggested in *Films in Review* that Lewis's antics were "reflections of some of the untoward aspects of our time" (Kass 119). For Kass, Lewis emblematized the otherness of "young America gone berserk" (123). From a more celebratory perspective, J. Hoberman proposes that "the young Jerry was America's id. His every cute outburst threatened to escalate into loss of control; the sight of his big mouth promised a kind of ecstatic self-annihilation" ("The Nutty Retrospective," *Village Voice,* 15 December 1988, 47). The uncontrolled eruptions of Lewis's body connected with the rebellious stirrings of a nascent youth culture, which would itself erupt into national and international

Lewis with replacement buddy Darren McGavin in *The Delicate Delinquent* (Don McGuire, Paramount, 1957). Courtesy of BFI Stills.

consciousness with the primal beat of rock 'n' roll. As Karal Ann Marling argues, "Like Elvis, Jerry Lewis seemed rebellious because he wouldn't stand still; he both projected and aroused strong emotion through motion" (176–77).

Capitalizing on the recent success of juvenile dramas such as *The Blackboard Jungle* (1955) and *Rebel Without a Cause*, *The Delicate Delinquent* flaunts Lewis's allegiance to the youth audience. At the same time, it also distances

him from the energetic and rebellious excess that marked his earlier performances. Rather than abandoning himself to the delights of sheer abandon, Lewis's delicate delinquent, Sydney Pythias, is searching (literally) for
direction. Mistaken for a gang member after a street rumble, the good
natured orphan is hauled off to the neighborhood precinct house, where he
encounters patrolman Mike Damon (McGavin). A reformed juvenile
offender himself, Damon has a mission to save slum kids from criminal
temptations. Sydney is perfect for such rehabilitation as he lacks social and
familial ties, or any other external context of self-definition. "How does a
guy know what he wants to be?" he asks Damon. "Especially somebody like
me? I'll tell you what I am—I'm a nowhere." The connection with Lewis's
post-Martin crisis of self-representation is most explicit when Sydney performs Lewis's current theme song, "By Myself," in a lonely alleyway. Sydney Pythias ultimately becomes "somebody" by becoming, like Mike
Damon, a cop who can reconcile the conscience of society with its heart.
Sydney's success suggests that a good heart will eventually triumph over
insecurity and sheer ineptitude. It also inspires a schematic change of heart
by Monk (Robert Ivers), the leader of the juvenile gang that initially
plagues and rejects him. Sydney begins his career as a law officer by
encouraging Monk and the gang away from their delinquent ways, dis-
pensing the very advice Damon had tendered him earlier.

For Bosley Crowther, Sydney's characteristically Lewisian eccentricities
sat rather uncomfortably with the idealized authority he is allowed at the
end of this "serious-message comedy":

> Mr. Lewis, as the star of his own picture, runs a gamut from Hamlet to clown.
> . . . Mr. Lewis warding off a judo wrestler or trying to fit odd-shaped blocks
> into odd-shaped holes is a delirious comedian. Mr. Lewis trying to act hard
> like a man, with a policeman's hat planted on his noggin is a mite incred-
> ible and absurd. The good intention of his message may be missed in this
> eccentricity.   (New York Times, 4 July 1957, 16)

Its evident personal ambitions notwithstanding, Lewis's first solo feature
is a relatively straightforward comedian comedy that uses the framework of
the contemporary juvenile delinquent film as a vehicle for articulating the
comic misfit's quest for identity. The two films Lewis made with director
Frank Tashlin in 1958 subject the comic outsider to a more expressly nonconformist process of identity-formation. As a gagman, writer, and director,
Tashlin was a distinctive creative force in American screen comedy, and Lewis
acknowledges the profound influence he exerted on his own style as a filmmaker (Lewis and Gluck 200).[3] And, in Lewis, Tashlin found the nearest possible human approximation of a cartoon figure. Impressed by Tashlin's work

Jerry Lewis plays a nurturing parent (with David Halper) in *Rock-a-Bye Baby* (Frank Tashlin, Paramount, 1958). Courtesy of BFI Stills.

on *Artists and Models* and *Hollywood or Bust*, Lewis enticed him back to Paramount for *Rock-a-Bye Baby*, the first of their six post-Martin collaborations.

Rock-a-Bye Baby aims to broaden Lewis's appeal by replacing the earlier partnership dynamic with a family-oriented set of relations, albeit highly unorthodox ones. Like *You're Never Too Young* and *Living It Up*, *Rock-a-Bye Baby* freely adapts an earlier screwball comedy, Preston Sturges's wartime satire *The Miracle of Morgan's Creek* (1944). A composite of the roles played in the original by Betty Hutton and Eddie Bracken, Lewis's Clayton Poole has an extended engagement with parenthood when he agrees to take responsibility for the offspring of his former childhood sweetheart. Finding herself pregnant after a short-lived marriage to a recently deceased bullfighter, movie star Carla Naples (Marilyn Maxwell) tries to save her career by persuading Clayton to take her newborn triplets. Willingly embracing the domesticity Carla spurned, Clayton devotes himself tirelessly to raising the children of the woman he adores. The babies bring Clayton a sense of purpose previously lacking in his life, enabling him to move beyond his unrequited imaginings of perfection to discover new potentialities within himself. Through his nurturing skills, Clayton also manages to short-circuit established protocols of gender and parenthood. As he tends to the triplets, he is their breadwinner, their entertainer, their provider, and their nursemaid.

Spurning the Oedipal trajectory of most Hollywood comedian films, *Rock-a-Bye Baby* sanctions a more disorderly perspective on American manhood. Like *The Delicate Delinquent*, the film presents the Lewis figure triumphing over adversity, but it delivers a more purposeful disorientation of the conformist scripts of masculine achievement and cultural integration. The next Tashlin-Lewis collaboration, *The Geisha Boy*, similarly deals with the comic outsider's quest to realize his desire to "be" and to "belong" through a scenario of surrogate parenthood. As in *Rock-a-Bye Baby* the Lewis figure is subjected to a highly wrought succession of displacements and desiring potentialities, but *The Geisha Boy* adds to the earlier film's destabilizing of gender roles an intriguing negotiation across cultures. *The Geisha Boy* casts the Lewis figure as a refugee from home: magician Gilbert Wooley is unable to find acceptance or employment in the United States, and enlists on a USO tour of Japan.

Bernard Eisenschitz suggests that *The Geisha Boy*'s representation of Japan is remarkable by Hollywood standards as it is "neither racist nor patronizing" (170). With the exception of travelogue sequences composed of stock footage, the film was shot exclusively in Los Angeles. The only part of homeland America shown onscreen, however, is the drably functional space of the airport, while Japan is a seductive kaleidoscope of color and spectacle. *The Geisha Boy*'s vision of the East is vibrantly cinematic, and the film is jammed with the kind of self-reflexive cine-gags beloved of both its director and its star. Rendering the East a positive counterbalance to 1950s America, the film characterizes it as a zone of creativity, imagination, and the cartoon aesthetic. In America, Wooley is an "internal other," but when forced out to the alien otherness of Japan he discovers a landscape of surrealistic transfiguration that offers new possibilities for being and belonging.

Oppressed by the military, and by demanding women, Wooley finds refuge in a scenario of parental surrogacy with a six-year-old boy, Mitsuo Watanabe (Robert Hirano). *The Geisha Boy* evokes Chaplin's first feature-film, *The Kid* (1921), in which the comic outsider similarly achieves a new sense of purpose when he adopts a young boy. As in *Rock-a-Bye Baby*, the surrogate relationship provides the Lewis figure with a means by which he can transcend his initial insufficiency. Wooley is able to draw laughter from the sullen and withdrawn child, who in turn wishes the magician were his "father." Wooley's main goal after he arrives in Japan is to win and maintain Mitsuo's respect. As he tells Major Ridgely (Barton MacLane), he has found "a little boy who thinks I'm something. He thinks I'm something special. This is the first time in my life that anybody thought I was something. And I would love to prove to him that he's right."

The relationship between man and boy is more headily sentimental than Clayton Poole's adventures with the triplets, but the pathos operates through a tangled circuitry of emotional resonance. As in *The Kid*, the boy is not merely an external object, an other, but also functions as a mirror for the self. As an orphan raised by his aunt, Wooley's own story directly parallels Mitsuo's situation. The Japanese boy is an "alien other" who serves Wooley as a projection of his own otherness within U.S. culture. Mitsuo provides the motivation and alibi for a narcissistic economy of desire that protects the Lewis figure from sexual object-relations and other exterior definitional contexts. He embodies an alternative to Wooley's pet white rabbit (and best buddy) Harry, to WAF Sergeant Pearson (Suzanne Pleshette), who has romantic designs on him, and to Mitsuo's pretty aunt Kimi Sikita (Nobu McCarthy). Mitsuo is the one whose love is most worth having, whose love endows the greatest meaning. This scenario, of necessity, reverses the logic of Oedipal narrative, which tracks the progress from child to (male) adult. Risking cultural disapproval and exclusion, the clown-hero shows his courageous determination to remain a child or to become a child once again. This openly sentimental project of reversed self-definition harbors a more actively fantastical displacement of orthodox cultural priorities. By establishing his own meaning through the affinity with a child who is the projected image of himself, Wooley is able to elude the authority invested in American culture, in the army, and in women (Sergeant Pearson embodies all three contexts). *The Geisha Boy* wraps up with a last-minute multiple birth, but here it is a rabbit who produces the miraculous act of motherhood, which Wooley demonstrates when he pulls a profusion of little white rabbits from his magician's hat.

In the childlike vision of life celebrated at the end of the film, procreation is a magical rather than a sexual act. *The Geisha Boy* reworks the geographical and cultural otherness of the East to construct an idealized world in which adult heterosexuality is othered and denied a determinate role. The rabbit's shift of gender, from Harry to Harriet, illustrates that "Japan" is a place where "anything is possible," where the Western ordering of identity and sexuality can be transcended. To disavow the "seriousness" of this thematic play with otherness, identity, and cultural allegiance—and as a further tribute to the joys of metamorphosis—*The Geisha Boy* finishes with a cartoon-style gag where Lewis himself becomes a rabbit. He looks into the camera, chews on a carrot, and signs off, Bugs Bunny style, "That's All Folks."

NOTES

1. Recent books about Lewis include biographical works by Nick Tosches (1992), Shawn Levy (1996), and Lewis and Kaplan (2005); my critical monograph *Inventing Jerry Lewis* and the critical anthology *Enfant Terrible!* edited by Murray Pomerance (2002); and Chris Fujiwara's 2009 study of Lewis's self-directed films. The last few years have also seen two novels based on Martin and Lewis's career, by Ted Heller (2002) and Rupert Holmes (2003), the telefilm biopic *Martin and Lewis* (2002), and Atom Egoyan's adaptation of Holmes's novel *Where the Truth Lies* (2005).

2. For a more detailed account of Lewis's early solo films, see Krutnik, *Inventing Jerry Lewis* 101–120.

3. In the mid-1930s, Tashlin made animated shorts for Leon Schlesinger's unit at Warner Bros., where he helped nurture the career of his first comic star, Porky Pig (Prouty 198–201). He worked with flesh-and-blood comedians from the mid-1940s, devising gags for films starring the Marx Brothers and Bob Hope.

10 ★★★★★★★★★★★

Judy Holliday
The Hungry Star

PAMELA ROBERTSON WOJCIK

When Columbia pictures chief Harry Cohn purchased the rights to the Garson Kanin play *Born Yesterday*—for an almost unheard-of $2 million—he resisted casting the Broadway star, Judy Holliday. Initially hired as a last-minute replacement for Jean Arthur, Holliday had become an instant smash in the role of Billie Dawn and the focal point of the stage production for nearly four years. "That fat Jewish broad?" Cohn declaimed, and went on instead to consider such diverse—and slim—actresses as Rita Hayworth, Lucille Ball, Alice Faye, Barbara Stanwyck, and Gloria Grahame for the role. Cohn was finally persuaded to hire Holliday after her admirers—Garson Kanin, Katharine Hepburn, Spencer Tracy, and George

Courtesy of MovieStarNews.

Cukor—showcased her talents in a small performance in *Adam's Rib* (1949) as part of a deliberate maneuver to outwit Cohn and surreptitiously screen test Holliday. Finally won over, Cohn cast Holliday. Meeting her in his office (their second meeting, though Cohn gave no indication he recalled the first, when Judy was one of the sketch comedy troupe, the Revuers), Cohn broadcast his disparaging opinion of Holliday's appearance: "Well, I've worked with fat asses before" (Carey 95–107; Holtzman 133–37).

From a contemporary perspective, the 1950s appear to be the great era of the voluptuous woman, the era of Marilyn Monroe, Jane Russell, Lana Turner, and Kim Novak. The decade stands nostalgically as the moment when the full-figured gal prevailed, a moment sandwiched between the slim ideal of the 1930s and 1940s, exemplified by Marlene Dietrich, Greta Garbo, Joan Crawford, and Katharine Hepburn, and the arrival of the vogue for slim, even anorexic, boyish figures begun by Audrey Hepburn in the 1950s (see William Brown's essay in this volume) and typified in the 1960s by Twiggy and Mia Farrow. Judy Holliday herself proclaimed a shift in taste in a puff piece on "Women Men Like": "Girls, don't get discouraged if you are the curvy type—men seem to like us that way. It took a war to rediscover the feminine figure. Men were tired—and said so—of the boyish contours that greeted them from every billboard, stage and screen." Holliday's article, however, is more than a bit disingenuous, as she claims that when she reported to Columbia, "no one seemed to object to my curves" (5th Annual *Hollywood Album*, 1951).[1]

However, then as now, there was a distinction made between the voluptuous woman—full-bosomed, and full-hipped, but small-waisted—and the overly fleshy woman; between curves and fat. Regarding the pressure on women to uphold a slim ideal in the 1950s, witness Judy Garland's ongoing battle with the bulge, enacted most graphically across the body of *Summer Stock* (1950), whose beginning and middle feature her bloated and stuffed into gingham and overalls but whose ending features a slimmed-down siren in black hot pants and fedora singing "Get Happy" (a number filmed three weeks after principal shooting, and just shortly before MGM fired her, when Garland had undergone a speedy reduction plan). Vinne Young, the author of a self-help book from 1953 titled *It's Fun to Be Fat*, describes the struggle for "leanness, slenderness" as an American "obsession":

> We are desperately busy controlling our curves, or banishing them, getting rid of ugly fat, counting calories, going hungry, getting weighed, relaxing the pounds away on our relaxicisors, exercising the pounds away on our exercisors, and running to the nearest reducing salon for a siege in the steam cabinet or a tussle with the pummel and punch brigade.   (Young 15–16)

Against the "pattern of female beauty created by Hollywood," the author advises young women to accept themselves and become "plump beautiful" (32).

Much to Cohn's surprise, Holliday, "that fat Jewish broad," was able to make Billie Dawn sexy and appealing, if not quite "plump beautiful," as Holliday lost fifteen pounds during the film's two-week rehearsal schedule (though later she would claim she had dieted for months). Rather than body type, much of the character's sexiness stems from her frank sexuality, her sincerity and sweetness, and her wiggle—a rhumba-inspired strut Holliday copied off chorus girls at the Copacabana (Frank Rasky, "Judy Holliday: The Smartest 'Dumb Blonde' in Show Business," *New Liberty*, April 1952). Still, Holliday, like Garland, was a star consistently defined by fluctuations in her weight.

★★★★★ The Hunger Artist

As distinct from Garland, whose weight troubles were linked to her much-publicized depression and drug use, Holliday's fat was associated in the popular press with the pleasure of eating. "See how fat I am now?" she asks a reporter for *Quick* magazine. "That's because I love to cook and then I love to eat what I've cooked." But, Holliday makes clear, her pleasure in cooking and eating goes against the ethos of Hollywood: "When I was doing *Born* for Columbia, I had to diet for months. If I went on television, I'd have to be on diet and beauty treatments all the time. You think I'm nuts? I like living too much for that!" ("Judy Holliday: She Wasn't Born Yesterday," *Quick*, 19 February 1951). In popular discourse, Holliday figures as a woman of appetite who must constantly suppress her desire for food in service of a career. In certain cases, her interest in food sublimates her sexuality. The *Saturday Evening Post* reports a story in which Holliday poses for a "sexy" photo. Lips parted and moist, "I looked sick instead of sexy," Holliday says. Then, according to Holliday, one of the crew began discussing a meal he'd had at an Italian restaurant. "Suddenly there was a yearning look on my face. . . . After that, when they wanted me to look sexy, they just showed me a menu" (Virginia Bird, "Hollywood's Blond Surprise," *Saturday Evening Post*, 31 December 1955). Here, Holliday suggests that the image we see of her—in photos and films—is an image of hunger.

Holliday battled her weight before her arrival in Hollywood, living famously on Dexedrine and coffee before the opening of the stage version of *Born Yesterday*. Once she was under contract to Columbia, however, Holliday's weight fluctuations were generally mapped onto geography, as a contrast between her New York and Hollywood lifestyles, or between "home" in New York and "away" in Hollywood. The emphasis on her New York identity at once underscores and erases Holliday's Jewish identity. Similarly, the emphasis on her pleasure in eating ignores the way in which food can express an ethnic or cultural heritage. Whereas Cohn conflated "fat" and "Jewish" in his description of Holliday, most contemporary commentators ignore her Jewishness in favor of fat.

Holliday is consistently portrayed as a contradictory figure of discipline and excess, who can control her weight when she must, in Hollywood, but whose weight billows indiscriminately when she is in New York and isn't controlled by the studios. For example, *TV Guide* states, "She plans more movie work for Columbia, but says Hollywood depresses her. 'I like to eat,' she wails. 'Out there, they don't let a girl eat'" ("Happy Holliday," *TV Guide*, 26 February 1955). Emphasizing the battle between excess and control, the *Saturday Evening Post* suggests a parallel between Holliday's eating and alcoholism: "Another reason why she prefers Gotham is that Hollywood means dieting to her. Her weight leaps up and down, twenty-five pounds at a leap—lower when she is working; higher when she's at leisure. 'I hurry past restaurants the way reformed dipsos rush past saloons,' she said" (Bird, "Hollywood's Blond Surprise"). In a similar vein, an article in *This Week* joked:

> The truth might as well be told about Judy Holliday before the scandal magazines get hold of it: She eats! And once she starts off on a food jag it's a real lost weekend. Periodically, when she's making a picture, she straightens herself out, so to speak. Company guards see to it that not a single excess calorie reaches her plate. Back in New York, however, with the restraints lifted, she makes up for lost time.
>
> (Louis Berg, "Judy's Secret Sin," 14 July 1956)

And asked why she only made one or two pictures a year, Holliday "drew herself up indignantly. 'Who can diet more than that? Want me to starve to death?'"

In Franz Kafka's story "The Hunger Artist," the central character locks himself in a cage to starve for the amusement of the populace. In her gloss on the text, Maud Ellmann suggests that "the moral seems to be that it is not by food that we survive but by the gaze of others; and it is impossible to live by hunger unless we can be seen or represented doing so" (17). In the constant iteration of her hunger, Judy Holliday can be seen, on the one hand, as living by hunger, becoming a spectacle of starvation. At the same time, by drawing attention to the demands placed on her body by Hollywood, Holliday draws attention to the mechanisms of the gaze, and the need for women especially to be seen as thin, or hungry, which, in Holliday's case, amounts to the same thing. Holliday does not starve for the sake of starving, but enters into a state of starvation each time she enters a new character. Thus, her hunger can be seen as a suppression of her appetite, an erasure of her (bodily, ethnic, feminine) self.

In this sense, the reduction of self endemic to weight loss is part and parcel of the erasure of self attendant to acting. During rehearsals for the play *Laurette*, Holliday wrote the following diary entry: "I'm trying to eliminate every vestige of my own personality, style, approach, and get into somebody else's skin. Sometimes I feel I've accomplished it. But when I don't, I'm nobody at all, having left myself at home" (qtd. in Lee Israel, "Judy Holliday and the Red Baiters: An Untold Story," *Ms. Magazine*, December 1976). Here, Holliday suggests that acting requires her to inhabit someone else's body, or skin, and lose her own. At the same time, she does not totally disappear but leaves her self "at home." Holliday suggests that acting requires a staged spectacle of loss, a becoming "nobody," a nonentity that exists somewhere between the role performed and the self. Holliday suggests that she has not merely a dual identity but that her identity is in jeopardy, in flux, and unstable.

★★★★★ Eye Hunger

If Holliday is associated with physical hunger and the evasion of what Ellmann calls "the everyday catastrophe of eating" (36), she is also equally associated with a different kind of hunger, what Holliday refers to as "eye hunger," or "an insatiable, almost physical need to devour the printed word" (Carey 11). This characterization of Holliday's intellectual curiosity, her desire to read, employs the metaphor of ingestion—devouring the printed word—that is typical of much Western thought. Ellmann reminds us that "the *locus classicus* of the analogy is Genesis" (29), where both kinds of eating are tied together as female transgressions, as Eve eats the fruit from the tree of knowledge. Eating is the route to knowledge. Where the Bible suggests a fall from innocence, epistemology suggests that the subject comes into being through eating: through the mouth she learns to distinguish self from other, and inside from outside. However, Ellmann points to the "fundamental incompleteness of the subject" revealed through the link between eating and knowing: "If the subject is found in gestation . . . this also means his identity is constantly in jeopardy . . . the need to eat reveals the 'nothing' at the core of subjectivity" (30). Both eating and cognition aim to fill the subject, but the subject is never satiated, never complete.

As with Holliday's physical hunger, her "eye hunger," or intellectualism, is consistently remarked upon by the popular press, but, as with her physical hunger, it is represented as a repressed or hidden aspect of her personality, a feature obscured by the roles she plays. Time and again, contemporary articles reference Holliday's high I.Q. (of 172) and her intellectual pursuits. She is described as "a bonafide intellectual" (Rasky, "Judy Holliday: The Smartest 'Dumb Blonde' in Show Business"), who "reads books that are so deep that the average citizen might sink without trace into their pages" (Bird, "Hollywood's Blond Surprise") and famously plays double acrostics and Scrabble (Jon Whitcomb, "Judy and 'The Bells,'" *Cosmopolitan*, February 1960). But Holliday's intellectualism is always set in opposition to "usual portrayal of a dim-brained dame" (Bird, "Hollywood's Blond Surprise"), and especially the dumb blonde Billie Dawn. As Frank Rasky writes, "the worst possible libel against the flesh-and-blood Judy is the assumption that she is as dumb as the stage trollop she imitates" ("Judy Holliday: The Smartest 'Dumb Blonde' in Show Business"). For Rasky, Holliday is "the Svengali" who created Billie Dawn, but Dawn, like Holliday, is voracious: "[Holliday] is in danger of being swallowed up by her alter ego, and can do little about it." More than mere typecasting, Rasky views Dawn as a distinct and competing identity: "But Judy's personality is so inextricably confused in the public's affections with Billie Dawn that few will allow her to untangle the schizophrenia." As above, with respect to both eating and acting, the way Holliday handles the conflict between her intellectual hunger and her image is through the creation of a second self, different from the one "at home": "All I have to do is remember to be dumb when I'm out, and smart when I'm home" (Bird, "Hollywood's Blond Surprise").

The sense of Holliday as having multiple identities extends across her career. Most articles comment on her transition from being Judy Tuvim to the roughly translated less-Jewish-sounding name Holliday to becoming Mrs. David Oppenheimer. And critics emphasize Holliday's mobility among media, as she moves from New York revue ensemble artist to bit player in Hollywood to Broadway star to Hollywood star, then shifts back again to the stage, with forays into radio and TV, finally entering the music industry as a composer and singer with boyfriend Gerry Mulligan. Beyond those superficial changes, however, much of the discourse on Holliday emphasizes the changeability and indeterminacy of her identity. Lawrence Langer makes this most explicit when he describes Holliday as "not just one girl" but "at least seven" ("A Whole Week of Hollidays," *Theatre Arts*, March 1957). Langer argues that Holliday is an adolescent, comedienne, mimic, singer, dramatic actress, dancer, and vaudeville headliner. Even as he sorts her

Holliday was famed as a reader of books, an intellectual with an insatiable appetite for learning. Courtesy of MovieStarNews.

seven identities, he fractures them, offering that as a singer, actress, mimic, and comedienne she takes on numerous identities, moving freely between and among styles and adopting various personae, among them Ina Claire, Marlon Brando, Eddie Cantor, Al Jolson, Laurette Taylor, and George M. Cohan. Holliday is viewed as not just multifaceted but changeable. So, William Peters of *Redbook* (June 1957) identifies three "new" Judy Hollidays surfacing in 1957—one in the Broadway musical *Bells Are Ringing*, one in the film *Full of Life* (1956), and one who is newly content with her career as an actress.

★★★★★ Playing Nobody

To a large degree, the Judy Holliday character is a collaborative product that exceeds the star's input. The first four films she made at Columbia—*Adam's Rib, Born Yesterday, The Marrying Kind* (1952), and *It Should Happen to You* (1954)—were all directed by George Cukor and written by Garson Kanin, or in the cases of *Adam's Rib* and *The Marrying Kind*, Kanin and Ruth Gordon. Nonetheless, the persona in these films, defined as hungry and indeterminate, carries over into other films, such as Vincente Minnelli's *Bells Are Ringing* (1960) or the Richard Quine film *The Solid Gold Cadillac* (1956). Even more, the films play off of and intersect with views of Holliday in the popular press and the public's perception of the "real" Judy Holliday, as a star defined by hunger and a changing and indeterminate identity.

Ironically, *Adam's Rib*, the film used to convince Cohn to hire Holliday for *Born Yesterday*, explicitly weaves Cohn's critique of Holliday as fat into the role she plays as Doris Attinger. Doris shoots her husband Warren (Tom Ewell), who has been unfaithful to her. In court, he admits that he stopped loving his wife three years ago "because she got too fat" and, at one point during the proceedings, shouts at her, "Bite your tongue, fatso!" Interestingly, in this film—Holliday's first substantial film role after her first 1940s contract with Twentieth Century–Fox petered out—the Holliday character is characterized as incongruously hungry. The first time we see Doris, she is eating a candy bar while she nervously stalks her husband. When defense attorney Amanda Bonner (Katharine Hepburn) questions her about the events leading up to the shooting, Doris describes herself as first "mad" when she discovers that her husband has, once again, failed to come home, then "hungry" after she buys a gun: "So then I got very hungry . . . when I bought the gun. So I went in this hamburger place and I ate two rare. And one lemon meringue pie. . . . And then I was still hungry. . . . So then I bought some chocolate nut bars. . . . I kept eating the candy bars . . . then I followed him, and then I shot him." Asked how she felt after the shooting, Doris replies, "Hungry."

In Holliday's film roles, her character's weight is occasionally at issue. In *It Should Happen to You*, for example, her character, Gladys Glover, gets "canned" for her job as a girdle model "on account of 3/4 of an inch!"—a slight weight gain that makes her no longer eligible to model. More important than the weight gain, perhaps, is Gladys's association with the girdle—a garment associated with full-figured women and the need for restraining the body. Similarly, in *Bells Are Ringing*, Holliday's character has a past career as a model at the Bonjour Tristesse Brassiere Company. As a model for undergarments, Holliday's character is a contradictory figure—at once attractive enough to model, but also modeling the need to contain and discipline the unruly, even fat, body.

Rather than fat per se, the Holliday character is often associated with eating and preparing food. In *It Should Happen to You*, Gladys is introduced onscreen eating peanuts, just as Doris Attinger is shown eating a chocolate bar. Later, for a lunch date, Gladys cooks pork chops for boyfriend Pete Sheppard (Jack Lemmon). In *The Marrying Kind*, she also cooks pork chops for lunch. In *The Solid Gold Cadillac*, she brings her own lunch to work everyday. When her ex-boss Mr. McKeever (Paul Douglas) stops by, she offers him a sandwich of peanut butter and smoked salmon that she pulls from her desk drawer. In *Bells Are Ringing*, when a hung-over Jeffrey Moss (Dean Martin) expresses a desire for coffee, she pulls not only a cup of coffee but also a prune Danish out of her purse. While it may not be unusual for film characters to be shown eating or cooking, it is hard to imagine many of Holliday's blonde bombshell contemporaries—Monroe, Novak, Turner—eating, much less serving pork chops or peanut butter. But Holliday eats, cooks, and nurtures the men in her life with food.

Holliday's association with the homely arts of cooking, as well as her slight fleshiness, combine to make her seem appealingly ordinary. In films, she is usually cast as an average girl, and especially an urban working girl. Different from the glamorous career-girl image of the 1950s—the chic girls of publishing in *The Best of Everything* (1953), say—the Holliday character tends to work in relatively low and unglamorous positions—modeling girdles or bras or working as a telephone operator (*Bells Are Ringing*), chorus girl (*Born Yesterday*), or urban housewife (*Adam's Rib*, *The Marrying Kind*, *Full of Life*, *Phfft!* [1954]). In *The Solid Gold Cadillac*, she is a representative ordinary girl—a small stockholder who is bequeathed ten shares in a large corporation, International Projects, and becomes a liaison and proxy for other ordinary small stockholders.

In being ordinary, Holliday is represented as typical but not stereotypical. In *The Solid Gold Cadillac*, her Laura Partridge says she hasn't been able to get much work as an actress because "I'm an unusual type." In *It Should Happen to You*, ad man Evan Adams III (Peter Lawford) characterizes her as "the average American girl." At the same time, however, he recognizes that "the average American girl is unusual." The unusual aspect of the Holliday

Phffft (Mark Robson, Columbia, 1954) gave Holliday (here with Donald Randolph) a chance to play a wronged wife in a hilarious comedy of remarriage. Digital frame enlargement.

character partly relates to her lack of glamour. She is represented as potentially attractive but not stereotypically beautiful, and a bit of an oddity. In *Bells Are Ringing*, for instance, when Ella Peterson goes to a fancy party crowded with artists and writers, all the women wear sleek gowns in neutral colors while Ella wears a full red gown borrowed from an opera star appearing in *La Traviata*. As they name-drop Broadway and Hollywood stars, like Ethel Barrymore and Ava Gardner, Ella doesn't recognize the references; and then, when she begins to play the game, in the musical number "Drop That Name," she can only name-drop Rin Tin Tin and Lassie. In a different vein, in *Born Yesterday* Billie Dawn is also a bit of an oddity, marked as sexy and a little trashy, not appropriately conservative for Washington, D.C. Her drinking, manner of speech, mode of dress, manners, and especially her intelligence all come into question when she is placed amid D.C. political society. In *The Solid Gold Cadillac*, Laura Partridge is also inappropriate. She fails to recognize that small shareholders are meant to be invisible and silent, and she not only attends shareholder meetings but interrupts them, asks questions, and puts forward motions, generally making a nuisance of herself.

The combination of being both ordinary and unusual relates partly to Holliday's looks, including not just her chunky body but also her round eyes and thick nose. Her looks are "typically" Jewish but "unusual" against the dominant WASP norm. The characterization of her looks as "unusual" both acknowledges and conceals her ethnicity and difference from the norm. Holliday's performance style also contributes to her characterization as simultaneously ordinary and unusual. Her voice, especially, defines her. Holliday's voice is accented. She is a native New Yorker who usually adopts or exaggerates a Brooklyn accent. The Brooklyn accent signifies not only place but also ethnicity and class. Brooklyn signals a certain kind of authenticity at the same time that it relegates her to the margins of mainstream middle-class society as Jewish and working class. The films tend to play up place and class by frequently mentioning her Brooklyn origins and highlighting her class difference from others. But her Jewishness is never explicit, though it lurks in names like Gladys Glover. More than just accent, of course, is the way Holliday uses her voice. If Holliday is associated with being a dumb blonde, it may be in the way her voice slightly squeaks—one writer refers to it as a "toy whistle" (Betty Randolph, "An Intimate Talk with Judy Holliday," *TV and Movie Screen*, May 1955). But Holliday can also growl and squawk, manipulating her voice to bring out a grit and edge to her characters, an inability to modulate temperament.

Because she is ordinary, the Holliday character often perceives herself to be unimportant, a nobody. In *It Should Happen to You*, when Gladys is asked, "Who are you?" she answers, "Nobody, that's who!" In that film, Gladys wants to be "a name." She came to New York "to make a name for myself," but considers Gladys Glover "not much of a name because nobody ever heard of it." Gladys makes herself a name, literally, by hiring a billboard and putting her name on it, eventually garnering six signs and becoming a minor celebrity. However, her boyfriend Pete questions the value of being a mere name and questions her ability to know her own desires: "I sure hope you make a name for yourself. If that's what you want. If that's what you really want." Pete eventually educates Gladys, retraining her desire so that instead of wanting to be a name "above the crowd" she accepts being a "nobody," part of a crowd who may make her name *"stand for something."* Gladys's want, or hunger, for a name is thus represented as inappropriate and untamed. It requires discipline and education.

Just as Holliday imagines herself to be a "nobody" when she acts, a nonentity who has shed her self, her characters often seem to be between identities. In many films, the Holliday character is "nobody" not because she is insignificant but because her identity is indeterminate. For instance, in *It Should Happen to You*, Gladys, under fire from Pete, declares, "I haven't changed. I'm the same as before. Only in a different way." In *Bells Are Ringing*, Holliday's Ella Peterson adopts numerous personae as a telephone operator, tailoring each to the appropriate client. She plays Santa Claus for a little boy, for example; a French restaurateur for clients of a posh restaurant; a

In *It Should Happen to You* (George Cukor, Columbia, 1954), Holliday hams it up in a fat suit. Digital frame enlargement.

smooth-voiced receptionist for a dentist's office; and a little old lady named "Mom" for the needy composer Jeffrey Moss (Martin). As she begins to meddle directly in the lives of her clients, especially Jeffrey, with whom she is secretly in love, she invents a new persona, Melisande Scott. Ultimately, she beseeches, "Who is me? I don't know myself who I am." The bizarre grammatical structure here, a grammar not atypical for Holliday, suggests a crisis of identity. In the song "The Party's Over," Ella suggests that "who is me" does not exist or is "not": "He's in love with Melisande Scott / A girl who doesn't exist. / He's in love with someone you're not." When Jeffrey tells Ella he loves her, she says that because she is neither Melisande Scott nor "Mom," "I am nothing."

The indeterminacy of identity in Holliday films is tied to the character's cognition, her need to think clearly or know her own mind. *The Marrying Kind* offers the most extended discussion of the need for cognition. The newly married Florence Keefer explains to her mother and sister-in-law that on her honeymoon she discovered thought:

> Everybody gets in a rut. Take me. A rut. But down there in Atlantic City, I got into quite a lot of thinking. You know what I mean? I don't mean just stewing around. I mean thinking. And to tell you the truth I was surprised how enjoyable it was. You take most people, including me. They hardly ever get to do any thinking. When do they get the time? Or when you do get the time, there's the movies, or the radio, or you play a game of cards, but no thinking. . . . I made up a rule. I'm gonna do at least a half hour's of thinking everyday. All by myself. Just quietly.

Here, Florence develops a kind of "eye hunger," a desire for thinking itself. But Florence's newfound love of cognition never develops—it is a dream deferred. One senses that the demands of housewifery preclude her fulfilling her promise to seize time to think.

Born Yesterday makes the discovery of thought the plot. In an effort to make her more suitable for Washington society, Billie's mobster boyfriend, Harry Brock (Broderick Crawford), hires journalist Paul Verrall (William Holden) as a tutor. Paul teaches Billie about grammar, literature, history, and government. Initially, Billie claims to like being "stupid": "I get everything I want. I got two mink coats." Like Gladys, however, Billie has to be educated to want differently. Paul advises her, "As long as you know what you want." At first, Billie's efforts at thinking sublimate sex: she allows herself to be tutored by Paul because she has a "yen" for him and believes the way to him is through the mind. Eventually, however, she discovers herself really thinking: "Last night I went to bed. I started thinking. I couldn't fall asleep for ten minutes!" And she eventually revises her wants away from materialist desires and toward becoming a different sort of person: "I know one thing I never knew before. There's a better kind of life than the one I got." What Billie knows, or learns, leads her to become unstable and indeterminate: at film's end, she is set to leave one life, as mistress of a crook, to enter another, with the promise of a new romance with Paul. Yet what she is and what she wants are still somewhat up for grabs.

★★★★★ Whatever You Are, Be It!

Although Holliday would often work to distinguish her real-life persona from her film roles, and especially from Billie Dawn, frequently the boundaries between selves would blur. For example, Holliday famously played Billie Dawn when she went before the Senate Internal Subcommittee, an offshoot of the House Un-American Activities Committee, in a hearing on Subversive Infiltration of Radio, Television and Entertainment Industry. Holliday had been named in *Red Channels*, a list of 151 entertainers with alleged ties to communism produced by the publishers of a weekly anticommunist newsletter. Determined not to name names, Holliday accepted the advice of a friend, public relations man Robert L. Green (later fashion director at *Playboy*), who advised Holliday to play Billie Dawn: "What you don't want to do is appear intelligent. You represent a mistress, an absolutely darling piece of fluff. I would dress in dark clothes, a little sexy, not trashy. They'll be thrilled. They'll say, 'She's exactly what she is on screen'" (Holtzman 163; see also Israel, "Judy Holliday and the Red

Baiters"). The transcript of Holliday's testimony, from 26 March 1952, shows her answering questions from Senator Arthur Watkins and staff director Richard Arens with vague evasions and questions of her own that deflect theirs. In one exchange, for example, Holliday is asked if she had a picture taken with strikers:

> *Watkins*: Did any of your friends ask you to have that picture taken?
>
> *Holliday*: Somebody asked me.
>
> *Watkins*: Do you remember somebody asked you?
>
> *Holliday*: They must have, because I wouldn't wander over to strikers and ask to have my picture taken.
>
> *Arens*: Do you have any difficulty with your memory?
>
> *Holliday*: No. The only difficulty is that I met a tremendous lot of people and I get a lot of requests and phone calls. We get about 50 a day, and you just can't pay any attention to them unless you know them first.
>
> *Watkins*: This is back in 1946. Your prominence in the motion picture world has taken place largely since that time, has it not?
>
> *Holliday*: Yes.
>
> *Watkins*: Well, at that particular time you were on the way up. Do you not think you could remember?
>
> *Holliday*: If that is true. I'm not saying that it isn't, but so many things have been untrue. But, if that is true, then I was already in a play.

Throughout the Senate Internal Subcommittee hearing, Holliday baffles questioners with her refusal or inability to account for her own actions or those of her friends.

Adopting the circularity of her film grammar, Holliday not only brilliantly equivocates and saves herself from naming names, but begins to unravel any sense of a secure and knowable identity. When asked if she is sure that her friends Adolph Green and Betty Comden (her partners from the Revuers and the writers of *Bells Are Ringing*) do not have communist front records, Holliday replies, "I am as sure of that as I can be of anybody that isn't me." Asked, absurdly, whether she is aware of a communist front record for Albert Einstein or Thomas Mann, Holliday asserts: "Then I am sure they got into it the same way I did, because I am sure none of them are Communists. I mean, if you are a Communist, why go to a Communist Front? Why not be a Communist? Whatever you are, be it."

On the one hand, Holliday asserts the need to be true to one's identity—whatever you are, be it. But on the other hand, she opens up the possibility for identity to be multiple and changing—whatever you are (at the moment, in that incarnation, however vague and unknowable), be it. This ability to be at once authentic, not a front and indeterminate, may ultimately be the defining characteristic of Holliday's star text. Whatever, or whoever, Judy Holliday was—fat or hungry, dumb or smart, ordinary or unusual, nobody or somebody—she was it.

NOTES

1. All citations from fan magazines and mass-market periodicals come from the online Judy Holliday Resource Center, www.judyhollidayrc.com, and were accessed on 25 June 2008 (page numbers are not provided). Research for this essay is indebted to the hard work of webmaster Glenn McMahon, who compiled and posted the numerous articles, including Holliday's FBI transcript, on the site.

11

What a Swell Party This Was

Fred Astaire, Gene Kelly, Bing Crosby, and Frank Sinatra

ADRIENNE L. McLEAN

Fred Astaire, Gene Kelly, Frank Sinatra. From the author's private collection.
Bing Crosby. Courtesy of Paramount.

By the end of World War II, the Hollywood musical had become one of the industry's most enduring and enduringly popular genres, its films and stars landing frequently on lists of top box-office performers especially in the depths of the Depression and during the war itself. More of the films were being accorded critical acclaim as well, with the praise directed usually at the technical innovations of a particular number—Gene Kelly's "alter ego" dance with himself in *Cover Girl* (1944), for example—or on the lavish ballets that appeared with greater regularity in the postwar era. Fred Astaire had retired from filmmaking altogether in 1945 (his "final" film was *Blue Skies* [1946] with Bing Crosby), but he was lured back in 1948 to replace Gene Kelly in *Easter Parade* (Kelly had broken his ankle playing touch football), which was followed by a nostalgic reunion with Ginger Rogers in *The Barkleys of Broadway* (1949). Kelly helped move the Hollywood musical off the studio back lot the same year by shooting at least part of *On the Town* on location in New York City. Frank Sinatra, the idol of the bobby-soxers during the war years, was also in *On the Town*, and if middle-aged Bing Crosby was still riding high (he and Betty Grable, also one of the biggest musical stars of the 1940s, were tops at the box office in 1950),[1] it was assumed that Sinatra was the new all-around movie crooner of the day. The phenomenal tenor voice of Mario Lanza was even making films about opera popular again, too, with fan magazines reporting that *The Great Caruso* (1951), one of MGM's big-budget Technicolor biopics, was the "most popular film in the world." Overall, it did seem to be MGM's musicals, particularly those produced by Arthur Freed, that garnered the most official praise; but regardless of studio, by the early 1950s the genre had reached a heretofore unprecedented level of prestige and profitability.

At the 1951 Academy Awards ceremony on 28 March 1952, Freed won the Irving Thalberg Award for his "extraordinary accomplishment in the making of musical pictures" and for adding "stature to the whole industry," and Gene Kelly was awarded an honorary Oscar in "appreciation for his contribution to the creation and improvement of the motion picture musical film; not only because of his extreme versatility as an actor-singer, director and dancer, but because of his specific and brilliant achievements in the art of choreography on film" (qtd. in Fordin 344–45). Freed's and Kelly's *An American in Paris* even won the 1951 Oscar for Best Picture at the end of the evening; it was the first time a musical had been granted the award since 1936. Given the triumph of Freed, Kelly, and *An American in Paris* that night, it appeared that the 1950s was going to be a good decade indeed for musicals, one that could only build upon the success and approbation the genre had already achieved.

To be sure, things did not look great for everyone. Judy Garland made her first publicized suicide attempt in June 1950, slashing at her throat with a broken water glass after being fired by MGM following the completion of *Summer Stock* (which also starred Kelly) the same year. Garland quickly made a triumphant return to live performing, breaking records at the Palace and Carnegie Hall as well as the London Palladium, but her only other 1950s musical was the remake of *A Star Is Born* (1954), for Warner Bros. Moreover, even the stars and studios that began the decade with such high hopes were frequently in some sort of difficulty by the end of it. According to the tabloids, Mario Lanza "ate himself out of a career" and died in 1959 as a result of complications from diet drugs. Gene Kelly and Arthur Freed attempted to repeat the success of *On the Town* with a widescreen sequel, *It's Always Fair Weather* (1954); it is significant that the new film's plot satirized the medium of television with which movies were now openly competing and that, in contrast to the mostly joyous self-expression that the numbers in *On the Town* represented, the dances in *It's Always Fair Weather* were often motivated by alcohol, depression, or anger. Whereas *On the Town* was released to rapturous reviews and big box office, the later film made little stir and disappeared into drive-in theaters, double-billed with the western *Bad Day at Black Rock* (Fordin 436). In fact, by the dawn of the 1960s, the big-budget Hollywood musical had all but disappeared as a viable genre, replaced by adaptations of Broadway vehicles that often would not star musical performers at all (the film version of *West Side Story* [1959] featured leads who were neither singers nor dancers) or by lower-budget vehicles for young and newly popular radio and recording stars like Pat Boone and Elvis Presley. Even Frank Sinatra would not sign up for *It's Always Fair Weather*; he had become too big a star to perform as one of a trio of war buddies, even in an MGM musical.

The 1950s, then, can be seen as both the most glorious era in Hollywood musical history and also perhaps its grimmest, the decade during which the genre reached its penultimate glory and then began to sicken and die. Regardless of whether their careers had begun decades or just a few years earlier, there are relatively few musical stars whose fortunes were not wildly changed ten years later. The 1950s posed age and experience against youth and energy; spectacles of masculinity (especially dominant during the decade) against the great appeal of the singing and dancing women stars of the 1930s and 1940s (Ginger Rogers, Eleanor Powell, Betty Grable, Judy Garland, and Rita Hayworth); established versions of the popular and the folk (which had always involved absorbing and reconstituting but also drawing upon the status and cultural capital of "elite" arts such as opera and ballet, as well as co-opting and exploiting nonwhite or "jazz" forms of popular music and dance) against commercialized but fresh rock 'n' roll and a slightly more racially and ethnically heterogeneous "teen" culture; an industrially and culturally mandated reliance on romance against, and gradually giving way to, more overt physical expressions of sexuality.

This chapter focuses on some of the most famous and long-lived of the era's song-and-dance men, those who, like dancers Fred Astaire and Gene Kelly, remain associated with the Hollywood musical's canonical master-pieces, and others, like singers Bing Crosby and Frank Sinatra, whose careers represented alternative versions of the musical star as someone for whom film was simply another means, if a powerful one, for circulating the performer's fame among a number of different venues—radio, television, nightclubs and shows, the recording industry and its products. By the end of the 1950s, even older stars like Astaire and Crosby were working in tel-evision as much as in the movies; this is not particularly surprising, given the concomitant decline in the fortunes of the studio system generally dur-ing the decade, and wider social changes that made the musical's once appealing but always overtly simplistic ideology—conflicts, whether per-sonal, generational, or cross-cultural, can all be resolved through song, dance, and romance—less relevant. The popularity of the new teen idols, like Boone and Presley, seemed to be based less on a spectacular display of virtuosic talent and ability than on an aesthetic of personal expression and, at least in Presley's case, sexual appeal.

Of course, Kelly and Sinatra had partly positioned themselves as "ordi-nary" in contrast to the top-hat-and-tails image of Astaire or even the hyperbolic amiability and middle-classness of Bing Crosby. But, overall, the "original" Hollywood musical came to depend less and less on the framing of some extraordinary or noteworthy skill in a carefully tailored film vehi-cle and instead relied more and more upon a performer's preexisting mass-mediated celebrity, whether achieved in television, radio, or the recording industries. Where once Gene Kelly or Fred Astaire could be labeled as "triple-threat" singers, dancers, and actors (and, in Kelly's case, he also directed or co-directed some of his films), through the 1950s the same label would acquire a different meaning, such that the triple threat that Frank Sinatra, or younger cohorts such as Presley or Boone, represented meant that he was successful in movies, as a nightclub performer, and as a record-ing artist. The stories of Astaire and Kelly, Crosby and Sinatra in the 1950s serve as illustrations of the shifting value of the song-and-dance man, a value always inflected by the peculiarities of the male musical star's rela-tionship to bodily spectacle, to the suspicion directed at men whose careers, like those of "showgirls," were devoted to displaying themselves in front of an audience (see Cohan "'Feminizing'"). These stars also help us to understand the film industry's complex notions and negotiations of the musical, as adjective and as noun, as a peculiarly American form of *entertainment*, and how attitudes toward the musical's performing bodies in the 1950s engaged and represented hopeful and utopian as well as despairing or cynical visions of ourselves.

★★★★★ Ageless Astaire

"Anyone dancing on the screen today who doesn't admit his debt to Astaire," said Gene Kelly in a 1946 article, "is either a liar or a fool" (Isaacs 149). Astaire was born at the end of the nineteenth century and did not make his first film, which was for MGM, until 1933. He played himself in *Dancing Lady*, and MGM was not sufficiently impressed by his work to keep him under contract. Thus it remains astonishing that he was given so much control over the filming and editing of his screen dances at RKO, the studio where he began his legendary partnership with Ginger Rogers the same year. It was this control—over the choreography as well as framing and editing of his solos, in particular his insistence that the dances be filmed with a mobile camera in long takes and with the dancer's body in full view throughout—combined with a well-publicized interest in producing work that was "new" and "original" that helped turn the male tap-dancer/choreographer into a respectable film artist rather than a performing *artiste*. Moreover, Astaire arrived in Hollywood a happily married man around whom no rumors of scandal had ever circulated, and but for an occasional fan-magazine piece about his shyness, his perfectionism, and his appeal to women despite his somewhat odd looks, it is difficult to find much mass-market material on Astaire (even during the heyday of his partnership with Ginger Rogers) that is not about the preparation of his dances or else studio-produced publicity for the films in which they appear.

When Astaire announced that *Blue Skies* would be his last film, there was little obvious public consternation, just many adulatory farewells. He was, after all, pushing fifty, and he was planning to found a string of dancing studios across the country; it was rumored that he might also become a film producer. In another of his 1946 films he partnered Gene Kelly in a long and long-anticipated "challenge" number in MGM's revue *The Ziegfeld Follies*, and while Astaire generally got the better notices (some kindness was no doubt paid him because of his impending retirement), Kelly seemed the natural, if physically and stylistically dissimilar, successor to Astaire in terms of the art of screen dancing. Signally, Astaire never claimed to be retiring because of his "joints—which [were] as resilient as ever," as *Life* put it in a picture story on "Astaire's last dance" in *Blue Skies*—but because of an "apprehension that his inventiveness [was] running dry" (31 December 1945, 55). His relatively quick return in *Easter Parade* was met with a general critical consensus that he was "dancing at the top of his form" (*New York Times*); and since *Easter Parade* was a success at the box office, from that point on Astaire's age, or rather his agelessness, became an acknowledged feature of his star image.

Of the eight films—all musicals—that Astaire made in the 1950s, however, only a few have become part of the genre's canon, most if not all of them MGM films. Astaire's first 1950s film was supposed to be *Let's Dance*, with Betty Hutton, to fulfill a contractual obligation he had with Paramount, but the script was not yet ready so he made *Three Little Words* at MGM instead, partnering Gene Kelly's *On the Town* co-star, Vera-Ellen, in a profitable biopic of the songwriters Bert Kalmar and Harry Ruby. One wonders whether Astaire's 1950s career would have remained viable had *Let's Dance* been released first, for the frenetic Hutton was one of Astaire's least compatible co-stars and, in Astaire's own words, the film "just seemed to come and go" (Astaire 297). It was providential for Astaire that Arthur Freed at MGM had long admired him and was eager to have both him and Gene Kelly under contract at the same time, and throughout the decade, whether at MGM or elsewhere, Astaire and Kelly would not only share dancing partners—Cyd Charisse, Leslie Caron, Vera-Ellen—but become metaphorically a sort of shadow team themselves, the one the classy elder statesman in top hat and tails who subsumed effort under a veneer of grace and ease, the other the scrappy streetwise "regular guy" who made dance into a species of athletics to be performed in khaki pants, rolled-up sleeves, and loafers. The irony was that Astaire refused any association of his dancing with effeteness or the balletic, preferring to think of himself as "just a song-and-dance man" or a hoofer, while Kelly employed considerable amounts of classical ballet vocabulary and technique even in his most athletic tap numbers.

Certainly the budgets of Astaire's MGM films were far larger than he had been used to at other studios, and MGM was known for a high degree of visual stylization (all of his 1950s films were in color), especially in the big ballets that came to be part of so many musicals in the late 1940s. (*On the Town* may have been shot partly on location in New York City, but it of course also featured a long, expressionistic, and soundstage-bound dream ballet as well.) In *Easter Parade*, Astaire had experimented with dancing in slow motion, and in *The Barkleys of Broadway*, he did terpsichorean battle with ranks of rebellious animated shoes; both these numbers were singled out in virtually every review of the films. It would increasingly become the case, therefore, that individual numbers, and the film "tricks" or gimmicks that they employed, would attract as much attention in his 1950s films as Astaire's dancing as such—with some journalistic verbiage still devoted to the parlor game of predicting whether this or that star or starlet might be "the new Ginger." *Royal Wedding* (1951) is the film in which Astaire danced with a coat rack and on the ceiling, the process by which the latter illusion was accomplished featured in another *Life* magazine spread (the camera was bolted to the floor of a rotating room). In the period piece *The Belle of New York* (1952), his second and less successful partnering with Vera-Ellen, he dances among special-effects clouds as well as on the back-lot streets of Old New York.

Royal Wedding, which was originally intended to star Astaire with Judy Garland again, ended up pairing him with a much younger (by thirty years) co-star, Jane Powell. The plot was changed to make Powell his sister, an extratextual reference to Astaire's early stage career in which he was known as the lesser half of the team composed of himself and older sister Adele. But more significant, the strategy suggests some discomfort at the studio with the idea of Astaire as romantic partner to a much younger co-star. Notwithstanding the "unrealistic" elements of the average big-budget Hollywood musical as a genre, or of Gene Kelly's interest in dancing as an "average Joe," both Astaire and Kelly frequently played song-and-dance men in their 1950s musicals, with many of the numbers therein, even the dream ballets or fantasy set pieces, motivated narratively by their place-ment in some sort of a show-within-a-show. So for Astaire, the problem of his age, and his links to earlier and now outmoded forms of show business, remained; and *The Band Wagon*, probably his most famous and respected 1950s film, chose to tackle the situation head-on.

The Band Wagon's credit sequence rolls over a shot of a top hat, cane, and white gloves on a stand in a display box, and it turns out that they are being auctioned off along with other personal effects of an aging film star, Tony Hunter (Astaire). That nobody will bid on the items at any price sets up Hunter (and Astaire) as a relic of a by-gone age; the film's project is to reclaim him for "now," to turn him into "Tony Hunter, 1953." Jane Feuer has written extensively of *The Band Wagon*'s self-reflexivity as functioning conservatively, as a way for the MGM musical to establish, or reestablish, its relevance as entertainment in a changing world through a linking of the values of the present and past (the songs were virtually all older standards

Fred Astaire in the "Ritz Roll and Rock" (and top hat and tails) from *Silk Stockings* (Rouben Mamoulian, MGM, 1957). Courtesy of Loew's Incorporated.

from the songbook of Howard Dietz and Arthur Schwartz) as well as of entertainment and art, as represented by the classical credentials of co-star Cyd Charisse, playing a ballerina, and Jack Buchanan, as an affected but hammy British high-art showman (Feuer "Self-Reflexive"). Betty Comden, who wrote *The Band Wagon* with Adolph Green, remembered that they were "very nervous in the beginning about Fred's character because it was based in so many ways on his actual position in life. It was not a man down, out and broke, but a man midway in his career, a man thinking of possibly retiring, or continuing to look for fresh fields"; when they "timidly" presented the character to Astaire, they were relieved that he "loved it immediately" (Fordin 400).

Charisse had been at MGM since the early 1940s; already in her midthirties, and grave enough in demeanor to seem maturer than her years, she became one of the best-publicized assets of *The Band Wagon*, her obvious expertise as a dancer sparking any number of new rounds in the "Is she better than Ginger" debate. She adorned the cover of *Newsweek*, and the accompanying story ("Finklea & Austerlitz, Alias Charisse & Astaire," 6 July 1953, 48–50) made reference to *her* scandal-free private life and motherhood to two sons, her partnership with "the still-twinkling, 54-year-old Fred Astaire" (48) naturalized through their shared professionalism and devotion to the hard work of dancing. *The Band Wagon* was a success both critically and financially, with Astaire and Charisse in the long "Girl Hunt" ballet—a spoof of the hard-boiled novel of the Mickey Spillane sort and of what had not yet come to be called film noir—attracting particular attention. From then through the end of the decade the appellation "ageless Astaire" became applied more and more frequently.

Ironically, *The Band Wagon* was actually Astaire's last contracted film at MGM; as he writes in his 1959 autobiography, "Nobody seemed too anxious or excited about getting me to do another picture," so he planned to "fade gently out of action" and maybe return later "minus the old dancing shoes" to produce (Astaire 304). He made no other films for two years, and his next one was for Twentieth Century–Fox, *Daddy Long Legs*, with Leslie Caron. Astaire's persona had always been based on his reticence as well as his perfectionism, and the death of his wife in 1954 appeared to make him even less interested in being in any kind of spotlight; certainly there is very little publicity material to be found about him in the mid-1950s other than that tied to the release of *Daddy Long Legs* and, a couple of years later, *Funny Face* (1957) with Audrey Hepburn. In the first film, he portrays a playboy who falls in love with a friend of his college-age niece and financially supports her education and transition to adulthood from afar (a friend calls him her "Daddy Sugar") before identifying himself to her as her benefactor and asking her to marry him; again his co-star was thirty years younger than he was. In *Funny Face*, he plays a fashion photographer (modeled on Richard Avedon) who takes another young woman under his wing (Audrey Hepburn, three years older than Caron), arranging to have her rough edges polished off and turning her into a model and his photographic muse. If the romances in both these films provoke some queasiness among audiences today, at the time most reviews continued to pretend that Astaire was "ageless" ("Fred Astaire . . . is as nimble in 1957 as he was in 1927 when he danced a *Funny Face* on Broadway," declared *Life* [15 April 1957, 88]), and his star image became similar to the roles he played in these films—he was older, rich, experienced, kind, debonair, a bit sad, and sexually unthreatening, the opposite in many ways to, or perhaps a denial of, the teenage rebels attracting so much attention in the press who seemed less a continuation of paternal dominance than an affront to it.

After *Funny Face* he reunited with Cyd Charisse for *Silk Stockings* (1957), a big-budget color and CinemaScope adaptation of a Broadway musical (in turn based on a 1939 MGM nonmusical adaptation, *Ninotchka*), in which he and the pleasures of Parisian conspicuous consumption win over and transform dour Soviet womanhood. The penultimate song in *Silk Stockings,* which was Astaire's final MGM musical number in his final MGM musical film, is called "The Ritz Roll and Rock," and the lyrics proclaim that "rock and roll is dead and gone." Astaire performed it, of course, in top hat, white tie, and tails—even as on another sound stage at MGM Elvis Presley was gyrating and wailing away in a relatively low-budget black-and-white musical, *Jailhouse Rock* (also in CinemaScope). The latter film, aimed at a putatively smaller "youth audience," was much more profitable, the former's fair but lackluster performance becoming, literally and figuratively, one more sign of the impossibility of older established musical stars being able to reconcile the retrograde and the innovative in an increasingly fragmented industry and for an increasingly fragmented audience.

★★★★★ Gene Kelly: Man in Motion

The title of the 1946 *Theatre Arts* article in which Kelly acknowledges his debt to Fred Astaire is titled "Portrait of a Dancing Actor" (Isaacs), and it is a nice coincidence that about a decade earlier the same magazine ran a feature on Astaire whose title referred to him as an "actor-dancer." Similarities between Astaire and Kelly, as Hollywood stars, are clear enough—they both became famous, and remained so through the 1950s, as song-and-dance men in mostly big-budget musicals. At the same time, Kelly's star persona drew significantly on his *dis*similarity from Astaire, or, in fact, from any other type of male dancer. As *Theatre Arts* put it, "If you saw Gene Kelly walking down Broadway, you would not be likely to say, 'There goes a dancer.' With his Navy Lieutenant's cap thrust down on his head, his hands plunged deep into overcoat pockets, his walk tilted slightly forward, compact and purposeful, you might label him as a cop in civilian life, but not as a dancer" (Isaacs 149). Other articles about Kelly made much the same point; Kelly, unlike Astaire, was a "regular guy." The fan-magazine version of Kelly's life and career in the 1940s and 1950s describes him as falling into a performing career more or less through luck; his parents made him and his siblings learn to dance as children, and they performed professionally for a time. But in high school Kelly played football, baseball, ice hockey, and did gymnastics in addition to performing in school plays and talent shows; he liked to say that he did not know whether to pursue sports or dancing. He ended up with a college degree in economics and planned to be a lawyer; but he had also become a popular dance teacher in and around Pittsburgh, his hometown. In 1938, at the age of twenty-five, he decided to make a run on Broadway, and with virtually no missteps soon became a star in the title role of Rodgers and Hart's *Pal Joey* in 1940, after which Hollywood came calling and he signed a contract with MGM.

Kelly did not get to do much in his first films besides sing pleasantly and dance competently, and only when he was loaned to "poverty-row" studio Columbia in 1943 for *Cover Girl* was he allowed to experiment with the film medium in such a way that he could become a star not only as a male dancer but as an innovative "choreo-cinema-maker," as he was called by the end of the 1940s. "On the stage," Kelly told *Theatre Arts,* "I can walk around in rhythm for a minute or two doing nothing but grin at the audience . . . and they love it. . . . But on the screen that sort of thing leaves them cold" (Isaacs 153). To replace "the impact that sheer presence provides on the stage," Kelly would have to transmute his "natural" energy as a personality into the kinetic energy of dance movement, choreographic patterns, color, camerawork, and editing. How best to accomplish such a transmutation became the driving force behind Kelly's work through the rest of his career. And if Astaire's postwar musicals featured more tricks and special effects than had his earlier films, it was partly as a response to Kelly's fame as someone who was not interested in merely "executing a niftier buck-and-wing than the next one" (David Chandler, "Strictly from Hunger," *Photoplay,* February 1952, 55) but who was enjoined in a "battle between the dancer and the medium" (Isaacs 156).

Where Astaire's persona emphasized his modesty—false modesty, perhaps, but his relative absence from popular discourse does tend to create a persona defined by reserve rather than grandiosity—Kelly's star image is based, with very little variation, on energy, drive, and competitiveness. According to one writer in 1950, "There are those in Hollywood who describe Gene Kelly by saying, 'Everything the guy goes into, he expects to win, even if it's only a volleyball game in his back yard. He figures that fate is something you can shape the way you mold an aspic. On him, that kind of cockiness looks good, for most of the projects he pitches into with his dukes up seem to jell'" (Pete Martin, "The Fastest-Moving Star in Pictures," *Saturday Evening Post*, 8 July 1950, 24). And as Kelly proclaimed in 1952, "Movie-making is a true form of creative art, not just a money-making device. . . . We must produce the very best pictures that possibly can be made" (Jeanne Sakol, "Traveling Man," *Photoplay*, August 1952, 74). After the success of *On the Town* in 1949, and the tremendous response to *An American in Paris* in 1951 and *Singin' in the Rain* in 1952, Gene Kelly's reputation as a genius whose career had been "one success after another" seemed set.

Unlike Astaire, however, Kelly was intent not only on broadening the appeal and increasing the reputation of the musical but also on proving his versatility as an actor in nonmusical films. His first film of the 1950s, in fact, was the nonmusical *The Black Hand*, in which the Irish Kelly plays a curly-haired Italian mobster intent on avenging the death of his father; the film received little attention from the public or critics. Some five other of Kelly's fifties vehicles—*It's a Big Country* (1951), *Devil Makes Three* (1952), *Seagulls Over Sorrento/Crest of the Wave* (1954), *The Happy Road* (1957), and *Marjorie Morningstar* (1958)—were also mediocre straight films, as against his eight or so musicals. While Kelly was not a bad actor—he received his best reviews for his performance as the producer and older romantic interest of Natalie Wood in *Marjorie Morningstar*—his persona remained that of the brashly confident song-and-dance man. Kelly's "cockiness" had always bordered on narcissism; his sailor's pants were always tighter than anyone else's, his grin a little too self-consciously wide. And several critics had remarked on his propensity for performing saccharine and "charming" numbers with little old ladies, small children, or cartoon animals in his musicals, including *An American in Paris*; these numbers only supported the growing sense in U.S. culture that the musical was no longer an adult genre addressing adult concerns.

The problems that vexed Hollywood studios and their mode of working in the postwar era, the closeness and insularity of the Freed Unit notwithstanding, also affected the sorts of musical with which Gene Kelly was most associated in the 1950s. *Singin' in the Rain* was rapturously received by critics and audiences in 1952, but its "Broadway Ballet" was considered at the time to be less interesting and innovative than the "American in Paris Ballet" the year before. *Brigadoon* (1954), an adaptation of the Lerner and Loewe Broadway musical, represented Hollywood's increasing dependence on "pre-sold" properties and was meant to be made in Scotland. But MGM's

Ballet in loafers: Gene Kelly and Leslie Caron in a publicity photo for *An American in Paris* (Vincente Minnelli, MGM, 1957). Courtesy of Loew's Incorporated.

profitability was in marked decline, and in the end the entire film, exteriors included, was shot on a soundstage sporting fake heather and hills as well as a fake Scottish lass in the person of Cyd Charisse. *Brigadoon*'s disappointing returns, combined with those of *It's Always Fair Weather* the same year, had particularly demoralizing effects on Kelly,[2] and on one of Kelly's most ambitious and personal projects.

Before making *Brigadoon* and *It's Always Fair Weather*, Kelly had convinced MGM to allow him to make Hollywood's first "all-dance" film, *Invitation to the Dance*, in 1952, much of which *was* shot in Europe and which employed the talents of many of the best and most prestigious theatrical ballet dancers then working in the world. Kelly directed and choreographed the film as well, and performed—again, in one number animated by Hanna-Barbera, in a tight white sailor suit with a little boy and various cute animals—in some of the ballets. But rather than releasing the film upon its completion in 1954, MGM, worried about its reception in a world that seemed less and less interested in the expensive "prestige" musicals on which it had made its reputation, shelved it until 1956. The timing was unfortunate; Hollywood had not only changed but the art of dance, ballet specifically, had become more popular and better known across the United States by 1956. And it is ironic that Kelly himself had helped to popularize the formerly elite art in his early 1950s films especially (themselves made viable by the success of the British import *The Red Shoes* in 1948), so much so that it was the aesthetic failures of Kelly's choreography and dancing, their comparative conventionality and lack of stature, that doomed *Invitation to the Dance* upon its ultimate release.

Another feature Kelly had shared with Fred Astaire throughout the heyday of his Hollywood career was that of happily married husband and father. Virtually no popular article about Kelly does not refer to his devotion to his wife and young daughter. "Gene is so crazy about his family—his wife Betsy, his daughter Kerry—he talks about 'us' all the time, the way most actors talk about themselves. He's always thinking in terms of Betsy-Kerry-Gene" (David Chandler, "Strictly from Hunger," *Photoplay*, February 1952, 88). But in 1957 Kelly's wife, Betsy Blair, sued him for divorce, which attracted relatively little public attention in comparison to younger performers, like Presley, or more notorious womanizers, like Frank Sinatra, whose romantic exploits, real or imagined, made them more exciting sources of news. But it devastated Kelly, and his final MGM musical was *Les Girls* (1957), in which he played a playboy song-and-dance man. In it he is portly, a little tired, and stiff, his formerly light but pleasant singing voice now searching for keys that it seemed increasingly unable to find. By the end of the 1950s Kelly's reputation as the auteur of *An American in Paris* and *Singin' in the Rain* had earned him plaudits and fame in a genre in which he, like Astaire, could no longer really compete; and it was surely bittersweet that in 1962 the Museum of Modern Art, in a gesture guaranteed to make even the cockiest and most confident star feel old and passé, mounted a Gene Kelly dance film festival.

But it turned out that both Astaire and Kelly had a few tricks up their sleeves, and they involved the medium that Hollywood loved to loathe, television. Fred Astaire made two well-received hour-long variety specials at the end of the decade, "An Evening with Fred Astaire" (1958) and "Another Evening with Fred Astaire" (1959); both earned Emmy Awards and tremendous critical praise, and rumors circulated about a possible romantic relationship between Astaire and his new partner, Barrie Chase. Gene Kelly became a familiar face on television variety shows and specials, with one of his most influential and popular television efforts being an entry in the "Omnibus" series in 1958, "Dancing: A Man's Game," in which he worked very hard to make dance seem as masculine and athletic a form as professional sports. Once again, Kelly was referred to as a "gifted triple-threat man in films—dancer, director, actor" (Robert Lewis Shayon, "Shall We Dance?" *Saturday Review*, 16 May 1959, 61), and he continued directing films and Broadway shows for the next several years.

☆☆☆★★ Lucky Bing

As much as historians of the film musical have deified Fred Astaire and Gene Kelly, the fact remains that singing musical stars rather than dancing ones were always more popular with the public. And Bing Crosby was arguably the most popular singing star in Hollywood's history, the only star to be a top-ten box office attraction in the 1930s, the 1940s, and the 1950s, and the only one to be on the list for twelve years running—from 1943 to 1954. One encyclopedia of Hollywood stars maintains that "no one in the history of mankind has given so much pleasure to so many people as Bing Crosby, not even Chaplin" (Shipman 132). This "epitome of niceness," as the same writer puts it, was characterized throughout the 1940s in terms that are monotonous in their similarity: Harry Lillis Crosby, whose nicknames ranged from the Crooner to the Groaner to Der Bingle,[3] was born in 1903 (many accounts claim 1904) to parents of Irish descent and grew up in Spokane, Washington. He quit college to become part of a trio of singers (the Delta Rhythm Boys) in the 1920s and was discovered and put into his first film, *King of Jazz*, by Paul Whiteman in 1930, the same year that Crosby married film actress Dixie Lee, initially more famous than he was but who retired from the screen in order to raise their four sons. Crosby made an average of three pictures a year through the 1930s and 1940s, virtually always playing an easy-going guy with a slightly sardonic edge who appeared to be improvising at least some of his lines. He sang Irving Berlin's "White Christmas" for the first time in *Holiday Inn* (which also starred Fred Astaire) in 1942, and by 1945, when he won his Academy Award for playing a priest in *Going My Way* (1944), *Time* magazine reported that Crosby's voice "had been heard by more people than any voice in history" (since 1935, he had "averaged a new record every other week" ["World-Wide Groaner," *Time*, 26 March 1945, 88], with "White Christmas" becoming one of the best-selling songs of all time). What would eventually be seven "*Road to*" films with Bob Hope, beginning with *Road to Singapore* in 1940, turned Hope and Crosby into one of the most successful musical-comedy teams in film history.

Crosby's offscreen stardom seemed initially well aligned with the types of roles he played onscreen; "in person" he cultivated an image of lazy comfort and self-deprecation (his success was due to "luck"), loved practical jokes and wisecracking, had a hatred of "phoniness," and wore odd combinations of usually casual clothing whose bizarre hues he laid at his color-blindness. His hats were to cover his baldness, a baldness that, like Fred Astaire's, was rarely revealed in publicity photos. And finally, there are perpetual references in material about Crosby to his love of golf and the racetrack and his preference for staying at home over going out on the town; given his own way, the stories report, the happy-go-lucky Crosby, "the man nobody knows but who is everybody's best friend" ("Going His Way Is a Nation's Habit after Twenty Years of Crosby Song," *Newsweek*, 28 January 1946, 66), wouldn't care if he ever worked again.

In fact, Crosby, helped by his brothers, was a canny businessman who invested in everything from Minute Maid orange juice to oil fields to toy dogs. In 1953, when he published his "as told to" autobiography, *Lucky Bing* (which was serialized in the *Saturday Evening Post* as well), *Newsweek* noted that Crosby "was always the average, the representative, or the ideal figure, the average boy of an average family in Spokane, Wash., and now the average millionaire, or the average great success in show business. . . . Crosby pictures himself as a strictly representative figure. . . . In view of his movie career . . . Crosby could hardly be called an average movie star. But he does seem the 'average' lucky American among the legendary and exotic figures of the entertainment business" ("Lucky Bing," *Newsweek*, 29 June 1953, 92–93). In 1950, however, *Photoplay* published a story by Bob Thomas called "The Crosby Myth" that aimed to "explode a few truths about Bing," and it is apparent that Crosby's enormous wealth and box office clout had by then turned "the crooner" into something inspiring resentment and jealousy as much as affection. What had once appeared to be Crosby's unassailable popularity was also made an easier target by the comparative failure of *A Connecticut Yankee in King Arthur's Court* in 1949 (for the first time

in five years Crosby was not the top box-office star in the nation—Bob
Hope was). "Bing Crosby is not an American legend put together by a string
of radio and movie writers. He's a mature citizen," Thomas writes. "But
because he does not act according to [the characters he plays], people are
disappointed, disillusioned and angry" (*Photoplay*, June 1950, 95). In the
1950s, Crosby is still "shy," but also "sullen" and characterized by "a chilling stare that is a masterpiece," an arrogance that often pained his friends
(Crosby refused to show up at a testimonial dinner for Bob Hope, which
"genuinely hurt" him and "marked a break" in their "fabulous friendship"
[95]), and a disdain for the press, especially photographers, because they
took up too much of his "valuable time." Although the article praises
Crosby's donations to charities, his love for singing, and his devotion to his
family, it is clear that he had become an institution whose multi-media success and power were increasingly difficult to reconcile with an image based
on ordinariness, being a regular guy, and wanting "to live as normal a life
as he can."

If the 1940s had been Crosby's heyday, the 1950s could best be
described as uneven. His popularity rebounded after *A Connecticut Yankee* in
a successful Frank Capra racetrack remake aptly titled *Riding High*. Although not a musical, it included, like many if not all of Crosby's "straight"
films, a couple of songs that Crosby could also record and which were
played on the radio. But *Mr. Music* (also 1950), an apparently appropriate
title that Crosby reportedly disliked (Shipman 135), was disappointing to
fans and critics, and Crosby slipped further in the box office rankings. But
the next few films were all quite popular: *Here Comes the Groom* (1951) and
Just for You (1952), both musicals with Jane Wyman; *Road to Bali* (1952), the
first color film with Hope and perennial "love interest" Dorothy Lamour,
but which "more than one critic pointed out [was] rather like two indul-
gent uncles and an aunt dressed up for a children's party" (Shipman 135);
Little Boy Lost (1952), a nonmusical in which Crosby nevertheless sang four
songs; *White Christmas* (1954), a hugely successful remake of *Holiday Inn*
(and the first film released in VistaVision) with Danny Kaye, Rosemary
Clooney, and Vera-Ellen; *The Country Girl* (1955), in which he convincingly
and affectingly played a broken-down musical star opposite Grace Kelly in
a nonmusical film (Kelly won an Academy Award); the Cole Porter musical
High Society (1956), another successful remake, this time of *The Philadelphia
Story*, but one in which most of the plaudits went to his co-stars Frank Sinatra, Grace Kelly, and Louis Armstrong; and another nonmusical, *Say One for
Me* (1959), in which he again played a priest and sang a few songs. There
were several unbilled guest appearances in the decade as well—in *The Great-*

est Show on Earth and Hope's *Son of Paleface* (both 1952), Dean Martin and Jerry Lewis's *Scared Stiff* (1953), and *Alias Jesse James* (1959).

By mid-decade, most publicity stories about Crosby referred to how rich he was and the fact that, in middle age, he was "unique among ranking American entertainers in that he feels no strong compulsion to keep his name in lights. He is, as everyone knows, a wealthy man" ("With $15,000,000, Bing Wants to Bow Out Slowly," *Newsweek,* 4 January 1954, 40). Although he was still making records, films, and a television special here and there, he seemed to be shifting gears toward a "gradual retirement." Events in Crosby's personal life also changed his offscreen image over the course of the decade; his wife Dixie Lee died in 1952, and although Crosby's genial image depended strongly on the notion of a happy marriage and family, public spats had begun to generate rumors of marital discord before his wife's death. In one article, Crosby is named "a catch, possibly the biggest marital catch in the business," but he is also referred to as seeming old, tired, both "in search of the old Bing" and "looking for a future" (James Hunt, "Bing Walks Alone," *Photoplay,* February 1954, 48–49, 84). Toward the end of the decade, part of Crosby's "future" developed from his own sheer longevity in the entertainment business; he was frequently asked for his opinions about other performers, whether they were going to last as he had, and how his own work compared to theirs. Crosby was asked about rock 'n' roll ("It's really a new name for an old musical medium"), Elvis Presley ("Elvis is a phenomenon. He's a good-looking kid, he sings in tune and he's got good rhythm. He'll outgrow his grinds and bumps in time"), Pat Boone ("He's different from Elvis; his pelvis doesn't jerk, no sideburns, but he can pump out rock and roll"), and Frank Sinatra ("Frank's still a tremendous attraction in pictures, and . . . when he begins his own television show, in my opinion he'll qualify for the title of the world's greatest entertainer") (Pete Martin, "I Call on Bing Crosby," *Saturday Evening Post,* 11 May 1957, 39, 119–20). Crosby himself claimed that he was "not singing as well as [he] used to," and that his "recording days [were] about over, except for albums and old standards" ("Bing Crosby's in It," *Newsweek,* 8 July 1957, 89).

The big disruption in Crosby's smooth transition to "retirement" was his marriage in 1957 to Kathryn Grant, an "ambitious starlet" some thirty years his junior, and the increasing notoriety of his four mostly adult sons. The two events were continually linked: as a May 1959 article put it, "Old family friends say that relations between Bing and the boys really changed when Crosby married Kathy Grant. 'That made the break definite. Before that the boys had lost Dixie but they still had Bing'" (Leonard Slater, "Crisis for the Crosbys: What's Bothering Bing's Boys," *McCall's,* 112). The Crosbys had been "an American family," the subjects of "deep and far-reaching affection." The "public portrait" of Crosby himself "was invariably a candid pose of a pleasant, easy-sauntering man who divided his time among singing, acting, occasionally exchanging witticisms with Bob Hope, and being a homebody" (110). But at the end of the decade, the "Crosby family portrait" had gone "askew," the four sons often appearing "regularly and unflatteringly" on front pages and in gossip columns. "What's bothering them is perhaps a name—the name of Crosby—a household name that they are expected to live up to in a manner not always lived up to by the man who gave it to them. In his new, if not publicly popular, marriage, Bing Crosby can offer a revised portrait of himself" (113). And, the article concludes, there is "a huge audience that would dearly love to love all the Crosbys all over again" (113). As is probably well known by anyone who saw one of Crosby's latter-day Christmas specials featuring the three children he had with Grant, or their commercials for Minute Maid orange juice, the Old Groaner never did truly "bow out," and U.S. audiences did come to love "all the Crosbys" again; it was unfortunate for "Bing's boys" that "the Crosbys" came to mean not them and their father but the new, and newly promising, family constructed by his marriage to Grant.

★★★★★ Frank Sinatra: The Boy Comes of Age

In 1950, *Time* magazine reported that "Frankie Sinatra" had been a celebrity for "some seven years" and pondered his effect on the young female "bobby-soxers" who were known as his most ardent fans. It was not Sinatra's voice, the writer concluded, that made "young ladies . . . swoon in ecstasy, and . . . maturer matrons gurgle with protective delight," but his smile—the "shy, deprecating smile with the quiver at the corner of the mouth." Under Sinatra's "crashing self-assertion," the article continued, was still "only a child, frightened and whimpering in the dark" (*Time*, 31 July 1950, 47). The next year, journalist Lee Mortimer, whom Sinatra had punched in public after Mortimer called him a "Dago son of a bitch" (Hendler 50), wrote a notorious article in which he linked Sinatra's career in "night clubs and other branches of the amusement industry" in the 1940s both to communists and the "underworld" of the mob ("Frank Sinatra Confidential: Gangsters in the Night Clubs," *American Mercury*, August 1951, 29–36). Rather than being a result of either Sinatra's smile or voice, Mortimer claims the success of the "swaggering, flashy kid" was due largely, if not entirely, to "gangster wirepulling behind the scenes" (32). That such claims were taken seriously, with few rushing publicly to Sinatra's defense,

Frank Sinatra and Bing Crosby performing "Well, Did You Evah [What a Swell Party This Is]" in *High Society* (Charlie Walters, MGM, 1956). Courtesy of Loew's Incorporated.

suggests the extent to which Sinatra, in contrast to Astaire, Kelly, and even Crosby, was no longer seen as a valuable property in the new decade. Sinatra's career, whether in nightclubs, on radio, in the recording industry, or as a movie star, had apparently come and gone, with 1946 "the zenith," as several writers put it. While of course this turned out not to be true (in 1957 Bing Crosby claimed in *Newsweek* that Sinatra, along with Nat King

Cole, was "going on forever" [8 July 1957, 89]), it is remarkable how many accounts of Sinatra's career during the decade are posed as narratives of professional and—equally important—personal comeback.

Indeed, it is difficult to separate accounts of Sinatra's first 1950s professional decline from his 1951 divorce from wife Nancy, to whom he had been married since 1939. The family life of "Frankie and Nancy" and their three children had helped to stabilize Sinatra's image as both the "crooning idol of America's bobby-soxers" during the war years and the representation of what many suggested was a necessarily deferred desire for such a family—with a sexualized but comparatively docile male at its head—among his female fans. Sinatra's nicknames included Frankie Boy, Croonatra, the King of Swoon, and the Voice, and he often played roles in his 1940s films—for example in *On the Town*—that made his physical scrawniness combined with the deep and deeply soothing baritone voice into the object of sometimes hysterical female desire. It was not just that Sinatra, a professed Catholic of Italian ancestry from Hoboken, New Jersey, divorced his devoted wife, the wife who had supported him through his rise from singing waiter to big-band singer to idol of the "Sinatra fainters" to movie star; but that the divorce was caused partly by Sinatra's much-publicized affair with Ava Gardner, whom he married the same year.

"Almost any movie-goer can tell you," stated one journalist, "that Sinatra had become a virtual has-been" by 1952; Sinatra "completely revitalized his career recently by playing tough little Private Maggio in the motion picture *From Here to Eternity*. . . . And its success was like money from home to a Sinatra whose name was still in the papers only because of his volcanic marital disturbances" (Evelyn Wells, "The Rise and Fall and Rise Again of Frank Sinatra," *Good Housekeeping*, August 1954, 56). In *Eternity* (1953) the Italian American Maggio—whom screenwriter Daniel Taradash claimed "looked so thin and woeful and so pitifully small" (Hendler 52)—is beaten to death, and, as Mitch Miller put it, it was as if Sinatra "by getting stomped to death in that movie . . . did a public penance. . . . You can chart it. From the day that movie came out, his records began to sell" (qtd. in Hendler 237n11). Sinatra also won the Academy Award for Best Supporting Actor, which helped to rejuvenate his film career as well.

By the mid-1950s, then, Sinatra was "back," his image that of a reckless and once ungrateful but now chastened star whose attempts to reconcile with both his wife and Ava Gardner—their public battles and breakups and reconciliations had become legendary—as well as his vigorous assumption of the role of responsible father helped lay "Frankie Boy" and his "quivering smile" to rest. "The Boy Comes of Age," as *Tempo* put it (12 July 1954);

and now, "although his marriage to Ava has ended [they would not divorce until 1957], Sinatra has taken his rightful place among the giants of the entertainment field. He knows where he is going and he knows what he wants. In fact, the string-bowed juvenile with the peg pants and multi-colored socks has suddenly become a man . . . and his fans love it" (30). From being strictly a musical star Sinatra, like Crosby, was now a respected actor; and, like Crosby, throughout the decade Sinatra alternated musicals, or films in which he sang a few songs, with straight dramatic films. In the first category were *Double Dynamite* and *Meet Danny Wilson* (both 1951), *Young at Heart* (1954, with Doris Day), *Guys and Dolls* (1955, a film he felt miscast in; he should have played not Nathan Detroit but Sky Masterson), *The Tender Trap* (1955, singing the title song only), *High Society* (1956, in which Crosby's character calls him "one of the newer fellas" as they sing "Well, Did You Evah [What a Swell Party This Is]" together), *The Joker Is Wild* (1957), *Pal Joey* (1957, in Gene Kelly's original role and in which the "older woman," Rita Hayworth, was in fact two years Sinatra's junior), and *A Hole in the Head* (1959). In the latter category were *From Here to Eternity* and also *Suddenly* (1954), *Not as a Stranger* (1955), *The Man with the Golden Arm* (1955, Otto Preminger's then-daring film about heroin addiction), *Johnny Concho* (1956), *The Pride and the Passion* (1957), *Kings Go Forth* (1958), *Some Came Running* (1958, based on another novel by James Jones, who had written *From Here to Eternity*), and *Never So Few* (1959). And again like Crosby, Sinatra showed up in cameos or guest spots in any number of other films, among them *Around the World in 80 Days* (1956) and *Meet Me in Las Vegas* (1956), a Cyd Charisse–Dan Dailey musical. Although never the number-one star in the country, Sinatra appeared in top-ten lists from 1956 to 1960 (returning for one last time in 1962).

Where Sinatra differed from Crosby was in remaining a free agent as a film actor and never signing another long-term studio contract; in more fully embracing television, appearing regularly in specials and in his own series ("The Frank Sinatra Show" ran for twelve episodes in 1957 and 1958); and in becoming, or returning to being, a staple headliner in night-clubs and other live performance venues, especially Las Vegas. Capitol Records had put Sinatra under contract in 1952 and helped him to produce a regular string of hit singles and albums through the following decade. Again, in the mid-1950s several articles were glowing in their praise of Sinatra's talent and his newly humble attitude. In one, Sinatra is quoted as saying, "I guess in the old days I hurt a few people . . . I don't suppose it helps to say I didn't mean to" (Lou Larkin, "Frankie, You've Changed," *Motion Picture*, August 1955, 61). But the honeymoon did not last long; and as Sinatra's power and authority as an entertainer who could write his own ticket increased, so did the attention paid to his tempestuous romances, his frequent tantrums, and his feuds—with stars like Marlon Brando on the set of *Guys and Dolls*, but especially with the press.

It is hard to judge how much of the moody, defensive, impatient, ungrateful, and pugnacious Sinatra portrayed in press accounts in the latter half of the decade is itself a result of his antagonistic relationship with all but a few of the journalists who wrote about him.[4] Many of the articles contain familiar versions of Sinatra's life story before they turn to considering whether he is ever going to stop being in or causing trouble, and Sinatra, unlike Astaire, Kelly, and even Crosby, also became a favorite subject of newly influential tabloids such as *Confidential, Inside Story*, and *On the QT*. Some regular fan magazines, like *Photoplay*, that were still part of Hollywood's publicity machinery kept working doggedly to turn Sinatra into someone who "has found himself at last. He is more mature, more calculated about his career, less hot-headed, and less prodigal in expending his emotions and money" (Adela Rogers St. Johns, "The Nine Lives of Frank Sinatra," *Photoplay*, May 1956, 89, which also advertises the forthcoming *High Society*). But generally, Sinatra's offscreen image became one defined almost exclusively by "Talent, Tantrums and Torment," to employ the title of the first part of *Look*'s 1957 three-part "life story of Frank Sinatra" (the other parts were called "Why Frank Sinatra Hates the Press" and "Blondes, Brunettes and the Blues" [Bill Davidson, "The Life Story of Frank Sinatra," *Look*, 14 May 1957, 28 May 1957, and 11 June 1957). Other titles are also suggestive: "God's Angry Man," *Movie Secret* (August 1956), "Frank Sinatra: The Man Nobody Knows," *Photoplay* (November 1957), "Frank Sinatra: Hollywood's No. 1 Problem Child," *Inside Story* (December 1957 ["Sinatra's terrible tantrums have studio bosses tearing their hair—and wishing they could tear his!"]). A long story in *Good Housekeeping* is called "The Enigma of Frank Sinatra" (Richard Gehman, July 1960, 58–60, 179–84), and while the conjunction of Sinatra and *Good Housekeeping* may seem strange, the fact was that despite the tantrums and the bad press he had become arguably the most powerful star in the United States, if not the world.

As *Good Housekeeping* reported, "Sinatra's power is not merely personal; it is also fiscal. Because he is ranked high among the top-drawing film attractions, he can demand a share in the production of the film from all major studios that ask for his services—and practically all of them are constantly asking for his services. . . . What all of this means to you is that Francis Albert Sinatra exercises a most powerful control over much of what you enjoy (or don't enjoy) in films, on television, on records, on the radio, in nightclubs—indeed, in every medium of entertainment except newspapers and magazines. To Sinatra's apparently intense disgust, there is very little he can do about controlling the press" (179–80). Moreover, *Good Housekeeping* was disturbed by Sinatra's "vast and growing personal power," which it felt "should be a cause of concern to all who watch and listen to popular records, radio and television shows, movies, and nightclub acts"; it would be bad enough, the article concludes, if such "enormous power were in the hands of a completely stable and predictable human being. When it is in the hands of a man torn by emotions that he apparently either cannot or does not care to control, it is something to view with alarm" (184).

Given his longevity as a popular icon since the 1950s, it is easy to agree with Bing Crosby's characterization of Frank Sinatra in 1957 as "the world's greatest entertainer"—a characterization that would seem less suitably to apply to Crosby himself, despite Crosby's equivalent, if not superior, popularity as a movie star and recording artist in the 1940s and 1950s, and his ubiquity on television and as a holiday icon in subsequent decades.[5] And regardless of Sinatra's personal demons and depressions, in the end I find his image less elegiac or melancholic than those of Astaire, Kelly, and even Crosby. Perhaps it is that time always seems more predatory in the case of dancers and their bodies, even dancers who keep on dancing with women half (or a third) their age. Or it may be that it is almost impossible to imagine a place in commercial cinema for an Astaire or a Kelly today. But it could also simply be that Sinatra's rashness and pugnaciousness, if not his talent, make him similar to so many who came after him or who themselves became representative icons of 1950s masculinity—Brando and James Dean as well as Elvis Presley and his ilk.

In his study of stars and masculinity in the 1950s, Steven Cohan found it "easy enough to bracket off" discussion of the era's song-and-dance men, because despite the "open acknowledgment in musicals that masculinity and femininity are equally performative," this performativity and/as spectacle turns out to be a "fundamental insight" of the Hollywood star system in general (Cohan, *Masked Men* xvi). But, for male as well as female musical stars of the era, it was Hollywood itself, and the musical genre that had once sustained it, that increasingly became "bracketed off" from new, or at least newly powerful, regimes of professional entertainment. Astaire, Kelly, and Crosby retained a nostalgic appeal through the ends of their lives, respected and respectable but no longer particularly relevant except as representatives of the extraordinary in a less complicated and more utopian past.[6] Sinatra's talent made him extraordinary, too; but his ultimate legacy may be that, finally, the talent came to attract less attention than the tantrums, the power, the bad behavior, and the headlines, a situation that, for better or worse, is with us still.

NOTES

1. The polls I use here were published annually in the *International Motion Picture Almanac* (New York: Quigley Publications), and have been reprinted online at http://reelclassics .com/Articles/General/quigleytop10-article.htm.

2. The biggest disappointment of Kelly's career was MGM's refusal to allow him to play Sky Masterson in *Guys and Dolls* for Samuel Goldwyn. "A part like Sky comes along once or twice in a lifetime," Kelly said. "It happened to me with *Pal Joey*, and miracle of miracles, Goldwyn was about to make it happen a second time. I was born to play Sky the way Gable was born to play Rhett Butler. But the bastards at MGM refused to loan me out" (Hirschhorn 245).

3. The name "Bing" came from his childhood fondness for a comic strip called "The Bingville Bugle."

4. One cannot discount Sinatra's well-known stance against racism of all kinds, which was folded by some journalists into his reputation as a "troublemaker." As Jane Hendler writes, Sinatra had "made a number of public appearances on the subject. Even his damaging altercation with Lee Mortimer, which thanks to Hearst newspapers threatened to discredit Sinatra further by implicating him in both left-wing and Mob activities and rehashing his 4-F status during the war, produced an alternative reading. Another paper claimed that Sinatra's aggressive response to being called a 'dago' 'must have warmed the hearts of millions' by purportedly striking a blow against 'race prejudice'" (qtd. in Hendler 44).

5. In recent years, Sinatra's "Rat Pack" has become newly famous thanks to publicity surrounding George Clooney's and Steven Soderbergh's remakes of Sinatra's 1960 film *Ocean's 11*. Sinatra's entourage was also referred to at the time as "The Clan," and, to quote *Good Housekeeping* again, "when the members of the Clan who are performers—Dean Martin, Sammy Davis Jr., Peter Lawford, and Joey Bishop—get together with Sinatra for a public appearance, they reverently call him 'The Leader,' and he speaks of the gathering as 'The Summit Meeting.' This is a joke, but at bottom it is not; it is kidding on the square" (Gehman 60).

6. Astaire died in 1987, Kelly in 1996, Crosby in 1977 (after a round of golf), and Sinatra in 1998.

In the Wings

R. BARTON PALMER

What was the heritage of 1950s cinema, especially in terms of the long-established institution of star performers, in the next decade? To understand what (and who) was waiting in the wings as the 1950s drew to a close, it is useful to begin by recalling some points about postwar Hollywood made throughout this book.

The 1950s was a period of rapid change for Hollywood's filmmakers, as the model of vertical integration that had sustained the business for more than three decades was gradually dismantled following a series of Supreme Court consent decrees that forced the studios to divest themselves of their first-run theatrical holdings. Though rapidly declining, movie attendance remained high enough to make it possible for many to continue to find steady employment in the industry, as the individual case histories in this volume eloquently establish. But increased uncertainty was the lot for all in Hollywood, both those in the creative end of the business and technicians of various kinds. By the end of the 1950s, stars were for the most part no longer studio employees, but rather individual contractors. The last actor to enjoy the benefits (and suffer from the restraints) of an exclusive studio contract was Sandra Dee, who signed with Universal in 1957 as a teenager. Hollywood has since suffered through, and successfully adapted to, no other change of such magnitude. By the end of the 1960s, the traditional studio system had disappeared, to be replaced by the assimilation of these once-independent players into larger, increasingly diverse corporate entities. But by the end of the 1960s, the system had disappeared that, if not bringing them into being, had allowed stars to be constructed and to flourish. Stars continued to be important as the building blocks of the attraction that films must exhibit in order to be successful in the marketplace.

After the 1950s, the studio star system lived on, with many of the stars who had been groomed in the previous two or three decades continuing to play an important role within the industry as major box-office attractions. A number of the well-established stars discussed in these pages continued to be prominent and bankable featured performers in the next decade. Consider

246 R. BARTON PALMER

Jimmy Stewart. As we have seen here, Stewart remade his career in the 1950s while not abandoning his earlier screen persona as a virtuous man of the people, the living exemplar of small-town values. He did this largely through branching out into what was for him a new genre (the western) and exploring collaboration with premier directors he had never (or hardly) worked with before (Anthony Mann, Alfred Hitchcock), who each interestingly drew at times on the darker aspect of his all-American image. In the 1960s, Stewart built further on these new career directions by concentrating on the western and making three films with the acknowledged master of the genre, John Ford (*Two Rode Together* [1961], *The Man Who Shot Liberty Valance* [1962], *Cheyenne Autumn* [1964, in a brief supporting role]), and two others with an emerging western specialist, fresh from success in series television: Andrew V. McLaglen (*Shenandoah* [1965] and *Bandolero!* [1968]). Produced under the package-unit system, these films were financed, made, and released in a fashion somewhat different from those of the studio era. But Stewart's role in them, as both protagonist and box office attraction, is thoroughly traditional.

It is true that, because of the shift to package-unit production and the particular nature of U.S. income tax laws, a number of stars incorporated as individuals, thus becoming in effect the producers of their own films. In the landmark film *To Kill a Mockingbird* (1962), for example, Gregory Peck not only signed on to play the main character, Atticus Finch, but also invested significantly in the project through his company Brentwood Productions. He was rewarded with significant control over the film's final cut. Other stars in the 1960s achieved a power over how their images and performances were circulated that harkened back to the freedom enjoyed by star/filmmakers of the pre-studio era such as Charlie Chaplin and Douglas Fairbanks. At the same time, the decline in the number of films issuing from Hollywood, as well as the volatility of employment brought on by the package-unit system, made it more difficult for performers to build toward star status or to succumb to such a process of construction as engineered by directors, studio heads, and agents. With its roots in the 1950s, this career trend accelerated in the 1960s. But it is also true that there were a significant number of actors who, getting a start in filmmaking during the 1950s (even coming over from television to do so), managed to become bona fide stars during the following decade.

The road to stardom in the 1960s, however, was made more difficult by a substantial change in Hollywood's conception of its product, which made stars increasingly less essential than they had been in previous decades. Joan Hawkins usefully traces the emergence of a new consumption aesthetic in the period, a growing interest on the part of filmgoers in "the ability of a film to thrill, frighten, gross out, arouse, or otherwise directly engage the spectator's body" (4). Films catering to these alternative tastes, as Hawkins suggests, might belong to a number of different genres, from "B" horror productions to French New Wave releases such as Jean-Luc Godard's *Alphaville* (1965). Historian Paul Monaco agrees with Hawkins that a central development during the 1960s was the emergence of a "cinema of sensation." This new film type, he suggests, was inaugurated by Alfred Hitchcock's *Psycho* (1960). Anticipated by Hollywood's concern during the 1950s with offering viewers an experience different from what they could enjoy on their small black-and-white televisions, the cinema of sensation, as Monaco suggests, would eventually come to be defined essentially by "speeded-up pacing," "the sweep of color production," and "an increased reliance on graphic visual and sound effects" (190). The cinema of sensation would replace (or at least reduce substantially in prominence) the cinema of sentiment, Hollywood's traditional approach to engaging its customers, in which emotions are aroused and satisfied by compelling narrative, sympathetic characters, and the prominence of charismatic, culturally evocative stars.

But the sensational film is innovative, Monaco contends, in more than its abandonment of classic visual style and its embrace of medium-specific wizardry. Such a change in concept transforms the role of characters and, by implication, that of stars as well. *Psycho* exemplifies this new approach to audience appeal, for it "breaks entirely from the demands of classical Hollywood film that placed a primacy on the narrative. It also bypassed the conventions of scripting characters as opposing forces that guided the viewer toward clearly empathizing with one of them" (190). What the sensational film offers instead is carefully orchestrated affect, groundbreaking in its depth and complexity. In arousing, organizing, and satisfying audience sympathies, the star, as both character and familiar persona, had long been thought crucial. In its place, Hitchcock offers the shocking violence of the unanticipated shower stabbing scene at the hands of an only barely glimpsed monstrous presence, a creepy anatomizing of the discontents of voyeurism, an insoluble enigma of gender and sexual desire, and the convention-breaking failure of the therapeutic and legal establishments to explain away psychopathic motive and energy. In a gesture that can be read as a dismissal of the necessity of the star system (a system that, ironically enough, had sustained his immensely successful period of filmmaking in the 1950s), Hitchcock eliminates his one well-known performer (Janet Leigh) before the halfway point of the film, allowing his careful manipulation of suspense, image, and theme to carry the remainder of the picture. With this daring and provocative move was born, according to Monaco, "the dominant motion-picture aesthetic of the late twentieth-century" (190). *Psycho* in fact seems to invite a reading that emphasizes its embodiment of the industry's move away from a star-based production strategy, with Hitchcock (callously? confidently?) throwing away his single established star to focus on a lesser known and unconventional rising performer (Anthony Perkins).

This emerging aesthetic eventually manifested itself during the 1970s in what Justin Wyatt has termed "high concept" filmmaking, whose "style is based upon two components: a simplification of character and narrative, and a strong match between image and soundtrack throughout the film" (16). And thus one of "the most striking results" of high-concept filmmaking is "a weakening of identification with character and narrative," as, "in place of this identification with narrative, the viewer becomes sewn into the 'surface' of the film, contemplating the style of the narrative and the production" (60). This surface, to be sure, does not necessarily obviate the presence of the star, who may well constitute one (but only one!) of the multifarious "channels" that create a surface "excess." As Wyatt suggests, moreover, high-concept films usually depend upon the "linkage of a star's persona with a concept," a simplifying transformation that turns the performer into little more than one of the film's marketing hooks (10).

Wyatt's earliest examples of high-concept films are drawn from later 1970s releases, including, most notably, *Jaws* (1975), *King Kong* (1976), *Star Wars* (1977), and *Saturday Night Fever* (1977), all extremely popular films that, although in some cases not lacking for name performers, do not feature established stars who were expected to be a focus of viewer interest and pleasure. But a number of successful 1960s productions fit into this same category, especially the so-called "youth films" of the last years of the decade: *The Graduate* (1967) and *Easy Rider* (1969), as well as *Midnight Cowboy* (1969), all three of which were marketed as taboo-breaking in terms of their engagement with the discontents of the sexual life. Similarly, *The Wild Bunch* (1969) features a number of aging stars (preeminently Ernest Borgnine, William Holden, and Robert Ryan), whose presence aptly reinforces the film's thematizing of the "closing of the frontier." Here are stars linked, as Wyatt suggests, with a single concept, no longer appearing as presences interesting in and of themselves. In any event, the marketing of this film foregrounded its radical revision of the ways in which Hollywood had traditionally represented violence. Also high concept in a somewhat different sense were productions that emphasized the appeal of their narrative and spectacle, using a number of well-known or star performers as part of an ensemble (*The Longest Day* [1962] and *The Great Escape* [1963]). Such films continue a trend toward gigantism of different kinds (including the mass concentration of star appeal) that was already well exemplified in the 1950s (notably in the decade's "epic" productions, including *The Greatest Show on Earth* [1952], *The Ten Commandments* [1956], and *Around the World in 80 Days* [1956]).

It must be noted, however, that in contemporary Hollywood the high-concept film (with minimal or no reliance on star presence in the classical sense) contrasts with more traditional releases in which narrative, character, and thus stars continue to offer one of the most important sources of viewer pleasure. This was also true of the 1960s, and so, even if the tried and true methods for developing stars had largely disappeared, there was a continuing demand for new stars to replace those of the previous three decades who were either retiring or moving into character roles. Old Hollywood, however, hardly disappeared overnight, with a good number of major studio performers of the 1940s enjoying an often amazing professional longevity. Among actors, Ernest Borgnine, Lee J. Cobb, Cary Grant, Henry Fonda, Clark Gable, Van Heflin, Ray Milland, Edmond O'Brien, Walter Pidgeon, Anthony Quinn, Spencer Tracy, Van Johnson, and John Wayne remained bankable headliners during the closing years of the studio era in the late 1960s. Others, including such luminaries as Claudette Colbert, Dick Powell, Ronald Reagan, and Loretta Young, turned increasingly to the small screen in order to find work.

Conversely, a number of actors who enjoyed only limited success in the 1950s rose to prominence in the 1960s, sometimes by modifying their approach in accordance with changing trends in the industry and taking their careers in radically different directions. First a success as a musical performer, and then as a gritty character actor (*From Here to Eternity* [1953], *The Man with the Golden Arm* [1955]), Frank Sinatra surprisingly became one of the 1960s' most bankable action heroes, especially in war (*Von Ryan's Express* [1965]) and detective (*Tony Rome* [1967]) films. Skilled supporting performer Rod Steiger (*The Harder They Fall* [1956], *Cry Terror!* [1958]) became a featured lead of amazing versatility, with acclaimed roles as diverse as those of a Holocaust survivor (*The Pawnbroker* [1964]), a redneck sheriff (*In the Heat of the Night* [1967]), and a serial killer of many disguises (*No Way to Treat a Lady* [1968]). Similarly, Tony Curtis, who began the 1950s mired in bit parts suited to his pretty-boy looks yet soon showed himself to be a capable performer in costume epics (*The Black Shield of Falworth* [1954], *The Vikings* [1958]), message pictures (*Sweet Smell of Success* [1957], *The Defiant Ones* [1958]), and comedy (*Some Like it Hot* and *Operation Petticoat* [both

1959]), would continue to develop his range in the 1960s, eventually delivering a startling performance as a serial killer in *The Boston Strangler* (1968).

In the 1960s, Hollywood proved, as Paul Monaco understates, "more agreeable" to male actors. This palpable masculinization of the Hollywood cinema meant that featured roles for women grew increasingly scarce, as, in a perhaps surprising development, one of the most financially and critically successful films of the period was what came to be called a "buddy picture." In *Butch Cassidy and the Sundance Kid* (1969), Robert Redford and Paul Newman are the "couple," with Katharine Ross playing a secondary role whose main purpose seems to be to establish the heterosexual bona fides of the desperado duo. Many of Hollywood's most bankable female stars had by the early 1960s switched, because of increasing age, to character roles (Joan Crawford, Bette Davis), lost prominence because their physical type or their favored genre lost popularity (Cyd Charisse, Janet Leigh, Kim Novak, and Gene Tierney), or left the business through marriage, death, disappointment, or the opportunity to work more steadily on television (Joan Bennett, Grace Kelly, Judy Holliday, Jayne Mansfield, and Marilyn Monroe).

Some prominent young actresses of the 1950s found suitable roles harder to come by in the next decade. Despite some success in featured parts (in *Exodus* [1960], *36 Hours* [1965], and *Grand Prix* [1966]), Eva Marie Saint was never given the opportunity to fulfill the immense promise she had shown in *On the Waterfront* (1954) and *North by Northwest* (1959). The industry's failure to take full advantage of the female talent developed during the 1950s is perhaps most obvious in the case of Joanne Woodward, who during the following decade was given little opportunity to repeat the kind of bravura performance she delivers as three different personalities uneasily resident in the same woman in *The Three Faces of Eve* (1957). Typically, in *The Fugitive Kind* (1960), Woodward is reduced to playing a two-dimensional stereotype, a promiscuous playgirl who briefly appeals to Marlon Brando before he discovers Anna Magnani. There were notable exceptions, of course, to this disappointing general development for talented actresses. Both Natalie Wood and Elizabeth Taylor successfully made the transition from child and then ingénue roles to more serious character portrayals. In *Who's Afraid of Virginia Woolf?* (1966), Taylor delivers what is arguably the most nuanced and powerful female performance of the decade, while Wood's portrayal of adolescent angst and sexual hysteria in *Splendor in the Grass* (1961) is as impressively affecting as that of more frequently praised Method-trained male actors in the era.

As noted in the introduction, during the postwar era the conventional leading man, equally adept in dramatic or comic roles but not suited for physically demanding parts, continued to be required by the industry. In fact, one of the actors to emerge from secondary roles to prominence during the 1960s, Jack Lemmon, certainly fits this traditional type and appeared in some of the decade's most notable comedies and dramas, especially for director Billy Wilder, arguably postwar Hollywood's most talented portraitist of manners: *The Apartment* (1960), *How to Murder Your Wife* (1965), *The Fortune Cookie* (1966), and, most famously, *The Odd Couple* (1968). William Holden was another, emerging from mostly light dramatic parts in the 1940s to play conventionally handsome romantic leads on into middle age in the late 1960s and early 1970s. More versatile than Lemmon (who was suited only to "parlor" genres), Holden could hold his own in drawing room comedy (*Sabrina* [1954]), but was equally at home playing cynical outsiders (*Stalag 17* [1953], *The Wild Bunch* [1969]), objects of sizzling female desire (*Picnic* and *Love Is a Many-Splendored Thing* [both 1955], *The World of Suzie Wong* [1960], *Paris—When It Sizzles* [1964]), and edgy action heroes (*The Bridges at Toko-Ri* [1954], *Bridge on the River Kwai* [1957], *The Horse Soldiers* [1959], *The Devil's Brigade* [1969]).

Holden's beefy good looks point toward an emerging type of the era. During the 1950s, the conventions delineating the ideal leading man began to shift decisively, as the action and dramatic films of the period required more physical, more energetic performers who were not conventionally fine-featured (Kirk Douglas, Charlton Heston, Burt Lancaster, and Robert Mitchum chief among them). All these actors started their careers in conventional, rather melodramatic roles in the early postwar era, but moved during the 1950s to more physical roles (often appearing bare-chested, in fact, to show off their impressively athletic physiques). These actors continued to enjoy substantial success in action roles, and also in the occasional dramatic film, during the 1960s. However, a new kind of male protagonist challenged them for prominence, what Monaco terms a "darker, more complex, 'antiheroic' type," best exemplified perhaps by Lee Marvin and Steve McQueen—quirky, only problematically sympathetic performers who appeared in a number of eminently forgettable secondary film roles during the 1950s and so were forced to earn a living through work in anthology television drama (Monaco 138). By the end of the decade, both had become main characters in long-running small-screen series: Marvin in "M Squad" and McQueen in "Wanted: Dead or Alive." During the 1960s, the two followed the lead of Paul Newman. Newman transformed himself from a conventional 1950s leading man eager for success and romantic fulfillment (*Until They Sail* [1957], *The Long Hot Summer* [1958], *The Young Philadelphians* [1959]) into a cynical outsider angry at the establishment, which he refuses even in the end to join, rising to critical and popular prominence in a number of important 1960s films: *The Hustler* (1961), *Hud* (1963), and *Cool Hand Luke* (1967).

McQueen went on to become one of the most successful actors of the decade in a series of Newmanesque roles: *The War Lover* (1962), *The Sand Pebbles* (1966), and, preeminently, *The Thomas Crown Affair* and *Bullitt* (both 1968). And Marvin excelled at the portrayal of a gallery of anti-establishment types (some more villainous than antiheroic) in a number of the era's most loved films: *The Killers* (1964), *Cat Ballou* (1965), and *Point Blank* (1967). Such releases suited the era's growing taste for the rejection of conventional values, middle-class lifestyles, even the need to relate meaningfully to others except through manipulation and violence. Nurtured in the Hollywood of the 1950s, McQueen and Marvin blazed the trail for the antiheroic types (strong, taciturn alpha-males appalled by the banality of respectability and the pervasiveness of corruption) who turned on, tuned in, and dropped out in the youth movement films that were such a striking innovation at the end of the 1960s.

But, as it turned out, the end of that decade sounded the death knell for most actors whose appeal was defined, and of course limited, by the notion of type. The most noteworthy actors of the generation that would take the places of studio-era performers, among its number such luminaries as Robert De Niro, Dustin Hoffman, Al Pacino, and Meryl Streep, would arguably depend less on good looks and charm and more on talent. In part, this generation has been strongly attracted to, and trained in, the archly naturalistic style of inner-directed character portrayal—the so-called Method in its many guises—that had its first flowering in 1950s Hollywood. In one sense, that is the most notable legacy of the decade as far as American practice of screen acting is concerned. But it is worth noting that all the actors noted above have also shown great skill at one time or another in the various forms of one-dimensional impersonation that was the stock-in-trade of their predecessors during the heyday of classic Hollywood in the 1950s.

WORKS CITED
☆☆☆☆☆☆☆☆☆☆★

Fan magazine and other primary or archival materials are cited in the text of individual essays.

Anderson, Chris. *The Long Tail: How Endless Choice Is Creating Unlimited Demand.* New York: Random House, 2007.

Anderson, Christopher. *Hollywood TV: The Studio System in the Fifties.* Austin: U of Texas P, 1994.

Astaire, Fred. *Steps in Time.* New York: Harper, 1959.

Auiler, Dan. *Vertigo: The Making of a Hitchcock Classic.* New York: St. Martin's, 1998.

Axelrod, George. *The Seven Year Itch.* New York: Random House, 1952.

———. *Will Success Spoil Rock Hunter?* New York: Random House, 1956.

Bacher, Lutz. *Max Ophuls in the Hollywood Studios.* New Brunswick, N.J.: Rutgers UP, 1996.

Balio, Tino, ed. *Hollywood in the Age of Television,* London: Unwin-Hyman, 1990.

Banner, Lois W. "The Creature from the Black Lagoon: Marilyn Monroe and Whiteness." *Cinema Journal* 47:4 (2008), 4–29.

Banninger-Huber, Eva. "Prototypical Affective Microsequences in Psychotherapeutic Interaction." *What the Face Reveals: Basic and Applied Studies of Spontaneous Expression Using the Facial Action Coding System (FACS).* Ed. Paul Ekman and Erika L. Rosenberg. New York: Oxford UP, 2005. 512–28.

Baron, Cynthia, and Sharon Marie Carnicke. *Reframing Screen Performance.* Ann Arbor: U of Michigan P, 2008.

Baron, Cynthia, Diane Carson, and Frank P. Tomasulo, eds. *More than a Method: Trends and Traditions in Contemporary Film Performance.* Detroit: Wayne State UP, 2004.

Barthes, Roland. *Mythologies.* Trans. Annette Lavers. London: Vintage, 1993.

Bazin, André. "Beauty of a Western (Beauté d'un western)." *Cahiers du cinéma* 55 (January 1956). Reprinted in *Cahiers du Cinéma: The 1950s: Neo-Realism, Hollywood, New Wave,* ed. Jim Hillier, trans. Liz Heron. London: Routledge/BFI, 1985. 165–67.

Bell-Metereau, Rebecca. "1953: Movies and Our Secret Lives." *American Cinema of the 1950s: Themes and Variations.* Ed. Murray Pomerance. New Brunswick, N.J.: Rutgers UP, 2005. 89–111.

Boddy, William. *Fifties Television: The Industry and Its Critics.* Urbana: U of Illinois P, 1993.

Bogdanovich, Peter. "The Last Innocent." *Premiere* 13:3 (November 1999), 124–29, 140.

———. *Who the Devil Made It.* New York: Knopf, 1997.

———. *Who the Hell's in It: Portraits and Conversations.* New York: Knopf, 2004.

Bolan, Peter, and Lindsay Williams. "The Role of Image in Service Promotion: Focusing on the Influence of Film on Consumer Choice within Tourism." *International Journal of Consumer Studies* 32:4 (2008), 382–90.

Bordwell, David, Janet Staiger, and Kristin Thompson. *The Classical Hollywood Cinema: Film Style and Mode of Production to 1960.* London: Routledge, 1988.

Bosworth, Patricia. *Montgomery Clift: A Biography.* New York: Harcourt Brace Jovanovich, 1978.

Brando. Dir. Mimi Friedman and Leslie Greif. Turner Classic Movies and the Greif Company. Aired 26 July 2008.

Brett, Simon. "Audrey Hepburn." *Films and Filming* 10:6 (March 1964), 9–12.

Bruck, Connie. *When Hollywood Had a King: The Reign of Lew Wasserman, Who Leveraged Talent into Power and Influence.* New York: Random House, 2003.

Bruzzi, Stella. *Undressing Cinema: Clothing and Identity in the Movies.* London: Routledge, 1997.

Bukatman, Scott. "Paralysis in Motion: Jerry Lewis's Life as a Man." *Camera Obscura* 17 (Fall 1988), 194–205.

Butler, Jeremy G., ed. *Star Texts.* Detroit: Wayne State UP, 1991.

Butler, Judith. "Imitation and Gender Subordination." *The Second Wave: A Reader in Feminist Theory.* Ed. Linda Nicholson. New York: Routledge, 1997. 300–315.

Byars, Jackie. "The Prime of Miss Kim Novak: Struggling over the Feminine in the Star Image." *The Other Fifties: Interrogating Midcentury American Icons.* Ed. Joel Foreman. Urbana: U of Illinois P, 1997. 197–223.

Capua, Michelangelo. *Montgomery Clift: A Biography.* Jefferson, N.C.: McFarland, 2002.

Carey, Gary. *Judy Holliday: An Intimate Life Story.* New York: Seaview Books, 1982.

The Celluloid Closet. Dir. Jeffrey Friedman and Arnold Glassman. DVD. Culver City, Calif.: Columbia Tristar, 1996.

Clarke Keogh, Pamela. *Audrey Style.* London: Aurum, 1999.

Cohan, Steven. "'Feminizing' the Song-and-Dance Man: Fred Astaire and the Spectacle of Masculinity in the Hollywood Musical." *Screening the Male: Exploring Masculinities in Hollywood Cinema.* Ed. Steven Cohan and Ina Rae Hark. New York: Routledge, 1993. 46–69.

———. *Masked Men: Masculinity and the Movies in the Fifties.* Bloomington: Indiana UP, 1997.

Cook, Pam. *Fashioning the Nation: Costume and Identity in British Cinema.* London: BFI, 1996.

Corliss, Richard. *Lolita.* London: BFI, 1994.

———. "Serene Majesty." *Film Comment* 29:2 (March/April, 1993), 4–5.

Coursodon, Jean-Pierre. "Jerry Lewis." *American Directors, Volume II.* Ed. Jean-Pierre Coursodon and Pierre Sauvage. New York: McGraw-Hill, 1983. 189–202.

Croce, Arlene. *The Fred Astaire and Ginger Rogers Book.* New York: Galahad Books, 1972.

Custen, George F. *Twentieth Century's Fox: Darryl F. Zanuck and the Culture of Hollywood.* New York: Basic Books, 1997.

Day, Doris, with A. E. Hotchner. *Doris Day: Her Own Story.* New York: William Morrow, 1975.

DeAngelis, Michael. *Gay Fandom and Crossover Stardom: James Dean, Mel Gibson, and Keanu Reeves.* Durham, N.C.: Duke UP, 2001.

Derry, Charles. "Jerry Lewis." *The International Dictionary of Films and Filmmakers. Volume 2: Directors.* Ed. Laurie Collier Hillstrom. 3rd ed. Detroit: St. James, 1997. 602–06.

Doane, Mary Ann. "Film and the Masquerade: Theorising the Female Spectator." *Screen* 23 (1982), 74–87.

Druxman, Michael B. *Charlton Heston.* New York: Pyramid, 1976.

Durgnat, Raymond. *Films and Feelings.* Cambridge, Mass.: MIT Press, 1967.

Dyer, Richard. "Never Too Thin." *Sight and Sound* 3:12 (December 1993), 59.

———. *Stars* [1979]. New ed. London: BFI, 1998.

Eames, John Douglas. *The Paramount Story.* New York: Random House, 1987.

Eckert, Charles. "The Carole Lombard in Macy's Window." *Stardom: Industry of Desire.* Ed. Christine Gledhill. London: Routledge, 1991. 30–39.

Ehrenreich, Barbara. *The Hearts of Men: American Dreams and the Flight from Commitment.* Garden City, N.Y.: Anchor, 1983.

Eisenschitz, Bernard. "*The Geisha Boy.*" *Frank Tashlin.* Ed. Roger Garcia and Bernard Eisenschitz. London: Éditions du Festival International du film de Locarno/Éditions Yellow Now/BFI, 1994. 170–71.

Ekman, Paul. *Telling Lies: Clues to Deceit in the Marketplace, Politics, and Marriage.* New York: Norton, 2001.

Ellis, John. *Visible Fictions.* London: Routledge, 1982.

Ellmann, Maud. *The Hunger Artists: Starving, Writing, Imprisonment.* Cambridge, Mass.: Harvard UP, 1993.

Endy, Christopher. *Cold War Holidays: American Tourism in France.* Chapel Hill: U of North Carolina P, 2004.

Everson, William K. *The Hollywood Western.* New York: Citadel, 1992.

Eyman, Scott. *Lion of Hollywood: The Life and Legend of Louis B. Mayer.* New York: Simon & Schuster, 2005.

Farson, Daniel. "They Made Me a Myth: Funny Men Dean Martin & Jerry Lewis." *Sight & Sound* 22:1 (July–September 1952), 30–31.

Feinstein, Herbert. "My Gorgeous Darling Sweetheart Angels: Brigitte Bardot and Audrey Hepburn." *Film Quarterly* 15:3 (Spring 1962), 65–68.

Feuer, Jane. *The Hollywood Musical.* 2nd ed. Bloomington: Indiana UP, 1993.

———. "The Self-Reflexive Musical and the Myth of Entertainment" (1977). In *Film Genre Reader.* Ed. Barry Keith Grant. Austin: U of Texas P, 1986. 329–43.

Fishgall, Gary. *Gregory Peck: A Biography.* New York: Scribner, 2002.

———. *Pieces of Time: The Life of James Stewart.* New York: Scribner, 1997.

Fordin, Hugh. *The World of Entertainment: The Freed Unit at MGM.* New York: Doubleday, 1975.

Fox, Patty. *Star Style: Hollywood Legends as Fashion Icons.* Santa Monica, Calif.: Angel City, 1995.

Francke, Lizzie, and Elizabeth Wilson. "Gamine Against the Grain." *Sight and Sound* 3:3 (March 1993), 30–32.

Freud, Sigmund. "A Letter from Freud." *American Journal of Psychiatry* 107 (April 1951), 786–87.

Fried, Michael. *Absorption and Theatricality: Painting and Beholder in the Age of Diderot.* Berkeley: U of California P, 1980.

Fujiwara, Chris. "Jerry Lewis." *Senses of Cinema.* *www.sensesofcinema.com/contents/directors/03/lewis.html.* 2003. Accessed 1 July 2008.

———. *Jerry Lewis.* Urbana: U of Illinois P, 2009.

Gaines, Jane. "Costume and Narrative: How Dress Tells the Woman's Story." *Fabrications: Costume and the Female Body.* Ed. Jane Gaines and Charlotte Herzog. London: Routledge, 1990. 180–211.

Gaines, William M. *Son of Mad.* New York: Warner Books, 1959.

Garcia, Roger, and Bernard Eisenschitz, eds. *Frank Tashlin.* London: Éditions du Festival International du film de Locarno/Éditions Yellow Now/BFI, 1994.

Gehman, Richard. *That Kid: The Story of Jerry Lewis.* New York: Avon Books, 1964.

Gibbs, John. *Mise-en-Scène: Film Style and Interpretation.* London: Wallflower, 2002.

Gledhill, Christine. "Signs of Melodrama." *Stardom: Industry of Desire.* London: Routledge, 1991. 207–29.

Godard, Jean-Luc. *Godard on Godard.* Ed. and trans. Tom Milne. New York: Da Capo, 1972.

Gosselin, Pierre, Gilles Kirouac, and Françoise Y. Doré. "Components and Recognition of Facial Expression in the Communication of Emotion by Actors." *What the Face Reveals: Basic and Applied Studies of Spontaneous Expression Using the Facial Action Coding System (FACS)*. Ed. Paul Ekman and Erika L. Rosenberg. New York: Oxford UP, 2005. 243–70.

Gottlieb, Sidney, ed. *Alfred Hitchcock: Interviews*. Jackson: U of Mississippi P, 2003.

Grihault, Nicki. *Film Tourism: The Global Picture*. Mintel Reports, 2003.

Gunning, Tom. "The Cinema of Attractions: Early Film, Its Spectator and the Avant-Garde." *Early Cinema: Space, Frame, Narrative*. Ed. Thomas Elsaesser and Adam Barker. London: BFI, 1990. 56–62.

Handyside, Fiona. "Beyond Hollywood, into Europe: The Tourist Gaze in *Gentlemen Prefer Blondes* (Hawks, 1953) and *Funny Face* (Donen, 1957)." *Studies in European Cinema* 2:1 (October 2004), 77–88.

————. "'Paris isn't for changing planes, it's for changing your outlook': Audrey Hepburn as European Star in 1950s France." *French Cultural Studies* 14:3 (October 2003), 99–108.

Haney, Lynn. *Gregory Peck: A Charmed Life*. New York: Carroll & Graf, 2005.

Harris, Thomas. "The Building of Popular Images: Grace Kelly and Marilyn Monroe." *Stardom: Industry of Desire*. Ed. Christine Gledhill. London: Routledge, 1991. 40–44.

Haskell, Molly. *From Reverence to Rape: The Treatment of Women in the Movies*. Chicago: U of Chicago P, 1987.

————. "Our Fair Lady." *Film Comment* 27:2 (March 1991), 9–17.

Hatch, Kristen. "1951: Movies and the New Faces of Masculinity." *American Cinema of the 1950s: Themes and Variations*. Ed. Murray Pomerance. New Brunswick, N.J.: Rutgers UP, 2005. 43–64.

Haver, Ronald. *A Star Is Born: The Making of the 1954 Movie*. New York: Knopf, 1988.

Hawkins, Joan. *Cutting Edge: Art-Cinema and the Horrific Avant-Garde*. Minneapolis: U of Minnesota P, 2000.

Heller, Ted. *Funnymen: A Novel*. London: Abacus, 2002.

Henderson, Brian. "Cartoon and Narrative in the Films of Frank Tashlin and Preston Sturges." *Comedy/Cinema/Theory*. Ed. Andrew Horton. Berkeley: U of California Press. 153–73.

Hendler, Jane. *Best-Sellers and Their Film Adaptations in Postwar America*. New York: Peter Lang, 2001.

Herzog, Charlotte. "'Powder-Puff Promotion': The Fashion Show-in-the-Film." *Fabrications: Costume and the Female Body*. Ed. Jane Gaines and Charlotte Herzog. London: Routledge, 1990. 134–59.

Heston, Charlton. *The Actor's Life: Journals 1956–1976*. New York: E. P. Dutton, 1976.

————. *In the Arena: An Autobiography*. New York: Simon & Schuster, 1995.

Higham, Charles. *Brando: The Unauthorized Biography*. New York: New American Library, 1987.

Hirsch, Foster. *A Method to Their Madness: The History of the Actors Studio*. New York: Da Capo, 2002.

Hirschhorn, Clive. *The Films of James Mason*. Secaucus, N.J.: Citadel, 1977.

————. *Gene Kelly*. Chicago: Regnery, 1974.

Hofler, Robert. *The Man Who Invented Rock Hudson: The Pretty Boys and Dirty Deals of Henry Willson*. New York: Carroll & Graf, 2005.

Holmes, Rupert. *Where the Truth Lies*. New York: Random House, 2003.

Holtzman, Will. *Judy Holliday: A Biography*. New York: Putnam's, 1982.

Hudson, Rock, and Sara Davidson. *Rock Hudson. His Story*. New York: Da Capo, 1986.

Inge, William. *Four Plays by William Inge*. New York: Grove & Weidenfeld, 1990.

Isaacs, Hermine Rich. "Gene Kelly: Portrait of a Dancing Actor." *Theatre Arts* 30 (March 1946), 149–56.

Jameson, Fredric. "Globalization as Philosophical Issue." *The Cultures of Globalization*. Ed. Fredric Jameson and Masao Miyoshi. Durham, N.C.: Duke UP, 1999. 54–79.

Jarvie, Ian. "Audrey Hepburn: The Performer and the Star." www.arts.yorku.ca/phil/jarvie/documents/documents/HepburnAudrey.doc. 1990. Accessed 5 October 2008.

———. "Free Trade as Cultural Threat: American Film and TV Exports in the Post-War Period." *Hollywood & Europe: Economics, Culture, National Identity 1945–95*. Ed. Geoffrey Nowell-Smith and Steven Ricci. London: BFI, 1998. 34–46.

———. "The Postwar Economic Foreign Policy of the American Film Industry: Europe 1945–1960." *Hollywood in Europe: Experiences of a Cultural Hegemony*. Ed. David W. Ellwood and Rob Kroes. Amsterdam: VU UP, 1994. 155–75.

JAS Productions, Inc. *Martin & Lewis: Their Golden Age of Comedy*. "Part 1: The Birth of the Team." Disney Channel, 1992.

Jennings, Wade. "Nova: Garland in *A Star Is Born*." *Quarterly Review of Film Studies* 4:3 (Summer 1979), 321–37.

Johnson, Steven. *Emergence: The Connected Lives of Ants, Brains, Cities, and Software*. New York: Scribner, 2001.

Johnston, Claire, and Paul Willemen, eds. *Frank Tashlin*. Edinburgh: Edinburgh Film Festival/Screen, 1973.

Kael, Pauline. *Reeling*. New York: Warner Books, 1976.

Kanfer, Stefan. *Somebody: The Reckless Life and Remarkable Career of Marlon Brando*. New York: Knopf, 2008.

Kass, Robert. "Jerry Lewis Analyzed." *Films in Review* 4:3 (March 1953), 119–23.

Kaufman, David. *Doris Day: The Untold Story of the Girl Next Door*. New York: Virgin Books, 2008.

King, Barry. "Articulating Stardom." *Stardom: Industry of Desire*. Ed. Christine Gledhill. London: Routledge, 1991. 167–82.

Krämer, Peter. "'Faith in relations between people': Audrey Hepburn, Roman Holiday and European Integration." *100 Years of European Cinema: Entertainment or Ideology*. Ed. Diana Holmes and Alison Smith. Manchester: Manchester UP, 2000. 195–206.

Kreidl, John Francis. *Nicholas Ray*. Boston: Twayne, 1977.

Krutnik, Frank. "The Handsome Man and His Monkey: The Comic Bondage of Dean Martin & Jerry Lewis." *Journal of Popular Film & Television* 23:1 (Spring 1995), 16–25.

———. *Inventing Jerry Lewis*. Washington, D.C.: Smithsonian Institution Press, 2000.

———. "Jerry Lewis: The Deformation of the Comic." *Film Quarterly* 48:4 (Fall 1994), 12–26.

———. "Sex and Slapstick: The Martin & Lewis Phenomenon." *Enfant Terrible! Jerry Lewis in American Film*. Ed. Murray Pomerance. New York: New York UP, 2002. 109–21.

Krutnik, Frank, ed. *Hollywood Comedians: The Film Reader*. London: Routledge, 2003.

LaGuardia, Robert. *Monty: A Biography of Montgomery Clift*. New York: Avon, 1984.

Landy, Marcia, ed. *Imitations of Life: A Reader on Film and Television Melodrama*. Detroit: Wayne State UP, 1991.

Lang, Robert. *American Film Melodrama*. Princeton, N.J.: Princeton UP, 1989.

Laurents, Arthur. *Original Story By*. New York: Applause Theatre Books, 2000.

Lesser, Wendy. "The Disembodied Body of Marilyn Monroe." *His Other Half: Men Looking at Women through Art*. Cambridge, Mass.: Harvard UP, 1991. 193–224.

Lev, Peter. *The Fifties: Transforming the Screen, 1950–1959*. Berkeley: U of California P, 2003.

Levy, Shawn. *King of Comedy: The Life and Art of Jerry Lewis*. New York: St. Martin's, 1996.

Lewis, Jerry, and Herb Gluck. *Jerry Lewis in Person*. Athenaeum: New York, 1982.

Lewis, Jerry, and James Kaplan. *Dean and Me (A Love Story)*. New York: Doubleday, 2005.

Lewis, Jon. "1955: Movies and Growing Up . . . Absurd." *American Cinema of the 1950s: Themes and Variations*. Ed. Murray Pomerance. New Brunswick, N.J.: Rutgers UP, 2005. 134–54.

Lindner, Robert. *Must You Conform?* New York: Holt, Rinehart and Winston, 1956.

Lippe, Richard. "Kim Novak: A Resistance to Definition." *CineAction!* (December 1986), 4–21.

Mailer, Norman. "The Homosexual Villain." *Sexual Revolution*. Ed. Jeffery Escoffier. New York: Thunder's Mouth, 2003. 477–85.

Maltby, Richard. *Hollywood*. 2nd ed. Oxford: Blackwell, 2003.

Manso, Peter. *Brando: The Biography*. New York: Hyperion, 1995.

Marling, Karal Ann. *As Seen on TV: The Visual Culture of Everyday Life in the 1950s*. Cambridge, Mass.: Harvard UP, 1994.

Marx, Arthur. *Everybody Loves Somebody Sometime (Especially Himself): The Story of Dean Martin and Jerry Lewis*. London: W. H. Allen, 1975.

Massumi, Brian. *Parables for the Virtual: Movement, Affect, Sensation*. Durham, N.C.: Duke UP, 2002.

May, Elaine Tyler. *Homeward Bound: American Families and the Cold War Era*. New York: Basic Books, 1988.

McCann, Graham. *Rebel Males: Clift, Brando, and Dean*. New Brunswick, N.J.: Rutgers UP, 1991.

McLean, Adrienne L. *Being Rita Hayworth: Labor, Identity, and Hollywood Stardom*. New Brunswick, N.J.: Rutgers UP, 2004.

———. "1958: Movies and Allegories of Ambivalence." *American Cinema of the 1950s: Themes and Variations*. Ed. Murray Pomerance. New Brunswick, N.J.: Rutgers UP, 2005. 201–21.

———. "Wedding Bells Ring, Storks Are Expected, the Rumors Aren't True, Divorce Is the Only Answer: Stardom and Fan-Magazine Family Life in 1950s Hollywood." *A Family Affair: Hollywood Calls Home*. Ed. Murray Pomerance. London: Wallflower, 2008. 277–90.

Mitchell, Lee Clark. *Westerns: Making the Man in Fiction and Film*. Chicago: U of Chicago P, 1996.

Monaco, Paul. *The Sixties: 1960–1969*. Berkeley: U of California P, 2001.

Morley, Sheridan. *James Mason: Odd Man Out*. London: Weidenfeld & Nicolson, 1989.

Moseley, Rachel. "Audrey Hepburn." *Journeys of Desire: European Actors in Hollywood—A Critical Companion*. Ed. Ginette Vincendeau and Alastair Phillips. London: BFI, 2006. 293–96.

———. "Dress, Class and Audrey Hepburn: The Significance of the Cinderella Story." *Fashioning Film Stars: Dress, Culture, Identity*. London: BFI, 2005. 109–20.

———. *Growing Up with Audrey Hepburn*. Manchester: Manchester UP, 2002.

———. "Trousers and Tiaras: Audrey Hepburn, A Woman's Star." *Feminist Review* 71 (2002), 37–51.

Mulvey, Laura. "*Gentlemen Prefer Blondes*: Anita Loos/Howard Hawks/Marilyn Monroe." *Howard Hawks, American Artist*. Ed. Jim Hillier and Peter Wollen. London: BFI, 1996. 214–29.

———. *Visual and Other Pleasures*. Bloomington: Indiana UP, 1989.

———. "Visual Pleasure and Narrative Cinema." *A Critical and Cultural Theory Reader*. Ed. Antony Easthope and Kate McGowan. Toronto: U of Toronto P, 1992. 158–66.

Nancy, Jean-Luc. *Au fond des images*. Paris: Galilée, 2003.

Naremore, James. *Acting in the Cinema*. Berkeley: U of California P, 1988.

Neibaur, James L., and Ted Okuda. *The Jerry Lewis Films: An Analytical Filmography of the Innovative Comic*. Jefferson, N.C.: McFarland, 1995.

Newton, Esther. *Cherry Grove, Fire Island: Sixty Years in America's First Gay and Lesbian Town*. Boston: Beacon, 1993.

Nowell-Smith, Geoffrey. "The Beautiful and the Bad: Notes on Some Actorial Stereotypes." *Hollywood & Europe: Economics, Culture, National Identity 1945–95*. Ed. Geoffrey Nowell-Smith and Steven Ricci. London: BFI, 1998. 135–41.

O'Neill, William. *American High: Years of Confidence, 1945–1960*. New York: Free Press, 1989.

Oppenheimer, Jerry, and Jack Vitek. *Idol, Rock Hudson: The True Story of an American Film Hero*. New York: Villard Books, 1986.

Palmer, R. Barton. *Harper Lee's To Kill a Mockingbird: The Relationship between Text and Film*. London: A & C Black, 2008.

Paris, Barry. *Audrey Hepburn*. London: Orion, 1997.

Pearson, Roberta. "A Star Performs: Mr. March, Mr. Mason and Mr. Maine." *Screen Acting*. Ed. Alan Lovell and Peter Krämer. London: Routledge, 1999. 59–74.

Phillips, Alastair, and Ginette Vincendeau. "Film Trade, Global Culture and Transnational Cinema: An Introduction." *Journeys of Desire: European Actors in Hollywood—A Critical Companion*. Ed. Ginette Vincendeau and Alastair Phillips. London: BFI, 2006. 3–18.

Polan, Dana. "Being and Nuttiness: Jerry Lewis and the French." *Journal of Popular Film and Television* 12:1 (Spring 1984), 42–46.

Pomerance, Murray. *Enfant Terrible! Jerry Lewis in American Film*. New York: New York UP, 2002.

———. *An Eye for Hitchcock*. New Brunswick, N.J.: Rutgers UP, 2004.

———. "Introduction: Movies and the 1950s." *American Cinema of the 1950s: Themes and Variations*. New Brunswick, N.J.: Rutgers UP, 2005. 1–20.

Powdermaker, Hortense. *Hollywood: The Dream Factory*. Boston: Little, Brown, 1950.

Prouty, Howard. "Documentation." *Frank Tashlin*. Ed. Roger Garcia and Bernard Eisenschitz. London: Éditions du Festival International du film de Locarno/Éditions Yellow Now/BFI, 1994. 185–240.

Pudovkin, V. I. "Film Acting." *Star Texts*. Ed. Jeremy G. Butler. Detroit: Wayne State UP, 1991. 34–41.

Ray, Nicholas. *I Was Interrupted*. Berkeley: U of California P, 1993.

Rivette, Jacques. "The Genius of Howard Hawks." Trans. Russell Campbell and Marvin Pister. *Cahiers du Cinéma: The 1950s: Neo-Realism, Hollywood, New Wave*. Ed. Jim Hillier. London: Routledge/BFI, 1985. 126–31.

———. "The Naked Spur." *Cahiers du cinéma* 29 (December 1953), 60.

Rizzo, Domenico. "Public Spheres and Gay Politics since the Second World War." *Gay Life and Culture: A World History*. Ed. Robert Aldrich. New York: Universe, 2006. 197–221.

Rosen, Marjorie. *Popcorn Venus*. New York: Avon, 1974.

Rosendorff, Neal Moses. "Be El Caudillo's Guest: The Franco Regime's Quest for Rehabilitation and Dollars after World War II via the Promotion of US Tourism to Spain." *Diplomatic History* 30:3 (June 2006), 367–407.

———. "'Hollywood in Madrid': American Film Producers and the Franco Regime, 1950–1970." *Historical Journal of Film, Radio and Television* 27:1 (March 2007), 77–109.

Rushton, Richard. "What Can a Face Do? On Deleuze and Faces." *Cultural Critique* 51 (Spring 2002), 219–37.

Russo, Vito. *The Celluloid Closet: Homosexuality in the Movies.* New York: Harper & Row, 1987.

Santopietro, Tom. *Considering Doris Day.* New York: St. Martin's, 2007.

Sarris, Andrew. *The American Cinema: Directors and Directions, 1929–1968.* New York: E. P. Dutton, 1968.

Schatz, Thomas. *Boom and Bust: American Cinema in the 1940s.* Berkeley: U of California P, 1997.

Shaviro, Steve. *The Cinematic Body.* Minneapolis: U of Minnesota P, 1993.

Shipman, David. *The Great Movie Stars: The Golden Years.* New York: Bonanza Books, 1970.

Sikov, Ed. *Laughing Hysterically: American Screen Comedy of the 1950s.* New York: Columbia UP, 1994.

Simpson, Mark. "The Straight Men of Comedy." *Attitude* (December 1994), 64–68.

Sklar, Robert. "'The Lost Audience': 1950s Spectatorship and Historical Reception Studies." *Identifying Hollywood's Audiences: Cultural Identity and the Movies.* Ed. Melvyn Stoker and Richard Maltby. London: BFI, 1990. 81–92.

Smith, Dina M. "Global Cinderella: Sabrina (1954), Hollywood, and Postwar Internationalism." *Cinema Journal* 41:4 (Summer 2002), 27–51.

Spigel, Lynn. *Make Room for TV: Television and the Family Ideal in Postwar America.* Chicago: U of Chicago P, 1992.

Spoto, Donald. *Enchantment: The Life of Audrey Hepburn.* London: Arrow, 2007.

———. *Marilyn Monroe: The Biography.* New York: HarperCollins, 1993.

Springer, Claudia. *James Dean Transfigured: The Many Faces of Rebel Iconography.* Austin: U of Texas P, 2007.

Stacey, Jackie. *Star Gazing: Hollywood Cinema and Female Spectatorship.* London: Routledge, 1994.

Staiger, Janet. "The Package-Unit System." *The Classical Hollywood Cinema: Film Style and Mode of Production to 1960.* Ed. David Bordwell, Janet Staiger, and Kristin Thompson. New York: Columbia UP, 1985. 330–37.

Stam, Robert, Robert Burgoyne, and Sandy Flitterman-Lewis. *New Vocabularies in Film Semiotics: Structuralism, Post-Structuralism, and Beyond.* London: Routledge, 1992.

Steinberg, Corbett. *Reel Facts: The Movie Book of Records.* Harmondsworth: Penguin, 1981.

Studlar, Gaylyn. "'Chi-Chi Cinderella': Audrey Hepburn as Couture Countermodel." *Hollywood Goes Shopping.* Ed. David Desser and Garth S. Jowett. Minneapolis: U of Minnesota P, 2000. 159–78.

Taylor, John Russell. "Jerry Lewis." *Sight & Sound* 34:2 (Spring 1965), 82–85.

Thomas, Tony. *A Wonderful Life: The Film and Career of James Stewart.* Secaucus, N.J.: Citadel, 1997.

Thomson, David. *A Biographical Dictionary of Film.* London: Andre Deutsch, 1994.

Tobin, Yann. "Audrey, la jeunesse." *Positif* 385 (March 1993), 54–56.

Tosches, Nick. *Dino: Living High in the Dirty Business of Dreams.* New York: Doubleday, 1992.

Truffaut, François. *The Films in My Life.* Trans. Leonard Mayhew. New York: Simon & Schuster, 1978.

Trumpbour, John. "Audrey Hepburn, ou la politique des actrices." *Positif* 365–366 (July 1991), 100–102.

————. *Selling Hollywood to the World: US and European Struggles for Mastery of the Global Film Industry, 1920–1950*. Cambridge: Cambridge UP, 2002.

Turim, Maureen. "Designing Women: The Emergence of the New Sweetheart Line." *Fabrications: Costume and the Female Body*. Ed. Jane Gaines and Charlotte Herzog. London: Routledge, 1990. 212–28.

Vineberg, Steve. *Method Actors: Three Generations of an American Acting Style*. New York: Schirmer Books, 1991.

Viviani, Christian. "Entre Audrey Hepburn et moi, cela remonte à loin." *Positif* 385 (March 1993), 57–59.

Welsch, Janice R. *Film Archetypes: Sisters, Mistresses, Mothers and Daughters*. New York: Arno, 1978.

Whyte, William H. Jr. *The Organization Man*. New York: Simon & Schuster, 1956.

Wilder, Billy. *Billy Wilder: Interviews*. Ed. Robert Horton. Jackson: UP of Mississippi, 2001.

Willemen, Paul. *Looks and Frictions: Essays in Cultural Studies and Film Theory*. Bloomington: Indiana UP, 1994.

Wilson, Elizabeth. "Audrey Hepburn: Fashion, Film and the 50s." *Women and Film: A Sight and Sound Reader*. Ed. Pam Cook and Philip Dodd. London: Scarlet, 1993. 36–40.

Wollen, Peter. *Singin' in the Rain*. London: BFI, 1992.

Wyatt, Justin. *High Concept: Movies and Marketing in Hollywood*. Austin: U of Texas P, 1994.

Young, Vinne. *It's Fun to Be Fat*. New York: A. A. Wyn, 1953.

CONTRIBUTORS
★★★★★★★★★★★★

WILLIAM A. BROWN is a Lecturer in Film Studies at the University of St. Andrews. He has published work in various journals (*New Review of Film and Television Studies, Animation: An Interdisciplinary Journal*, and *Studies in French Cinema*) and various collections (*The British Cinema Book*, 3rd ed., *Film Theory and Contemporary Hollywood Movies*, and *Film Festival Yearbook 1: The Festival Circuit*). His research interests include technology and cinema, cognitive approaches to cinema, and stars.

FOSTER HIRSCH, a professor of film at Brooklyn College, is the author of numerous books on film and theater including *Kurt Weill on Stage from Berlin to Broadway* and *Otto Preminger: The Man Who Would Be King*. He is a frequent host/moderator at the American Cinematheque, the Harvard Club, the National Arts Club, the Players Club, the Film Forum, and the American Film Institute, among others, and has lectured on film in India, China, Israel, Dubai, England, France, Germany, New Zealand, and at sea.

FRANK KRUTNIK is a Reader in Film Studies at the University of Sussex. He has published in leading screen studies journals since the early 1980s. His books include *Popular Film and Television Comedy* (co-author, 1990), *In a Lonely Street: Film Noir, Genre, Masculinity* (1991), *Inventing Jerry Lewis* (2000), *Hollywood Comedians: The Film Reader* (editor, 2003), and *"Un-American" Hollywood: Politics and Film in the Blacklist Era* (co-editor, 2008). He is currently working on a new monograph, *Out of the Shadows: Recontextualizing Postwar Hollywood, US Popular Culture, and Film Noir*.

AMY LAWRENCE is a professor of film and media studies, women's and gender studies, and comparative literature, and also chair of the department of Film and Media Studies at Dartmouth College. Among her many works on film are *The Films of Peter Greenaway* (1997) and *Echo and Narcissus: Women's Voices in Classical Hollywood Cinema* (1991).

ADRIENNE L. McLEAN is a professor of film studies at the University of Texas at Dallas. She is the author of *Being Rita Hayworth: Labor, Identity, and Hollywood Stardom* (2004) and *Dying Swans and Madmen: Ballet, the Body, and Narrative Cinema* (2008). She is co-editor, with Murray Pomerance, of the Star Decades series.

R. BARTON PALMER is Calhoun Lemon Professor of Literature and director of Film Studies at Clemson University. He is the author, editor, or general editor of more than forty books on various literary and cinematic subjects, including most recently *Harper Lee's To Kill a Mockingbird: The Relationship between Text and Film* and (with Robert Bray) *Hollywood's Tennessee: The Williams Films and Postwar America*. He serves with Linda Badley as general editor of the Traditions in World Cinema series (Edinburgh) and is the founding general editor, with Tison Pugh, of New Perspectives on Medieval Literature (Florida).

MURRAY POMERANCE is a professor in the Department of Sociology at Ryerson University and the author of *The Horse Who Drank the Sky: Film Experience Beyond Narrative and Theory*, *Johnny Depp Starts Here*, *An Eye for Hitchcock*, *Savage Time*, and *Magia D'Amore*, as well as of the forthcoming *Michelangelo Red Antonioni Blue: Eight Reflections on Cinema*. He has edited or co-edited more than sixteen volumes including *Cinema and Modernity*, *City That Never Sleeps: New York and the Filmic Imagination*, *American Cinema of the 1950s: Themes and Variations*, and *A Family Affair: Cinema Calls Home*. He is founding editor of the Horizons of Cinema series at the State University of New York Press and the Techniques of the Moving Image series at Rutgers University Press, and, with Lester D. Friedman and Adrienne L. McLean, respectively, of the Screen Decades and Star Decades series at Rutgers.

TISON PUGH is an associate professor in the Department of English at the University of Central Florida. He is the author of *Queering Medieval Genres* and *Sexuality and Its Queer Discontents in Middle English Literature*, as well as the co-editor of two film collections: *Race, Class, and Gender in "Medieval" Cinema* (with Lynn Ramey) and *Queer Movie Medievalisms* (with Kathleen Kelly).

BARRY SANDLER is an associate professor of film at the University of Central Florida. He has written and produced over twenty feature films. His work as a Hollywood screenwriter began with the story credit for *Kansas City Bomber* while he was a graduate student at UCLA. Subsequent screenwriting credits include *The Duchess and the Dirtwater Fox*, *Making Love*, *Gable and Lombard*, *The Mirror Crack'd*, *Evil Under the Sun*, and *All American Murder*. He produced and wrote *Crimes of Passion* for director Ken Russell.

MATTHEW SOLOMON is an associate professor of cinema studies at the College of Staten Island, City University of New York. He is author of *Disappearing Tricks: Silent Film, Houdini, and the New Magic of the Twentieth Century* (2010) and editor of *Méliès' "Trip to the Moon": Fantastic Voyages of the Cinematic Imagination* (2010).

SUSAN WHITE is an associate professor of film and comparative literature in the Department of English at the University of Arizona. She is the author of *The Cinema of Max Ophuls* as well as numerous essays on gender and cinema, and is the film editor of *Arizona Quarterly*.

PAMELA ROBERTSON WOJCIK teaches film at the University of Notre Dame, where she is also the director of Gender Studies. She has published widely on stardom, performance, and gender. She is the author of *Guilty Pleasures: Feminist Camp from Mae West to Madonna* and the forthcoming *The Apartment Plot: Urban Living in American Film and Popular Culture, 1945 to 1975*. She coedited *Soundtrack Available: Essays on Film and Popular Music* and edited *Movie Acting: A Reader*.

I N D E X
☆☆☆☆☆☆☆☆☆☆

Note: Featured stars in boldface; page numbers for illustrations in italic.